THE MARIAN MYSTERY

Visit our web site at
www.stpauls.us

or call 1-800-343-2522
and request current catalog

THE MARIAN MYSTERY

The Outline of a Mariology

Denis Farkasfalvy, O.Cist.

ST PAULS

Library of Congress Cataloging-in-Publication Data

Farkasfalvy, Denis M., 1936-
  The Marian mystery: the outline of a Mariology / Denis Farkasfalvy, O. Cist.
    pages cm
  Includes bibliographical references and index.
  ISBN 978-0-8189-1358-7 (alk. paper)
  1. Mary, Blessed Virgin, Saint–Theology. 2. Catholic Church–Doctrines. I. Title.
  BT613.F37 2013
  232.91–dc23

                              2013018119

Produced and designed in the United States of America by the
Fathers and Brothers of the Society of St. Paul,
2187 Victory Boulevard, Staten Island, New York 10314-6603
as part of their communications apostolate.

ISBN-13: 978-0-8189-1358-7

First Printing 2014

Current Printing 2019

TABLE OF CONTENTS

Table of Contents

Biblical Abbreviations

OLD TESTAMENT

Genesis	Gn	Nehemiah	Ne	Baruch	Ba
Exodus	Ex	Tobit	Tb	Ezekiel	Ezk
Leviticus	Lv	Judith	Jdt	Daniel	Dn
Numbers	Nb	Esther	Est	Hosea	Ho
Deuteronomy	Dt	1 Maccabees	1 M	Joel	Jl
Joshua	Jos	2 Maccabees	2 M	Amos	Am
Judges	Jg	Job	Jb	Obadiah	Ob
Ruth	Rt	Psalms	Ps	Jonah	Jon
1 Samuel	1 S	Proverbs	Pr	Micah	Mi
2 Samuel	2 S	Ecclesiastes	Ec	Nahum	Na
1 Kings	1 K	Song of Songs	Sg	Habakkuk	Hab
2 Kings	2 K	Wisdom	Ws	Zephaniah	Zp
1 Chronicles	1 Ch	Sirach	Si	Haggai	Hg
2 Chronicles	2 Ch	Isaiah	Is	Malachi	Ml
Ezra	Ezr	Jeremiah	Jr	Zechariah	Zc
		Lamentations	Lm		

NEW TESTAMENT

Matthew	Mt	Ephesians	Eph	Hebrews	Heb
Mark	Mk	Philippians	Ph	James	Jm
Luke	Lk	Colossians	Col	1 Peter	1 P
John	Jn	1 Thessalonians	1 Th	2 Peter	2 P
Acts	Ac	2 Thessalonians	2 Th	1 John	1 Jn
Romans	Rm	1 Timothy	1 Tm	2 John	2 Jn
1 Corinthians	1 Cor	2 Timothy	2 Tm	3 John	3 Jn
2 Corinthians	2 Cor	Titus	Tt	Jude	Jude
Galatians	Gal	Philemon	Phm	Revelation	Rv

FOREWORD

One of my most important reasons for writing a survey of Mariology is to provide an adequate textbook for college-level courses and formation programs for priestly and religious life.

Mariology is a special subject of theology. Every theology course needs a solid biblical foundation and a well constructed systematic presentation. In Mariology the question about "the development of dogma" is particularly important, and the correct way of discussing the apologetic aspect is also essential.

With a special emphasis on early patristics this book presents the primary texts and tries to provide a continuous narrative leading the reader from a careful reading of the biblical material to the peaks of the "Golden Age of Patristics" in the 4th and 5th centuries. As I experienced many times in my reading and my teaching, recent biblical trends have been extremely harsh to the first chapters of Matthew and Luke, and have led to Mariological minimalism which, in its turn, has obscured the meaning and the coherence of the Church Fathers' legacy.

As it happens in the intellectual and moral life, "abyssus abyssum invocat" – one extreme calls forth the other. Also in Mariology one extreme (minimalism) brings about excesses of the opposite kind (maximalism). This book makes a special effort to carefully explain, by keeping equal distance from both extremes, the earliest roots of our Marian patrimony, the teaching of the first Christian centuries about Mary's virginal motherhood.

I dedicate this book to my world-wide Cistercian community, consisting of both monks and nuns, Cistercians and Trappists, with their faithful adherence to a Marian heritage of 900 years, and to the young members of the monastery of Our Lady of Dallas in the last ten years, so eagerly attentive to what the Spirit is telling the Church in the third millennium.

I am especially grateful to Fr. Stephen Harding Gregg, O.Cist. of Dallas who has helped me with the final redaction of the text and provided me with his advice in editing this book.

Denis Farkasfalvy
June 28, 2013
Feast of St. Irenaeus

THE MARIAN MYSTERY

CHAPTER ONE

INTRODUCTION

The General Purpose of this Book

For any topic in Catholic theology, the inquiry must be rooted in revelation as known from Scripture and Tradition. Moreover, it should remain demonstrably connected with the *sensus fidei* of the faithful, expressed in their faith life, worship, and the moral decisions and attitudes that animate their spiritual life. Exploring the faith about Mary, the Mother of Jesus, assessing the ties linking this topic to other theological disciplines, and thus animating Marian devotion, are important tasks for contemporary theologians. Especially when done in service of priestly and catechetical formation, this reflection greatly contributes to building up (we might simply say, "edifying") the Church.

The Second Vatican Council led to a certain de-emphasis of both Mariology and Marian devotion. These developments were not unexpected, although at the same time much of it was not intended.[1] The famous debate at the Council's First Session about whether to insert a chapter into the Council's document on the Church or write a separate document about Mary made it clear early on that there was a "progressive" wing at the Council, critical of Catholic popular devotion to Mary, which it hoped to curb. These critical tendencies especially targeted Latin countries (Italy, Spain, and Latin America)

---

[1] For a historical survey of the debates on Mary at Vatican II, see René Laurentin, *La Vierge au Concile* (Paris: Lethielleux, 1965), 8-50.

and aimed at correcting certain forms of Marian devotion, perceived as exaggerations. The debate, sometimes described as taking place between "minimalists" and "maximalists," became, at one point, an alarming threat to the unity of the Council.[2] In retrospect, it is hard to avoid the conclusion that the Council left Mariology a bit scathed and in a vulnerable state. In the cited essay, Ratzinger sees the historical vote that split the Council Fathers almost evenly between the two tendencies as a tell-tale event. It manifested a lack of integration and a high level of tension between a "progressive" biblical-liturgical theology and spirituality, becoming a leading force in the Church after the Second World War, and a popular, devotionally based, more traditional, conservative, and – according of what theology meant in earlier times – a more "theological" trend reflecting closely the handbooks of the first half of the 20th century, chiefly produced and used in the Pontifical Universities of Rome, but also in many seminaries throughout the world. Despite claims to the contrary by many of the Council Fathers, Mary was not perceived by the majority as the "Mother of Unity" but as a problem for ecumenism, at least within that brand of ecumenism which sought to produce quick results through dialogue with the leading Protestant denominations.[3]

Even more significant were the changes affecting Catholic theology after the Council. The "mood" of the theologians – insofar as this can be judged from their publications – underwent a sudden change. While in the decades that preceded Vatican II, almost every Catholic theologian of name and fame, including those who even-

---

[2] The vote on October 29, 1963 resulted in a victory by a very small margin in favor of the progressives: 1,114 votes "in favor" of inserting a chapter on Mary, against 1054 votes in favor of a separate chapter on Mary. Cardinal J. Ratzinger in an essay "Thoughts on the Place of Marian Doctrine and Piety in Faith and Theology as a Whole" [Hans Urs von Balthasar-Joseph Cardinal Ratzinger, *Mary, the Church at the Source* (San Francisco: Ignatius Press, 2005)] says that "the significance of this vote can hardly be overestimated" (p. 22), but he later adds: "the immediate consequence of the victory of the ecclesiocentric Mariology was the collapse of Mariology altogether" (p. 24). These words appear to be extremely harsh. We intend to say more about it below in Chapter IX.

[3] One must note right away that there have been some very positive results in Mariology coming from ecumenism. An excellent example would be the book by a member of the famous and successful ecumenical French monastery of Taizé, Max Thurian, *Mary, Mother of All Christians* (New York: Herder, 1962).

tually became part of "the progressive wing" of the Council,[4] published a book about Mary; this swell in Mariological literature came to a rapid halt. From among the best known progressive leaders, only Hans Urs von Balthasar and Joseph Ratzinger sustained their interest in Mariology after the Council.[5] Unfortunately, they were the first to be re-classified, alongside some well-known specialists in Marian theology,[6] as turncoats relinquishing the progressive camp.

At the same time Mariology remained a compulsory subject for the formation of priests and deacons. Likewise, public interest in Marian devotion and spirituality did not vanish nor even regress in the Church, at least not immediately after the Council. No one had doubts about Pope Paul VI's sincere Marian piety, but the changes in exegesis and theology were beyond his personal control. During the long pontificate of John Paul II there was even more evidence that the Pope's deep filial piety toward the Virgin Mary was a shining example for those vocations to the priesthood which his many pastoral trips helped to nurture. But for reasons more difficult to explain, studies of biblical and patristic topics in Mariology did not keep up with changing needs and interests. In both biblical and patristic studies Marian topics were avoided or handled with suspicion as being insufficiently "scientific," more devotionally than intellectually

---

4   Yves Congar, Henri de Lubac, Karl Rahner, Hugo Rahner, Hans Urs von Balthasar, Jean Galot, Cipriano Vagaggini, Otto Semmelroth, Louis Bouyer, Edward Schillebeeckx etc. See these names in the bibliography.

5   The post-Conciliar publications on Mariology by K. Rahner, Y. Congar and H. de Lubac became low in number, although high in quality. About some additional names and publications see Chapter IX.

6   Most important is to name René Laurentin. He provided a critical edition of the documents related to the events at Lourdes and authored some outstanding books on Luke's infancy narratives [R. Laurentin, *Luc I-II* (Paris: Gabalda, 1954); Id., *Jésus au Temple. Mystère de Pâques et foi de Marie en Luc 2,48-50* (Paris: Gabalda, 1966)]. At the Council still an enthusiastic "progressive," reporting about it relentlessly session-to-session in the French newspaper *La Croix*, he soon became ostracized and summarily classified as a conservative or even a failed exegete for his views on the Infancy Narratives, the Marian apparitions and the origin of the Gospels. His short treatise on Mariology [*Court traité sur la Vierge Marie* (Paris: Lethielleux, 1967)], although belatedly translated into English [René Laurentin, *A Short Treatise on the Virgin Mary* (Washington, NJ: AMI Press, 1991)], never obtained enough international recognition and quickly fell into oblivion. Needless to say, it failed to make a significant impact on American Marian theology.

3

motivated. In the manner of all self-fulfilling prophecies, the quality of Marian theology, especially the biblical and patristic material, left much to be desired.

Mariology courses were offered less frequently and mostly by aging professors whose outdated textbooks were not replaced. As they retired, their courses also disappeared from the college catalogues. The classic works of the 1960's and 70's also disappeared and were not translated or reprinted in a marketable way.[7] By the end of the millennium Mariology looked like an old mansion in serious disrepair, crying out for remodeling.

The Motivation Behind this Book

My personal encounters with the "rise and fall of Mariology" go back to the decade of my initial formation, 1956-62. In those years, reading the young Karl Rahner's essays on Mary, attending seminars on Ambrose's and Origen's Mariology under Cipriano Vagaggini, reading the yearly bulletins on Mariology by René Laurentin and scanning a good number of books and essays on biblical and patristic Mariology gave me the false impression that Marian theology was securely included among the favorite topics of *la théologie nouvelle*.

It was in the late 1970's that I first suspected that seminarians might be ordained without having been taught Mariology. In most cases, the neglect was not intentional, but came about as if by default. Many syllabi of Christology or Ecclesiology contained a unit on Mariology at the end, but as it often happens in higher education the last topics were omitted or unduly reduced for lack of time. This is when, trusting my background and interest, I prepared a course in Mariology and taught it to graduate seminarians at the University of

---

[7] Illustrative of the new trend is the story of Laurentin's excellent although by now antiquated "Short Treatise" of Mariology, published in four subsequent editions in French. It was translated into English twice, once in Ireland from its second edition of 1952, then a second time from the expanded and improved fourth edition in 1991. Although the second translation was done by Charles Neumann, a fine American expert on St. Ambrose's Mariology, it received little publicity.

Introduction

Dallas, where I am still an adjunct professor. The course produced
mixed results. I did not find suitable resources and the course was
handled by both the students and the Department as of marginal
importance. In the next fifteen years my other occupations gave me
little chance to reflect on the matter. Yet at the turn of the century,
when asked again to teach Mariology, I was alarmed by the state in
which Mariology stood. In the first decade of the third millennium,
at the invitation of the Secretariat for Christian Unity, I participated
in ecumenical dialogues with Protestant groups. Unlike the Angli-
can-Catholic Dialogue, these programs paid little intention to Mary
and, in any case, the Catholic teams included no members who could
have addressed the topic. An ecumenical Faculty Seminar in North
Texas, focusing mainly on historical theology in the 2nd century with
four yearly sessions, has, through its exceptionally long existence of
forty years, touched on all conceivable subjects and authors, but the
subject of Mary in the 2nd century had never yet been the topic of a
session. My serious return to the study of patristic Mariology began
in such a setting. I discovered that – contrary to my previous notions
– the *Proto-evangelium Jacobi* had finally been published already in
the 1960's in a superb bilingual critical edition of which, however, I
had heard no mention from my colleagues and found no copy in the
theological libraries I frequented. I also discovered that this piece of
literature is neither an apocryphal Gospel nor just another worthless
Gnosticizing fantasy piece, but a document with important data, not
about details of history, but about the 2nd century's interest in Mary.
My second and third attempts to teach Mariology in 2005 and 2007
convinced me that we need a "reconstruction" of this theological discipline mostly from the primary sources of the biblical and patristic tradition but with less emphasis on speculative discussions held
in the scholastic and post-scholastic periods. These considerations
prompted me to write an article about "Reconstructing Mariology"
in which I attempted to identify the methodological issues anyone
encounters when trying to revive a seemingly moribund theological
discipline.[8]

---

[8]   Denis Farkasfalvy, "Reconstructing Mariology," *Communio* 37 (2010), 47-68.

Methodological Considerations

The word "renewal" means many things: catching up, reaching back, or extending newly acquired tools of research and systematization, or just starting all over again. "Recovery," a word overused by theologians of conservative leaning, does not signify much more than the need to re-read some old works that had been hastily buried in the fast-paced theological developments following Vatican II. The book I present here is not a renewal book, nor does it aim at a simple recovery. Rather, it tries to follow up on the initial attempts I recently made when forming a set of proposals for "reconstructing Mariology." The basic idea is to retrace the steps of the development of Catholic doctrine about the Virgin Mary. Thus the book begins with a biblical and patristic inquiry about the place and meaning of Mary in salvation as offered to man in Christ. Rather than making a microscopic study of the New Testament for an "objective portrait" of "the Mary of history," it begins with a canonical reading of the Savior's Virgin Mother as presented in the New Testament in conscious reference to the Hebrew Scriptures and with images and language based on the Old Covenant. The first biblical chapter aims to avoid frustrating the readers with efforts to calibrate the degree of historicity with which an "objective, historical-critical exegesis" would do the impossible: convincing suspicious believers and skeptical non-believers with certainties about what *really* happened. Instead I try to use the tools of biblical research with an exercise of a "faith with eyes" (*oculata fides*) for what God's word is saying about the mysteries of our salvation through the sacred books of the Canon – a Canon that the Church presents us along with an interpretive tradition in the context of various shades of emphasis and certainty, accents, exclamations, and question marks prompting further reflection. This approach to the Scriptures is open and receptive to the patristic tradition, which I try to access mostly for guidance and instruction and not for the sake of exercising the authority of a modern critical approach formulated from the privileged plateau of our present-day historical consciousness. But at the same time I use historical criticism as best I can as a tool for reaching the authentic voice of the Church Fathers, concretized in the context of their particular historical period and cultural milieu, but without letting slip from sight the overriding concern of the faith which we share and the Church we try to build up (i.e. to "edify").

This approach made more than clear to me that the emergence of the dogma of Mary's perpetual virginity requires a revised narrative beginning with the Gospels and the 2nd century reception of Matthew and Luke. My research opened my eyes to the damage a more than century-old biased reading of the Synoptic Gospels has done to our views on nascent Mariology by assigning, with pejorative implications, a late origin to the Infancy Narratives and handling them as if they were products of apocryphal imagination and creativity. In this regard, many commentators, Catholic and Protestant alike, ignored the importance that both Jesus' origins and the ongoing presence of his relatives had for the oldest church communities.[9] In this context I realized two things. First, the Mariological content of Matthew 1-2 and Luke 1-2 is inaccessible as long as they are read in isolation from the Mariological tradition of the 2nd century. Second, the Mary/Eve parallel found in Justin Martyr and Irenaeus is not just a peculiar curiosity of 2nd century exegesis of Genesis 3, where antiquated notions about the origins of mankind, the tale of Adam and Eve, and of original sin appear as if arbitrarily combined with the Annunciation, but rather provides an authentic exegetical context, in which the Church's anti-Gnostic stance obtained its first formulation with regard to the creation of mankind, its universal need for salvation, and the Incarnation of the Son of God, as well as his suffering, death, and Resurrection, by which God provided for this need. The cradle of Mariology is found in the interpretation according to which the Mary/Eve parallel explained the Adam/Christ parallel of the New Testament, and which opted for coherence and harmony between Pauline and Johannine Christology (and soteriology), thus setting the foundation for Christian theology altogether.

---

9   See Richard Bauckham, *Jude and the Relatives of Jesus in the Early Church* (Edinburgh: T & T Clark, 1990).

In this it is neither negligible nor historically mistaken that Justin Martyr explicitly quotes Luke's text of the Annunciation and speaks of the "Memoirs of the Apostles," the Hellenistic term he uses to explain for Hellenistic readers that he is quoting a literature in which the authentic tradition of Jesus' disciples is contained.[10]

Mariology begins to soar in the latter half of the 2nd century on account of the importance assigned to Mary in the first theological synthesis marking a wide and broad historical encounter, both hostile and enriching, with Hellenism in St. Irenaeus' *Adversus Haereses*.[11] The link that these Church Fathers, in the footsteps of the evangelists, established between Christology and the role of Mary *as Virgin and Mother*, is the first Mariological thesis, further enlightened in a chain of theological advancements: Origen, Athanasius, and Ambrose with the general spring of Mariology in the second half of the 4th century. Mary's perpetual virginity as a universally professed and defended article of faith obtains its modalities and contours in the course of this development.

The modern crisis of Mariology came about and is still sustained by contesting the validity of this development. What happened first in the 4th century was re-introduced in the Reformation and was experimented with in the 20th century, both before the Council (the Mitterer/Rahner dispute) and after, in circles who lost sight of the mystery of Mary's virginal conception and tried to settle Jesus' origins in isolation from the mystery of the Incarnation. In the narrative of this book, Mary's virginal motherhood is not only the chronologically first Marian dogma but a guiding light for all Mariology, leading to a doctrine of Mary's sanctity and to a program-

---

[10] When Raymond Brown's *Introduction to the New Testament* (New York: Doubleday, 1997, p. 267) begins dealing with the date and authorship of Luke by examining the historicity of Luke's relationship to Paul, he leaves out Justin Martyr and begins with later witnesses of the 2nd century, like Irenaeus. But Justin Martyr, who died shortly after the middle of the 2nd century (160), belongs to the *first half* of the 2nd century; he himself dates the historical antecedent to his *Dialogue with Trypho* as following the Bar Kochba revolt (132-135). It is in this work (n. 100) that Justin quotes the story of the Annunciation and testifies to the reception of Luke as an "apostolic" Gospel.

[11] Usually dated around 185.

matic and practical understanding of God's great gift of virginal and celibate life as it had its first full-scale blooming in the Church beginning in the 3rd century.

This book therefore follows the development of the Church's Marian teaching by registering the intertwined progression of three themes: Mary the Virgin, Mary in the Incarnation (divine motherhood), and the emerging doctrine of Mary's sinlessness leading to the formulation of her Immaculate Conception.[12] In this presentation the material on Mary's relationship to Eschatology (Mary's Assumption and relation to the Church) has been treated with some *apparent* neglect and, in any case, delays dealing with these topics.

It was a matter of methodological concerns that made me narrate "the development of the Marian Dogmas" in a largely historical sequence from the New Testament to Vatican Two and the post-Conciliar decades. This ordering of the material defined the first nine chapters. However, in Chapter X, risking the danger of repeti-

---

[12] While I do not agree with the method of mere "speculative Mariologies" proceeding exclusively from the essential elements of the Magisterium's doctrinal statements, I recognize its legitimate place in systematic theology. For this reason those recent Mariologies using the "fundamental principle of Mariology" as an axiom, stated as a point of departure, leave readers not only cold and unengaged, but also suspicious that Mariology is based on a per se negligible scriptural material blown up by the exaggerated devotional response of the centuries, and that this material in the sources of revelation, once examined "scientifically," offers only little rational content for real theology. Instead, I undertook a journey through the centuries in the footsteps of the Church Fathers, carrying in my hand an open dossier of the data of the New Testament with a readiness to expand them canonically and patristically even if contemporary exegetes may be inclined to read these "texts" with a point-wise separation in the monotonous *staccato* of the critical method. But I also stopped time and again, looking back as a wanderer who needs to see the panorama of the previous phases of the journey in order to obtain new inspiration and insights about what still lies ahead in the continued exploration of God's revelatory word. Therefore, a few times I made partial summaries or recapitulations for the sake of assessing the contours of a more complete view. Therefore, much of this book may impress the reader as a "theological *Dogmengeschichte*" or a theological commentary on the history of the Mariological dogmas. I am convinced however that such an approach is needed today more than ever before and that this presentation will be taken as an invitation to further systematic explorations by other authors. Meanwhile, I used and can recommend works on Mariology in a more traditional style like that by Cyrill Vollert, *A Theology of Mary* (New York: Herder, 1965) or the recent synthetic book by Benoit-Dominique Soujeole, *Initiation à la théologie mariale* (Toulouse/Fribourg: Parole et Silence, 2007).

tion, I returned to the doctrinal topics in a more systematic and synthetic way, yet completing in some sense what their first exposition
entailed. My hope is that in this way both the sequence of the doctrinal development and the interconnectedness of the various doctrinal
statements could be shown with a result of understanding a potential
synthesis of Marian thought which may be further developed from
the material presented.

Likewise, this book's approach may seem to underestimate
the riches of the speculative theology of the Middle Ages, and to
be overly zealous when treating historical, critical, and often mere
textual issues. But in today's state of Mariology such considerations,
even if often apologetic, are greatly needed. The damage done, as
assessed by a most qualified authority on the issue, Cardinal Ratzinger, Pope Emeritus Benedict XVI, largely came in the form or dis-
guise of doubts and suspicions raised by historians and critics, who
were at times indeed at a loss how to distinguish facts and fiction in
Mariology.[13] May the reader continue to work on the issues presented
here for further re-building Mariology, ultimately *ad aedificationem
Ecclesiae.*

---

[13] He formulates the conclusion that the invasion of biblical, liturgical and patristic
studies by historicism, led first to "the victory of ecclesiocentric Mariology" and
then to "the collapse of Mariology altogether." Cf. the article quoted above in note
n. 2, p. 2.

CHAPTER TWO

THE BIBLICAL SOURCES ON MARY

New Testament[14]

Methodological Remarks

In the New Testament Mary is neither frequently mentioned nor negligibly peripheral. Regardless of the statistical evidences that one could marshal in support to this statement, the question of her importance in the biblical books – or that of any person or doctrinal issue – is not to be decided by mere statistics. Such a question does not depend on the number of occurrences we find for a particular name and person, or a specific term, in the Bible, but on the merit of the issues involved, which is usually defined by the Christological perspective and possibly also by a method the theologian has applied. In biblical studies, in fact, the *theological* importance of a subject is greatly determined by the way in which the exegete conceives the relationship between exegesis and theology.

---

[14] Biblical Mariology, especially Mary in the New Testament is treated by a variety of literature. However, the exegetical presuppositions are often not clarified. It is left unclear by many of the authors how they regard the relationship of history and theology or that of biblical and systematic theology. A disconnected presentation of biblical, theological and historical chapters makes this literature often valuable on details but problematic with regard to general conclusions. Such is, for example, the work of Juan Luis Bastero, *Mary the Mother of the Redeemer* (Dublin: Four Courts Press, 2011), which in fact remains a series of ultimately independent lectures. An excellent biblical Mariology is by Ignace de la Potterie, *Mary in the Mystery of the Covenant* (New York: Alba House, 1992). Much better known in America is Raymond E. Brown, Karl P. Donfried, Joseph Fitzmyer, and John Reumann (eds.), *Mary in the New Testament* (Philadelphia: Fortress; New York: Paulist, 1978), but its pursuit of denominational pluralism turns it into a problematic tool for Catholic theology. On this see more on pp. 256-258.

By limiting the exegetical investigation to the historically identifiable and explicit intention of the human author(s), a biblical scholar may end up harvesting precious little from his inquiry about "Mary in the Bible." Such investigations often speak only of "suggestions" found in certain texts about Mary's role in the plan of salvation. In such a perspective, for example, Galatians 4:4 ("born of a woman, born under the law") would appear mariologically irrelevant. Also Romans 1:2 ("from the seed of David according to the flesh") may appear unimportant for what the Bible says about Mary, or even worse: contradictory to the idea of her virginal motherhood.

An inquiry into the "historical Mary," locked into critical exegesis, notes only that she is mentioned by name only in three of the four Gospels: Matthew, Mark, and Luke. In the Fourth Gospel, Mary is mentioned twice, in the short narrative of the Wedding Feast of Cana (2:1-11) and at the crucifixion (19:25-27), but without being named. Yet from these data it would be exegetically false to conclude that "the mother of Jesus" was for John a merely symbolic figure. Symbolic significance and historical reality are not mutually exclusive. In the case of the Fourth Gospel, we see quite the contrary: the historicity of the events causes their symbolic significance to be rooted firmly in reality. And this reality is not some lifeless factuality now all gone and pertaining to the realm of the past, but rather a physical fact pointing beyond itself and into a spiritual realm that lasts. Following this line of thought, we discover that also in the Book of Revelation (chapter 12) the Mother of the Messiah is mentioned, but in this book the primary aspect is symbolic, speaking about the end of history in a language of images. But, of course it is of great importance that the Church is being symbolized by the cosmic image of the Messiah's Mother, indicating that just like Mary so also the Church is called to go through both suffering and glory.

The biblical sources of Mariology, therefore, are not a catalogue of data to be programmed into a system, nor statements organized by their logical connections so that "all biblical data" could be worked into thesis-formulas. Instead we must treat biblical passages about Mary as verbal expressions of truth, "revealed for our salvation,"[15] in the form of narratives and statements, about natural and supernatural realities, which – in the case of Mariology – are connected in the closest possible way to the mystery of the Incarnation and of the Trinity, the central truths of Revelation. The biblical text clearly manifests the special status of Mariology: it presents her as the person from whose individual human nature the Incarnation of God's Son took place. In Matthew and Luke, the two canonical Gospels that explicitly treat Jesus' human origins, Mary appears as the one human being from whom the humanity of Jesus was created, in body and soul, and inserted into the human race by God's direct and unprecedented intervention.

The Genesis of the Lord

A majority of biblical historians, when they set about reconstructing Christian origins, consider the development of an interest in Jesus' childhood as a rather late phenomenon, absent from the mind of the first Christian generation and, for that reason, from the oldest written Gospel, that of Mark. Since Mark's priority as the oldest Gospel is widely accepted as the principal hypothesis in Synoptic studies, many Biblicists accept this premise without question or objection. Of course, Markan priority remains a hypothesis, not yet accepted by all, and recognized by most contemporary authors as not fully proven. If Matthew were the first Gospel, then the origins of the Messiah would more convincingly appear to have been a matter of original interest for the evangelists. But a third approach is also possible, and it does not depend on any source theory of the Gospels. Let us closely consider Romans 1:1-4. As practically all Pauline scholars admit, St. Paul here cites a pre-Pauline formula he inherited from the apostolic community. The text also shows vivid interest in Jesus' origins:

> Paul, a servant of Jesus Christ, called to be an apostle,
> set apart for the Gospel of God, which he promised be-

---

[15] Cf. Dogmatic Constitution *Dei Verbum* of the Second Vatican Council, n. 12.

forehand through his prophets in the Holy Scriptures, the Gospel concerning his Son, *who was descended from David according to the flesh* and designated Son of God in power according to the Spirit of holiness by his resurrection from the dead, Jesus Christ our Lord...

In this tripartite description of the "Gospel," (in the Pauline sense of the word, meaning message and not book or text) the middle part is about the Son's fleshly origins, described in terms of Davidic ancestry. According to Paul, Jesus' origin fulfills the Scriptures and proves that he is a human being. As such, he is able to suffer and die in order, thereafter, to be exalted in glory. It is important to note the two references this passage makes to Jesus as "Son of God," one before mentioning his descendance from David, and one before his exaltation is stated. That is, Jesus is proclaimed Son of God even before his human birth, and not only after his exaltation. Thus it is God's Son who is here said to have become a descendant of David and thereafter to have died and risen from the dead. Since the Epistle to the Romans is dated with unanimity to about A.D. 56-58, and therefore antedates all the canonical Gospels, we are entitled to conclude that there is nothing unusual or "late" in Matthew's or Luke's interest in Jesus' origin. Incidentally, it is rather Mark's lack of such interest that should be regarded as anomalous.[16] One is, therefore, entitled to ask why Mark omits at his Gospel's beginning any treatment of Jesus' origins and starts his "story" with the ministry of

---

[16] Eusebius in his *Ecclesiastical History* (VI, 14-5-7) quotes from an otherwise lost work by Clement of Alexandria (*Hypotyposeis*) a saying by one of the "ancient presbyters" (meaning the immediate disciples of the Apostles) according to which the gospels with "genealogies" (i.e., passages about the origins of Jesus) are more ancient than those without such texts. This probably does not mean that Matthew and Luke are prior to Mark and John, but rather that the heretical editions of the gospels, like Marcion's edition of Luke and the gospel of the Ebionites based on Matthew, have illegitimately left out the infancy stories. Clement's saying is the oldest statement asserting that the narratives about Jesus' origins belong to the original integrity of the Gospel tradition. See Denis Farkasfalvy, "The Presbyters' Witness on the Order of the Gospel as Reported by Clement of Alexandria," *Catholic Biblical Quarterly*, LIV, 2 (April, 1992) 260-270.

John the Baptist.[17] Whichever way we answer this question, we must say that the way Matthew opens his book is well in accordance with Paul's summary of his Gospel's message in Romans.[18]

Let us then consider the opening of Matthew:

> The book of "genesis" of Jesus Christ, the son of David, the son of Abraham... (Mt 1:1)

We must leave the word "genesis" untranslated for the moment. For Greek-speaking Jews and Christians alike, "Book of Genesis" meant in the 1st century what it means today: the title of the first volume of the Pentateuch. But it was also the Greek equivalent of the Hebrew expression *sefer ha-toledot*, which refers to texts that explain the origins of something or somebody. In fact, Genesis uses this expression when referring to the creation or origin of heaven and earth (2:4), then the creation or origin of Adam (5:1), and the genealogical tables connecting Adam to Noah and further down all the way to Abraham (6:9, 9:12, 10:1). Thus, Matthew begins his book quite skillfully and appropriately as a new "Genesis" in which he will describe the beginnings of a new creation – the story of Jesus – by combining this opening with the genealogical list from Abraham to David and from David all the way down to Jesus. For Matthew it is very important to show the initial paradox of his message: on the one hand, Jesus is the son of David (cf. Mt 1:20 and 2:5-6, in fulfillment of Mi 5:2) but, on the other hand, Jesus was born by no act of human "generation" (that would be γεννήσις not γένεσις) from a Virgin by an action of the Holy Spirit, which again fulfilled Scripture (cf. Is 7:14 in Mt 1:22-23). Therefore, we can say that Matthew 1-2 expands on the theme that Paul so briefly enunciated using a pre-Pauline Christian

---

[17] This is not our subject to treat, but the answer lies in a comprehensive study of all the omissions which Mark makes of the traditional material of which he was certainly cognizant. Such are, for example the "Our Father" or a closer description of Jesus' temptations in the desert, which he mentions in a few words (1:13) but does not describe.

[18] More specifically, Matthew's opening lines correspond to the way Paul's *sources* (the Jerusalem community in the late 30's) presented its narrative about Jesus the Christ.

confessional formula when speaking of Jesus' human generation in Romans 1:2.

The narrative pericopes of Matthew 1-2 provide answers more specifically to three questions: Was Jesus a descendant of David? Was he born in Bethlehem of Judah? How is it that nonetheless he was known as Jesus of Nazareth? Each answer is rooted in some scriptural passage of the Old Testament which we will treat here one by one.

The first is Isaiah 7:14, in which Ahaz, a Davidide king of Judah, is told about a "sign" that God will give him: his (messianic) descendant named Immanu-El (God is with us) will be conceived by a virgin. If we read this in Matthew's perspective, we understand the role of Joseph. He is an important part of the sign precisely because he is not Jesus' physical father. It is through him that Jesus is legally a "Davidide," "the son of David," although not "of a Davidic descendant's seed," unless indirectly, if one assumes that Mary was also a descendant of David.[19] Matthew wants to demonstrate not only that, under the same breath, the virginal birth and the Davidic origin of the Messiah (the two poles of the paradox) were prophetically predicted, but also that Jesus is identical with the Immanu-El of Isaiah's book. The latter means that he is the person through whom God's presence and reign in the world are fulfilled. How this ultimately happens will become clear only at the end of the story: Jesus' own ongoing and everlasting presence among his faithful is predicted (Mt 28:20).

A second quotation is signaled in Matthew 2:15; it comes from Hosea 11:1. Through this text the evangelist first identifies Jesus' return from Egypt with Israel's Exodus under Moses. In both cases God calls his "Son" – Jesus corresponding to the Chosen People – and calls him out of Egypt back into the land of the forefathers. This quotation points beyond Jesus' fleshly origin, for Jesus incorporates in himself the whole people of Israel: he is in fact God's Son, fulfilling in himself what Israel and the Messianic King were expected to

---

[19] Matthew provides no basis or hint for making this assumption. But Ignatius of Antioch seems to suppose it (cf. *Letter to the Ephesians* 18:2).

do in the world, that is, to bring God's reign to the Chosen People and through them to the whole world. By being all at once God's Son and David's Son, Jesus brings about, not only a new Genesis, but also a new Exodus.

In Matthew 2:23 we encounter again an explicit reference to some prophetic text, but its identification is a bit more difficult. For in 2:23 Matthew concludes again about Jesus' origins but now with a puzzling connection between the name "Jesus of Nazareth" and the fact that he grew up in this Galilean town, by referring to something that, allegedly "the prophets" said about it. In the tradition, this allusion is most frequently interpreted as a reference Isaiah 11:1, although contemporary exegesis seems to lean toward Isaiah 4:3.[20] Matthew's text lacks clarity. Among other things, it is not quite clear how the adjective "Nazarene" is grammatically derived from either the Semitic or Greek name of the town of "Nazareth." The Greek text offers little help. The plural in "prophets" is also obscure, but it does not necessarily indicate that more than one prophetic text is involved; it only means that the text in question is representative of "the prophets" in a collective sense, i.e., the Old Testament as a whole.[21] In any case, we have here a triangular connection linking a geographic name (Nazareth) with a scriptural quotation and a descriptive or personal name applied to Jesus (*Nazaraios* or *Nazarenos*). Modern Matthean scholarship is inclined to speak here of an unsolvable dilemma. For the name of the town Nazareth is certainly not named in any text of Isaiah, nor by any other ancient prophet. But there is evidence sufficient to resolve the issue with strong probability. Jesus' name "Jesus of Nazareth" is widely attested in all branches of the Gospel tradition. Most clearly, John 1:45 tells Jesus' full name under which he was unambiguously identified: "Jesus, son of Joseph from Nazareth." As was usual in 1st century Palestine, his name consisted of three parts: "personal name / patronymic / prov-

---

[20] W.D. Davies and Dale C. Allison, *The Gospel According to St. Matthew* (Edinburgh: T & T Clark, 1991) I, 275-281.

[21] Matthew and most New Testament books use the expression "Law and Prophets" as standing for all the Scriptures of the Old Testament. Cf. Mt 7:12; 11:13; 22:40.

enance." John 1:45 reproduces, therefore, Jesus' "full legal name." On the other hand, the verb "he will be called," in Matthew 2:23, makes the reader understand that Matthew presents here not some attribute of Jesus but a name by which he was called by his contemporaries. Since Matthew already stated that the personal name "Jesus" was predetermined by a divine decision (Mt 1:21), and carried out by Joseph (Mt 1:26), it is logical to expect that the last component of the name – his provenance – would also be divinely arranged and then put into effect by Joseph.

We can go now to Isaiah 11:1. Here again the prophet refers to the Davidic offspring, the one who was called Immanu-El in Isaiah 7:14, but here is called *"nezer,"* i.e., a shoot. This word was probably pronounced in the 1st century like *"nazar"* and, therefore sounded quite similar to *"Nazara,"* the Aramaic form of Nazareth.[22] The Greek word in the text, *"Nazaraios,"* meaning "from Nazara," refers to the same word but provided with a Greek ending, just like the Latinized form *"Nazarenos"* which is also found in variant texts. Both mean "from Nazara." Thus Matthew seems to be telling us that the decision Joseph makes when moving to Nazareth – the decision that eventually determines Jesus' "last name" (the place of provenance) – did not happen by accident, but was likewise divinely willed and carries a theological significance. That for modern linguistics this is a "false etymology," since the name "Nazareth" does not in its view come from "flower," is beside the point. When calling him Jesus of "Nazara," his contemporaries were in fact fulfilling the Scriptures: they called him the "shoot," and Matthew sees here a third reference to a new beginning – after "new Genesis" and "new Exodus," now "the shoot" – by which God jump starts his *salvation plan.*[23] Thus when, due to political circumstances, Jesus and his family end up choosing to dwell in Galilee, the evangelist sees in

---

[22] In ancient Gospel manuscripts there are three main forms for Nazareth: Ναζαρὰ (Mk 4:13; 4:16), Ναζαρὲθ (Mt 21:11), or Ναζαρὲτ.

[23] The word "Nazarene" could also be linked to the word and concept of the "Nazarites" or "nazirs" as privileged holy men chosen to be religious leaders in Israel. This connection seems to be the least warranted by "prophetic texts."

this event the fulfillment of the Scriptures as it was foretold by some prophet: "He will be called a Nazorean."

God both hides and reveals Jesus' identity – hides for the contemporaries and reveals to the reader of the Gospel. Not only is he God's Son by nature and origin, but exactly when, seeking refuge in Egypt, he loses the transparency of his origins, he begins appearing as the one who incorporates into his personal destiny that of the whole people. Moreover, by being re-routed back to Galilee, a region unfit for David's sons, he indicates a radically re-shaped salvation plan as a new shoot in "Galilee of the Gentiles" (Mt 4:15).

It is at this point that we must make a theological connection to Paul's text, regardless of how much or little Paul may have known about the name or the person of Mary:

> But when the fullness of time had come, God sent his Son, born of a woman, born under the law, in order to redeem those who were under the law, so that we might receive adoption as children. (Gal 4:4-5)

Once we admit the canonical unity of the two Testaments, this theological connection is inevitable. The "fullness" of time necessarily refers to its counterpoint, the beginning. But further, when Paul refers to "the Law," he speaks of the Torah (the Pentateuch), which had *its* beginning, the Book of Genesis, and comes to its fullness when it is transcended, that is, at Jesus' birth. In Jesus' case "birth from a woman" means a birth like any other that followed the creation of Adam and Eve, and yet it is unlike any other birth because it meant a new Genesis beyond the Torah. Paul says that, born of a woman, Jesus is born into the order of the First Genesis, under the Torah. Matthew agrees: he is son of Abraham and David. Yet he is not a physical son to the Davidide man Joseph. Rather, his birth was the miraculous fruit of a unique, non-sexual reproduction from "the woman," chosen to be the one on whom the Holy Spirit descended for a new creation, to signify a new Genesis. This new beginning continues with a new Exodus that is re-routed to Galilee of the Gentiles, where Jesus is rooted and planted anew as the "shoot," prophesied by Isaiah. As Son of God, he redeems from the Law and establishes a new Israel, a new filial relationship: a sonship that is spiritual and universal. Paul indicates that the birth of Jesus results in the birth of all the redeemed so that we may become "children of God" with the Spirit dwelling in our hearts crying out "Abba, Father." Regardless of how explicitly Paul registered the implications of his text, Galatians 4:4-5 stands in parallel to Matthew 1:20. Both speak about a physical birth causing, at the same time, a new beginning in a spiritual sense as it leads, ultimately, to our non-physical birth or "regeneration" from God. But while in Matthew the birth from the Spirit primarily refers to Jesus' divinity, in Galatians the spiritual birth is explicitly that of the Christians in whom the divine life comes about through faith and baptism so that Jesus' own voice and word call out from within us to the Father.

The mariological content of Matthew 1-2 consists of the virginal conception of Jesus, linked in two antithetical ways to the "Book of Genesis." On one level, the word "Genesis" in Matthew 1:1 assumes the role of a title and links the New Testament's beginning to the beginning of the Old. It links Jesus' origins to the origins of all creation. On another level, this same word points out that Jesus' conception marks the appearance of a new creation. Insofar as it is virginal, the new genesis comes about without an antecedent, yet, insofar as it stands in succession to human generations, it brings to fulfillment the drama that God has kept on weaving through a particular salvation history, a path starting with Abraham and leading from generation to generation to Jesus.

We must keep in mind that in the various episodes of Matthew 1-2 Mary is never the central figure. She does not act or speak, but is only the "locus" where the Holy Spirit's power of causing Jesus' conception operates. Nothing in the narrative suggests a sexual or "quasi-sexual" link of Mary to the Holy Spirit or to any male human being. Neither Joseph nor the Spirit "begets" Jesus in Mary. It is the divine action of the Spirit that makes this new generation happen, an action that has no sexual or physical characteristics and is fully supernatural. Therefore, Jesus' conception, expressed by the passive voice of γεννάω (γεννήθη in v. 16 and γεννηθὲν in v. 20), cannot be validly transformed into sentences with the same verb in active voice because the divine agent is asexual. This makes the role of Joseph peculiar in these narratives. It is not enough to speak of Joseph's role in the story as a feature of the author's "narrative technique" introducing the reader gradually to the mystery of Jesus' conception. It would be more correct to say that Joseph, the only conceivable witness other than Mary, is entitled to learn the truth about Mary's uncompromised virginity, as he does from an angel, and is, therefore, the chosen recipient of this revealed truth. That the reader too is thus told about this mystery through the message of an angel confirms this statement: Joseph transmits what he learns; the one evangelized becomes an evangelizer. Of course, only Mary is drawn into the heart of the mystery of divine motherhood, which Matthew's narrative indicates only indirectly. Mary's witness is not based on her association with a single point in Jesus' life; rather it is based on the sum total of her life-time's experience that ultimately remains behind an impenetrable veil beyond the limits of human speech.

It is simply unacceptable to argue that the evangelist fabricated the stories about Joseph with no more historical information than Jesus' patronymic (cf. Jn 1:45) and an anonymously evolving theology of the Incarnation. Of course, the name of Joseph makes one think of the stories of Joseph, the patriarch whose proclivity to revelatory dreams and whose virtue of chastity are known from the Bible (Gn 39:1-23). It is quite possible, even plausible, that the cross-references to this patriarch are intentional, so that the Joseph cycle of Genesis might have shaped the figure of Joseph in the Gospel. But his role in Matthew 1-2 focuses on his reception (embraced with faith) of a divine revelation about the mystery of Jesus' bodily origins, something entirely absent from the stories of Joseph.

We must remain aware that the overture to the story of Jesus' origins is the summary statement in Matthew 1:1, which makes a triple reference to the Old Testament: "book of Genesis," "son of Abraham," and "son of David." Of these, the third is fulfilled specifically through Joseph. Although Jesus was conceived in a way that by-passed human paternity "according to the flesh," Joseph was, in an important sense, the "father of the Messiah." He was the person linking Jesus to the Davidic covenant and thus bringing about one of the basic "fulfillments" of the Scriptures. We face here one of the Christological paradoxes of the New Testament: Jesus is the Davidic Messiah and yet his origins surpass, yes, even contradict, the most important element in the concept of Davidic messianism: he was not conceived by the Davidic spouse of his mother. We will see how consistently Luke's text affirms the two sides of the same paradox.

The Portrait of the Mother of the Lord in Luke 1-2

1. About Luke's Sources

For the rest of the Church's teaching about Mary as well as for Christian Marian piety, the most important texts are found in the first two chapters of Luke's Gospel; two passages, the Annunciation at 1:29-38 and the Visitation at 1:45-57, are the only Gospel episodes with Mary in the center. Although the story lines of Matthew 1-2 and Luke 1-2 share important elements and exhibit some convergent aspects, they cannot be harmonized. In fact, any harmonization would risk missing the point of each narrative. But one may say that Luke's text represents a further and deeper delving into the mystery of the virginal conception already seen in Matthew, and especially into its implications for Mary's personal life, her call and role. Luke, we might say, was the first to transmit the special outlook and perspective that characterize Mariology.

The Lucan narratives about Jesus' origins and childhood do not isolate Mariology, but keep it embedded in the Gospel structure. This is clear if we realize that the Lucan account of Jesus' origins consists of stories parallel to stories about John the Baptist, as if expanding the analogy found in all four Gospels between Jesus' ministry and that of John the Baptist. When comparing the episodes of Jesus' and John's infancy in Luke, René Laurentin speaks of a "diptych" exhibiting a certain "limping" or "asymmetric" parallelism.

The episodes about John become shorter and lose importance while those about Jesus expand in size and significance.[24]

As is the case for Joseph presented by Matthew, so for Mary presented by Luke, some recent exegetes tend to reduce Luke's accounts to a composite of fictitious narratives based on reflections on Old Testament texts and thus eliminate the question of historicity in their regard. This tendency is based on a handful of findings, convincing neither individually nor cumulatively, providing little more than random possibilities.

An important issue debated in this context concerns Luke's sources. Does his text reveal a Hebrew or Aramaic "Vorlage"?[25] For literary critics, the most important aspect of the question has always been the peculiar literary language and style exhibited by the Infancy Narratives in Luke 1-2.[26] These two chapters (following the Prologue in 1:1-4) contain so many Hebraisms – more than the rest of the Gospel or most of Acts – that, in general, they are legitimately considered to be indicators of Semitic sources used by the evangelist. However a few important studies claim to have produced evidence to the contrary. These propose that the stylistic peculiarities like the Semitisms may come from conscious efforts of imitation of "the sacred language" of Scripture (in this case, its Greek translation) by Luke, who developed a technique of writing in the style of the Septuagint, the Greek translation of the Old Testament produced a couple of centuries before the birth of Jesus.

---

[24] *Luc I-II, Études bibliques* (Paris: Gabalda, 1958), 22-42. Raymond Brown also speaks of a (more elaborate) diptych well laid out in his *An Introduction to the New Testament, The Anchor Bible Reference Library* (New York/London/Toronto/Sidney/Auckland: Doubleday, 1996), 230-231.

[25] "Vorlage" is a technical term for a previous oral or written composition, which the author finds ready-made and uses as a basic framework for his text.

[26] Raymond Brown notes that the question about the origin of the Semitisms in Lk 1-2 can be traced back to the early 1800's. See *The Birth of the Messiah. New Updated Edition* (New York: Doubleday, 1993), 246, n. 39. Brown, however, dissociates himself from those who regard "these stories as historical" and "trace them back to family traditions" (ibid., 244-245). But his last word is that the "reconstruction of the pre-Lukan sources" is "enormously difficult" and thus he cannot say anything definite about them (ibid., 250.)

This thesis is not satisfactory.[27] Luke's Prologue, which the Infancy Narratives immediately follow, insists rather adamantly that his Gospel is based on eyewitness accounts. The supposition that, after such a Prologue, he would present fully fabricated stories by using a deceptive stylistic maneuver does not square with his stated purpose. Nor can one explain clearly why he bothered to state this purpose at all in the wholly different style of a well educated Greco-Roman historian, only to switch over immediately to a narrative loaded with Semitisms. We do not know of any similar work contemporary or prior to Luke's Gospel written in a similar manner. The extraordinary number of authentic Hebraisms in Luke 1-2, well exceeding what we find in the rest of Luke, would need a better explanation than the author's effort of mimicking scriptural style. In a similar manner, a more "Hebraistic" account of Jesus' ministry could have also come about under Luke's pen for the sake of a similar effect, i.e., for an artificially obtained impression of authenticity.[28] Why does Luke limit this concentration of "Septuagintal

---

[27] To quote a French specialist of the Gospel of Luke, François Bovon, "The question of the occurrence of Semitism is a difficult one." Bovon observes that Luke very often *avoids* the Semitism he finds in Mark's Gospel (which most authors believe is a source used by Luke). But he also notes that, in the Birth Narratives, "he employs Semitisms whenever he finds them tolerable." And he adds that in numerous sayings of Jesus Luke is not prone to modify material he takes from his sources (*Luke 1, Hermeneia*, Minneapolis: Fortress, 2000, 4). In his *Anchor Bible Commentary* Joseph Fitzmyer just attempts a list of the "Septuagintisms" in Luke's style; he assures us that the list is incomplete and finally notes Luke's "fondness for Septuagintisms." *The Gospel According to Luke I-IX, Anchor Bible* 28 (Garden City, NY: Doubleday, 1981), 114-116.

However, I. Howard Marshall, the evangelical author of a commentary on Luke, puts together these findings in a positive way and concludes in a manner that I find most convincing: "In some places [of the Gospel] a number of scholars suspect that the material proper to Luke is his own creation, since it displays his peculiar theological interests. This theory has been advanced particularly in respect of the birth stories.... But the general fidelity of Luke to his sources Mk and Q, where these can be certainly identified, makes one skeptical of the suggestions that he created material in the Gospel on any large scale." *The Gospel of Luke, The New International Greek Testament Commentary* (Grand Rapids: Eerdmans, 1978), 31.

[28] Different authors would present differently the proportion of underlying traditional material and Luke's own effort of expanding them into full-fledged stories. Typically a "middle-of-the road" position is followed by Luke Timothy Johnson, a Catholic author, who points out in general Luke's "fondness for archaizing." He surmises that Luke builds "entire scenes" from "biblical prototypes." But all the

style" to the episodes about Jesus' childhood? It is in the context of this unanswered question that Luke's references to *Mary keeping the memory of the events in her heart* take special significance. For after the episode of the nativity we read: "And Mary kept all these things, reflecting on them in her heart" (2:19). Then at the end of the childhood narratives, as Jesus is found in the Temple, the text concludes: "And his mother kept all these things in her heart" (2:51).

Of course, nowhere does Luke claim that he personally learned about any event from Mary, the mother of Jesus. Yet the two comments quoted above seem to express his conviction that what is known about Jesus' origins and infancy has been remembered from eyewitness sources, among them the most qualified witness of all, Mary herself. This makes us understand why Luke, and Luke alone, mentions her by name in the early post-apostolic Church: among the Apostles gathered at Pentecost, at the "infancy of the Church," when they receive the Holy Spirit. For, in fact, Acts 1:13-14 lists by name the eleven Apostles and Mary, and only then, without names, indicates the presence of other women as well as the brothers of Jesus (of whom we will need to speak later), all of them witnesses at the overture of the "apostolic preaching." On the other hand, besides the events of the infancy, nowhere does Luke's Gospel offer any episode of Jesus' life with a reference to Mary. From Luke's own perspective, Mary's presence at Pentecost would be irrelevant unless she were a witness to something important that was narrated in the "first volume" of the Lucan work. Just as the eleven names in Acts 1:13-14 constitute a reference to Luke 6:14-15, Mary's name is best explained in connection with Luke 2:19 and 2:51.[29]

---

examples he gives for these statements are from Acts. Luke Timothy Johnson, *The Gospel of Luke, Sacra Pagina*, Vol. 3 (Collegeville: Glazier/Liturgical Press, 1991), 12-13. Much more restrained, maybe even too shy, is I. Howard Marshall's sober approach in assessing Luke's historicity. He states that work on tradition-historical issues has only recently begun in earnest. "It may, therefore, seem rash to attempt any kind of historical appraisal of the origins of the traditions recorded in Luke." *The Gospel of Luke, The New International Greek Testament Commentary* (Grand Rapids: Eerdmans, 1978), 32.

[29] The literature opting for non-historicity of the Infancy Narratives explains these references to Mary as a "model" of behavior rather than a reference to an oral source. Brown states this in the first edition of his *The Birth of the Messiah* and

2. The Annunciation (Lk 1:26-38)

The passage constitutes a literary unit: it starts with the Angel Gabriel being sent and ends with the Angel departing. The main character in the narrative is Mary. Its literary structure follows that of other biblical birth announcements – of Samuel, Samson, and most obviously John the Baptist – but it resembles just as closely, if not more, the narratives of divine calls like the call of Abraham, Moses, Gideon, Isaiah, and Jeremiah. It contains a number of characteristics typical of the latter group of narratives: an opening that makes the person addressed wonder, a reference to awe and fear ("Do not be afraid"), the announcement of conception and birth (or a call), an objection by the person addressed, a word of assurance in response to the objection and, finally, the expression of consent by the addressee.

But equally important are the differences that make this narrative unique. In the parallel texts the conception and birth of the child is ardently desired by the woman in question and her husband expected to become the father. Here, the issue is exactly the opposite, as the question is stated: how can this happen, since Mary is a virgin and has no relations with any man? The divine assurance resolves this question by reference to the intervention of the Holy Spirit and not by reference to a man, although a spouse was explicitly named in the introductory words.

The description of the Child, contained in verses 32-33 and 35, is rich in Christological details. At this point the title "Son of God" is closely connected with attributes of a Davidic Messiah. However,

---

repeats it in an appendix in response to the "conservative" critics of his book (see pp. 429-430 and 680-681 in the updated edition quoted above in note 26). However, he erroneously claims that in light of the Dogmatic Constitution *Dei Verbum* of Vatican II Catholic scholars are now not expected to adhere to the historicity of the inspired books. He seems to forget about no. 19 of *Dei Verbum*: "Holy Mother Church has firmly and with absolute constancy held and continues to hold that the four Gospels just named, whose historical character the Church unhesitatingly asserts, faithfully hand on what Jesus Christ, while living among men, really did and taught for their eternal salvation until the day he was taken up to heaven (see Ac 1:1-2)." The expressions "did and taught" is technical: it summarizes in Ac 1:1-2 what Luke himself thought to be the content of his first volume.

the "royal attributes" of the messianic figure are clearly transcendental: "he will reign forever" and "of his reign there will be no end." Of
course, these terms can be applied in some sense to David's merely
human successors as we have them in some royal messianic texts,
especially if isolated from the rest of the narrative (e.g. Ps 45:6 or
89:28-29). But when the Angel specifically describes Mary's conception as happening through the "overshadowing" of the Holy Spirit,
there can be no doubt that this Child is the result of a supernatural,
divine act. He is called "Son of God" not in the sense of any Davidic
Messiah – in fact, it is just being explained how he would be born
without being inserted into David's lineage – but because the Spirit
will cause this conception as a novel beginning in a virginal womb
without and beyond any human generative force.

It is Mary's question that elicits the exposition of the second
set of the child's attributes, as she inquires: How can this be? The
meaning of Mary's objection is handled in modern times as a *crux
interpretum*. No matter how we answer the long-debated issue about
Mary's intentions or vows or plans or prospects or expectation or
readiness or non-readiness to remain a virgin, all exegetes agree that
the narrator (Luke) makes it crystal clear that the Child is not being conceived by Joseph, but in a miraculous way without the Virgin
"knowing a man."

At this point – which contains, in fact, the heart of its message
– the story of the Annunciation to Mary diverges from all parallels.
The "task" divinely assigned to the addressee by the angelic messenger is not an action or a chain of actions but an act of inner consent. Of course, just like in the case of Abraham, Moses, Gideon,
Isaiah, or Jeremiah (vocation stories and not birth announcements),
Mary's consent implies a commitment that defines her life and identity – in this case her role as the mother of the Messiah. Verses 32-33
portraying a Davidic Messiah are essential parts of the story. Yet the
focus of the narrative is Mary's reply in which, predictably yet freely,
she accepts the task and commits herself as "the handmaid of the
Lord" (1:35).

This reply of hers is another feature that makes the story utterly different from its biblical parallels. Although the narrative explicitly states that "with God nothing is impossible" – it is impossible with God (it is "inconceivable") that God's Holy Spirit would make Mary conceive the Son of God without her previous consent. Thus, while there is no doubt that God can make a virgin turn pregnant, God cannot do what is intrinsically wrong. Thus it is impossible for God to cause Mary's pregnancy without first asking for her free consent.[30]

When Mary objects to the Angel that she does not "know man," her words must be logically taken as an objection to the Angel's words about her offspring (vv. 32-33); for she rightly concludes that this Child would be a son of David and thus, in view of her engagement to Joseph, Joseph's son. This is indeed what the reader is also reasonably expected to conclude at the beginning of the passage, since in the first sentence we are told that she was espoused to a man of Davidic descent. Therefore, for her to become pregnant with a Child who is to sit on David's throne would imply not only to "know man" (cf. Gn 4:1 and 4:25) in a general sense, but to "know" this specific man, Joseph, to whom she is espoused. Conversely, when Mary states that she "does not know man," the phrase means not only that she has no sexual relations with any man, but, on account of the context, specifically not with Joseph.

Here the story comes to a point where ancient interpretation and modern exegesis part. While the logic of the text seems to imply that Mary does not intend to be in sexual relations with Joseph, modern exegetes cannot see how, in a Jewish context, a "virgin espoused to a man" could be thought of as someone intending to remain a virgin.[31] But the problem of interpreting the text remains the

---

[30] Since the 2nd century (the Talmud and the Roman pagan writer Celsus) there have been authors interpreting the virginal conception as a cover-up for illegitimacy. Recent studies time and again refuted this on a historical and critical basis. See M. Eugene Boring, *Mark, A Commentary: The New Testament Library* (Louisville/London: Westminster John Knox, 2006), 165-166.

[31] A survey of modern proposals of interpretation is found in John McHugh, *The Mother of Jesus in the New Testament* (Garden City, NY: Doubleday, 1975), 188-192. McHugh pays much attention to the interpretation of some German exegetes (specifically Haugg and Gächter, but also Audet, a French exegete, who joined their view with some variation). These authors claimed that if translated into Hebrew the Angel's message can be read as "behold you have conceived"

same. If Mary is espoused with the intention of entering into sexual relations with Joseph, her objection makes no sense: she would naturally have thought the Angel was speaking of a Child to be born of her relation with Joseph. The text must be allowed to suggest beyond what it directly states. In other words it is unavoidable to perceive the suggestion by Mary's reply to the Angel that she has no intention to consummate her marriage and live with Joseph as his wife. We may think we know enough about 1st century Judaism to conclude that this interpretation is historically improbable; but such an understanding of the text is the oldest we know. The so-called *Proto-evangelium of James*, an apocryphal text coming from the middle of the 2nd century, although with no assured credentials of historical tradition or credibility for historicity, uses both Matthew's and Luke's Infancy Narratives and supposes this interpretation.[32] It assumes that Mary has made a vow of virginity and, therefore, raises her objection to the Angel because she intends to live a life of consecrated virginity.[33] Luke's text certainly does not say anything clear or explicit about such a vow. One must admit, however, that only if her words are taken as expressions of an intention of ongoing virginity, do they constitute both a *specific and substantial* objection to the angelic message. *Specifically* the Angel spoke of her future Child as

---

(*hinnach harach*) with Mary's responding that she had no sexual relations with anybody, although her espousal to Joseph would allow sexual intercourse. There are two astonishing details in this, in case this was indeed the "state of art" reached by the middle of the 20th century in interpreting Lk 1:34. First, it assumes that the Son of God has already taken flesh in Mary, i.e., the Holy Spirit made her pregnant without previous notification, not to speak of her previous consent. Second, when in need of a particularly "flattening" (Mariologically deconstructing) interpretation, these exegetes are ready to assume that the text came from a Hebrew *Vorlage* and nobody seemed to remind them (and McHugh) that Luke had no Hebrew or Aramaic sources; he only uses "Septuagintisms" as a literary device in order to camouflage the lack of Hebrew sources.

[32] The *Proto-evangelium* gives evidence that its author lacked knowledge about the conditions of 1st century Palestine. It reflects, however, beyond doubt, what has been thought about the Lucan narrative in the 2nd century. In fact it is by far the earliest record of how Christians understood Mary's question to the Angel: she was committed to remain a virgin.

[33] To be fair about the difficulty of historicity, we must mention right here (we will repeat it further down) that the *Proto-evangelium* had, most probably, no Hebrew sources either.

a son of David, while the narrative started by saying that her spouse, Joseph, was from the house of David. And, of course, "knowing man" in the Bible is, ever since the first pregnancy of Eve (Gn 4:1), a necessary premise to becoming a mother. The *Proto-evangelium's* explanation is easily understood on account of the early 2nd century's institution of consecrated virginity in the form of *virgines subintro-ductae*, meaning virgins living under tutelage and supervision of ascetic men. However, quite possibly, as many commentators admit, such an arrangement was known much earlier, perhaps to Paul and to the Church in Corinth (1 Cor 7:25-40), and even earlier, as some Jewish antecedents to such or similar arrangements suggest.

In any case, a genuine understanding of the Annunciation must be based on what is unique in it and differs from the conception of John the Baptist by Elizabeth and from other Old Testament parallels. Mary is not a barren wife like Elizabeth or Anna, Samuel's mother; she is not hoping and praying for a child, but quite to the contrary, she is a virgin who, although espoused, when told about her future pregnancy, reminds the heavenly messenger of her virginity and asks: how will that be? Even if these words do not refer to any "institutional status" of virginity, they cannot indicate anything short of a desire to remain in the condition of virginity.[34]

All Mariological reflections that grew out of the account of the Annunciation are based on the insight that "the virgin named Mary," when facing God's will to receive the gift of a Child without marital relations and thus by retaining her virginity, perceived this message as a call or invitation to which she responded positively but in complete freedom.[35] In Catholic theology, the understanding that the grace of the Incarnation – God becoming man – is the root of all graces also implies that Mary's call and her response constitute the prototype of all human encounters with divine grace. A literary analyst may claim that the outcome of the story is clear from its beginning; a theologian may state that God's actual grace was granted

---

[34] Ignace de la Potterie proposes that, even if the culture in which Mary lived did not appreciate lifelong virginity, she desired to remain a virgin, an interpretation he finds in St. Thomas and Thomas' commentator Cajetan. See *Mary in the Mystery of the Covenant* (New York: Alba House, 1992), 25-29.

with the foreknowledge and certainty of its acceptance; but theologically it remains just as correct and important to say that, when giving her response, Mary represented (and acted on behalf of) all mankind as she welcomed God's Son into her womb. This is the basis of the comparison and contrast between Mary and Eve, calling Mary's response an act of obedience and opposing it to the disobedience of Eve that marked man's first sin. In the Church Fathers' perspective, not only the Angel Gabriel, but the whole world was eagerly expecting Mary's response. We quote this tradition in the classical and most eloquent formulation St. Bernard gave it, when addressing the Virgin Mary in his fourth homily "In Praise of the Virgin Mother":

> You heard, O Virgin, the fact and the way; both are miraculous, both are happy. Rejoice, O daughter of Zion, exult O daughter of Jerusalem. And because what you heard was a sound of happiness and joy, let us hear your reply of joy which we so desire in order that our humiliated bones may exultantly rejoice. You have heard the fact and believed, believe also in the mode in which this is going to happen. You heard that you will conceive and bear a son; you heard that it will not happen through a man but through the Holy Spirit. The Angel is waiting for a reply; it is time for him to return to the one who sent him. We too await a reply of mercy, O Lady, all we who are oppressed by a sentence of condemnation. And behold, the prize of our salvation is being offered to you: we will be redeemed as soon as you agree. We have all been created through the Eternal Word of God and yet we are dying. In your brief response we should be restored and

[35] At this point we cannot remain boxed in uncertainties about the practice of virginity around the first years of the Christian era. There is an immense list of important issues of pre-70's A.D. Judaism, about which we know very little or nothing. But we know – and with certainty – that God could not have turned Mary into the virgin mother of his Son without her consent. Thus Mary's choice of accepting her virginal motherhood was a real one. This is why at this point, I expand the interpretation of the Annunciation in the sense Christian tradition slowly but surely penetrated its meaning.

will be called back to life. This is what Adam asks of you in despair, with all his offspring born outside of paradise. This is what Adam and David ask and all the holy fathers ask, your own fathers, who are dwelling in the shadow of death. This is what the whole world is asking, kneeling before you and rightly doing so.[36]

Mary's reply expresses both a free consent and a profound sense of obedience. The expression "let it be to me" clearly indicates that her motherhood happens to her as an event which she cannot cause or *make* happen. Yet her role is not totally passive: as a handmaid she commits herself to a life of service. The event of the Annunciation is the paradigm for any act of grace: the initiative and the act which bring about supernatural results belong totally to God, yet the human response is equally essential. All other acts of divine grace have their source in this grace given to Mary. Tradition rightly applies to this event the verse of John's Gospel, coined for indicating the universal import of the Incarnation: "out of this fullness we have all received" (Jn 1:16).

3. *Visitation to Elizabeth and the Magnificat (Lk 1:39-54)*

This is the second pericope in Luke's Gospel with Mary as its central figure. The episode begins with her trip to Judaea. Elizabeth greets her with inspired prophetic pronouncements. They address, first, Mary, and only in second place her messianic Child. At the end, a fairly long canticle follows, which Mary recites to celebrate all the great things God has done to her. Only *in obliquo* does the *Magnificat* refer to Jesus.

Although the Visitation seems to be a separate unit, it is essentially linked to the Annunciation. The reason for the trip comes from the Angel's statement to Mary about Elizabeth's pregnancy, which is supposed to prove that "with God nothing is impossible" (Lk 1:36). Luke's delicate presentation avoids giving specific reasons

---

[36] *In laudem Virginis Matris* IV, 8, Sancti Bernardi Opera Omnia (Leclercq IV, 53).

for Mary's trip. We may only guess that Mary is prompted by a desire to share her joy rather than to check on the truthfulness of the Angel's word. It is only in the middle of the Visitation story that we learn from Elizabeth that Mary believed Gabriel's words (Lk 1:45), and so her trip was not motivated by doubt but by faith.

The central passage of the narrative contains three *makarismoi* or proclamations of "blessedness":

> *Blessed* are you among women, and *blessed* is the fruit of your womb. And why has this happened to me that the mother of my Lord comes to me? For as soon as I heard the sound of your greeting, the child in my womb leaped for joy. And *blessed* is she who believed that there would be a fulfillment of what was spoken to her by the Lord. (Lk 1:42-45)

These expressions exalt her as the "mother of my Lord." Addressing Mary in this way evokes the court language of the Books of Samuel,[37] and thus expresses homage to the Davidic prince and to his mother as the Queen Mother, carrying him in her womb. Immediately thereafter Elizabeth explains that she received revelation from the prophetic child whom she bears in her own womb: "the child in my womb leaped for joy" (Lk 1:44).

The opening verses of the Visitation describing Mary's walk from Galilee to "a town in Judah" in the vicinity of Jerusalem reminds the reader of a scene of the Old Testament about the Ark of

---

[37] There appear here two literary features that justify this suggestion. When Elizabeth addresses Mary as "the mother of my Lord," she switches from second to third person; moreover "the mother of my Lord" resembles the expression "my Lord, the king" the latter being used in a consistent and highly stylized manner in 1 S 22-24 and 2 S 3-24 more than thirty times. René Laurentin, in *Luc I-II* (Paris: Gabalda, 1957), 78-80, and David Stanley in "The Mother of my Lord," *Worship* 34 (1959-1960), 330-332, argue that this formula, used in the Books of Samuel with regard to Saul and David is intentionally inserted here and expresses Elizabeth's homage to the messianic king, or really an homage by John the Baptist. Since even a contemporary reader of the Bible in English can recognize the stylistic similarity, I see no reason why J. Fitzmyer should call the reference all too "subtle" to be valid. See *The Gospel According to Luke I-IX, Anchor Bible* 28 (Garden City, NY: Doubleday, 1981), 365.

the Divine Presence being carried on a similar route. John and then, of course, his mother whom he inspires to greet Mary, realize the meaning of this humble event that brings to fulfillment the old story of the Ark's arrival to Jerusalem from Kiriat Yearim[38] in which David subserviently humbles himself in a ritual dance (2 S 16:14-16).

The Visitation ends with a poetic text (Lk 1:45-55), the *Magnificat*, named after the first word of its Latin translation. Although carefully researched in every commentary on Luke, the origin and full theological significance of this text has remained elusive. In the canonical Gospels only in Luke 1-2 are some of the narratives interrupted by inserted hymns. However, we find a similar technique with similar compositions in several narrative episodes of the Old Testament.[39] The *Magnificat* is a pre-eminently Marian text: it is Mary's song of thanksgiving for being chosen as the Mother of the Savior. This poetic text, together with the canticles of Zechariah (Lk 1:68-79) and Simeon (Lk 2:29-32), is one of the strongest indicators that Luke has used for his Birth Narratives a special source, for he would have found ample reason to make up similar compositions in the rest of his Gospel or in various parts of Acts.[40]

The most important message of the *Magnificat* is that it combines Mary's exceptional dignity and blessedness with a most profound sense of humility. In her prayer, Mary sees herself in full unity with all who are lowly, while prophetically predicting that she will receive praise from all generations. While this statement is extended to all future mankind, Mary points out that these blessings are rooted in the promise made to Abraham. She refers back to the first of all divine promises as we find it in Genesis 12:2-3:

---

[38] Traditionally Holy Land pilgrimage routes for immemorial times located the home of Zechariah and Elizabeth in ancient Kiriat Yearim, today on the outskirts of the extended city of Jerusalem.

[39] See for example Gn 15:1-17; Dt 32:1-43; Jg 5:1-32; 1 S 2:1-10 and the insertion of the entire Ps 18 into 2 S 22:1-51.

[40] Commentators often point out that the *Magnificat* cannot be a Lucan composition but must have come from some outside source because it does not exactly fit its context. This is a valid insight, but only up to a point. That it sheds additional light on the narrative beyond what the story says is obviously the very reason for which the lyrical passage has been inserted.

I will make you a great nation; I will bless you and make
your name great; and you shall be a blessing. I will bless
those who bless you, and I will curse him who curses you;
and in you all the families of the earth shall be blessed.

4. *Circumcision and Presentation in the Temple (Lk 2:21-40)*

The coincidence is not planned, nor is the harmony intentional, but Luke narrates what Paul stated in Galatians 4:4: "When the
fullness of time had come, God sent his Son, born of a woman, born
under the law." For this reason after the birth of Jesus in "the city
of David" (Lk 2:11) the Child is circumcised on the eighth day (Lk
2:21), then, forty days after the birth, he undergoes with his mother
a ritual of purification (Lk 2:22-24; cf. Ex 13:2, 12-15).

Protestant exegesis made it fashionable not to notice these texts'
Mariological relevance. Yet, in the episodes of the Lucan Birth Narratives, the mother of the Lord plays an important role: she acts on
behalf of the infant Messiah in fulfilling the Scriptures or prompting some bystanders to utter prophetic words and take prophetic actions, which in turn anticipate what the Child came to accomplish.
In the scene of the Presentation, the roles of two elderly persons,
Simeon and Anna, who receive Jesus in the Temple, are charged
with symbolic significance. Simeon recognizes in the Child the messianic "Light for the Nations" of whom Isaiah spoke (Is 42:46), and
performs, after the *Magnificat* and the *Benedictus*, the third song of
the Infancy Narratives, the *Nunc Dimittis* (Lk 2:29-32). Then he
prophetically addresses Mary with words predicting suffering in
the future: "This child is destined for the falling and the rising of
many in Israel, and to be a sign that will be opposed so that the inner
thoughts of many will be revealed – and a sword will pierce your own
soul too" (Lk 2:34-35). Historical-critical exegesis had immense
difficulties with this text. What do "the sign," the "sword," and the
"piercing" of Mary's soul signify? Catholic popular piety went in the
opposite direction and found in the passage more symbolism than

it was able to handle. Baroque art usually represented Mary's heart (meaning her "soul") as pierced by seven swords. There is, however, less agreement about how to enumerate one by one Mary's seven sorrowful experiences. Ultimately, there can be little doubt that, at this point, Luke's account of Jesus' infancy alludes to the Cross of Jesus (redemptive death by crucifixion), rather than to other particular painful episodes – real or projected – that one might perceive in Mary's life with Jesus. That the Messiah encounters oppositions and contradictions to be interpreted as signs of his authenticity is an Old Testament theme, best known through the songs of the Suffering Servant. These reached their climax at the Cross. The "daughter of Zion" – the people of Israel, whom Mary certainly represents in Luke 1-2 – was brought to a crisis and was broken-hearted on account of Jesus. Mary's soul, representing both that of Israel and her individual internal sufferings, was torn as she participated thus in Jesus' suffering.

Up to this point, the perspective of Luke's text is reasonably clear. We might therefore conclude that, as the community of the disciples was tried and "sifted" by the crisis of Jesus' demise (cf. Lk 22:21), Mary also underwent deep suffering. But beyond this the parallelism is less clear. The disciples participate in the night of Gethsemane, but in the Synoptic Gospels Mary is not mentioned in the Passion Narrative. However, we see her under the Cross in John's Gospel, providing evidence of her persevering on Jesus' side until his last hour. This detail is all the more important because the Beloved Disciple also remains at Jesus' side in his final hours, a detail that appears to be contrary to what Matthew and Mark suggest.[41] Moreover, all the four canonical Gospels note that a group of women watched Jesus' execution.[42] Mary's presence at the Cross and her suf-

---

[41] In Matthew and Mark (Mt 26:56; Mk 14:50) "all" the disciples are said to have fled. Luke does not make such a statement. Rather, he emphasizes that Peter followed him from a distance (Lk 22:54); this is mentioned also in Mt 26:58 and Mk 14:45.

[42] There is here an evident apologetic aspect which the Gospels could not have neglected: the women accompanying Jesus saw him die and thereafter visited the empty tomb so that his true death is ascertained by the same eyewitnesses who first discovered the empty tomb.

fering cannot be described as a time of crisis for her faith. Rather, it is a form of "com-passion," a participative sharing in Jesus' Passion by a mother who, in a preeminent way, has no other purpose in her life than that her miraculously conceived only Son may accomplish his mission.[43]

5. Finding Jesus in the Temple (Lk 2:41-52)

As if following up on Simeon's prediction, the last episode of Luke's stories about Jesus' young years includes a detail in which Mary and Joseph jointly undergo sorrow and anxiety. Luke expresses this pain in Mary's own words: "Behold, your father and I have been looking for you anxiously" (2:48).[44] The same Greek word (ὀδυνώμενοι) is used by Luke in Acts when he describes the experience of the Christians of Ephesus saying good-bye to Paul in the harbor of Miletos and anticipating the Apostle's martyrdom: "And they all wept and embraced Paul and kissed, sorrowing (ὀδυνώμενοι) most of all because of the word he had spoken, that they should see his face no more" (20:37-38). As several commentators point out, Luke's story about Jesus found on the third day in the Temple has a paradoxical and pre-figurative meaning.[45] These events, therefore, point to Jesus' death and burial followed by his "being found" on the third day. We have every reason to extend this symbolic trajectory to the conclusion of Luke's Infancy Narratives:

> And his mother said to him, "Son, why have you treated us so? Behold, *your father* and I have been looking for you anxiously." And he said to them, "How is it that you

---

[43] Patristic and medieval tradition developed this theme as an explanation for the biblical text. See especially what we find about this in St. Bernard's Mariology: pp. 188-189.

[44] I do not suggest that Simeon's prediction is completely fulfilled in the episode, but that its fulfillment begins right away in the subsequent passages.

[45] René Laurentin, *Jésus au Temple. Mystère de Pâques et foi de Marie en Luc 2,48-50* (Paris: Gabalda, 1966). But according to J. Fitzmyer, "this is scarcely the foreshadowing of the resurrection." *The Gospel According to Luke I-IX*, Anchor Bible 28 (Garden City, NY: Doubleday, 1981), 441.

sought me? Did you not know that I must be in *my Father's* house?" And they did not understand the saying which he spoke to them. And he went down with them and came to Nazareth, and was obedient to them; and his mother kept all these things in her heart. (Lk 2:48-51)

Some authors think that this "lack of understanding" on the parents' part points to a pre-Lucan tradition which knew nothing of the Virgin Birth.[46] Such commentators assume that Luke (or, in any case, the final redactor) has inadvertently kept this remark in the text, or was not bothered by the inconsistency. For if the parents knew that Jesus was virginally conceived they would have well understood why he calls God his *real* father in opposition to what Mary's words suggest.[47] Other commentators dwell on Mary's "keeping all these things in her heart." This verse certainly echoes Mary's "pondering" the events that surrounded the birth in Bethlehem like the shepherds' visit and their report about the appearance of angels. Here, however, the word "kept" (διετήρει) refers even more explicitly to a function of memory: remembered, retained, and kept in store. Moreover, at this point both an episode (Jesus' self-revelation in the

---

[46] Raymond Brown thinks that "this story or a form of it may have well spread in circles ignorant of the annunciation and of the virginal conception." *The Birth of the Messiah*, 483. One must strongly disagree. That Mary refers to Joseph as "your father" makes sense for two reasons. First, because it is an important reminder of Jesus' Davidic descent, an issue on which each of the four canonical Gospels, including Luke (3:23) insist outside of the Birth Narratives. Second, it re-enforces an awareness of the irony which a double usage of the word "father" provides, by pointing out a double paternity: a divine and real one on the one hand and a perceived but only legal one on the other.

[47] Brown also thinks that "they did not understand *the event*," assuming that the Greek word *rhéma* is a Hebraism, signifying the whole "issue" and not only Jesus' words in reply (ibid., 477). Such suggestions are avoided by more faithful devotees of "redaction criticism," (cf. I.H. Marshall and E.E. Ellis) who realize that according to the rules of this method one must assume that Luke pays attention to his text's implications and avoids inconsistencies. In fact, the Finding in the Temple makes its point by the fact that Jesus surprises both Mary and Joseph by a reference to his own miraculous origins of which only Mary obtained knowledge before Jesus was even conceived. If the Virgin Birth was miraculous at the beginning, is it not equally miraculous that, first, the Child declares that he is aware of his identity and, second, that he goes "home" to Nazareth and lives with his "parents" in perfect obedience?

Temple) and a whole subsection of the book (the Infancy Narratives) come to a close. Therefore, a reference to a person who keeps the "words" (both the events and the sayings) obtains a rather special significance. Since Luke assures us in his Prologue (1:1-4) that his material comes from informed sources and, at the beginning of Acts, he presents Mary by name along with the list of the eleven witnesses to Jesus' ministry, it is in no way an exaggeration to assume that the Lucan author is presenting Mary as the one through whom these stories were "stored" or remembered.[48]

Mary in the Johannine Writings

As we have seen above, the paucity of episodes mentioning Mary cannot be taken to imply the unimportance of her person or role. The scarcity of explicit statements about the three divine persons in one divine nature, does not allow us to conclude that Trinitarian theology is an unimportant issue for the Christian faith. Positively, explicit statements about the divinity of Christ or about the Incarnation are rare and far between, but these teachings are central to the doctrinal content of the Scriptures. But even these issues are cited only for the sake of *some* analogy. Ultimately, the concept of "importance" for a doctrine remains vague and must be researched in some particular sense.

It is, therefore, rather surprising that, without repeating any of the stories which Matthew and Luke provided about Mary, and without even mentioning her name, John's Gospel adds new material, and does so at a location as important as the beginning (Jn 2:1-12) and the end (Jn 19:34-35) of Jesus' public life. But there is also a third reference to Mary, likewise silent about her name, at a place even more important, the Prologue (Jn 1:13), which most probably contains a reference to the Virgin Birth.

---

[48] "As in 2:19 there may be an allusion to the source of the narrative." I. Howard Marshall, *The Gospel of Luke, The New International Greek Testament Commentary* (Grand Rapids: Eerdmans, 1978), 130.

1. The Prologue on the Virgin Birth: John 1:13

John 1:13 carries an oblique reference to the virginal conception, or so it seems. A good number of scholars question this assertion. Yet one thing is agreed upon: a very old textual variant of the Fourth Gospel, which was known at large among Christians in the 2nd century, as testified to by Irenaeus, Tertullian, the *Vetus Latina* and several other patristic sources, carries a clear reference to the virginal conception of Jesus. The issue is mishandled, if the discussion shifts too quickly from the textual to the doctrinal side of the argument. Nor must we deal with it from a narrowly apologetic point of view. To Christians of the early 2nd century the doctrine of the virginal conception was widely known. At the same time, in the Fourth Gospel *allusions* or doctrinal hints are often used to make the reader discover in the text what he already knows from oral tradition or other sources.[49] There is also little doubt that a number of Church Fathers read the text of John 1:13 in the singular, i.e., as referring to the incarnate Son who *was* born "not from blood, nor of the will of the flesh, nor of the will of a man, but of God." The question, legitimately raised as an issue of textual criticism, is only this: How did this variant reading come about and spread around so early that it was known in both East and West in the 2nd century, and yet subsequently disappeared from circulation so rapidly that no extant Greek manuscript of the Fourth Gospel contains it? The variant is in the singular and clearly designates the mode in which the Word was made flesh:

> He [the Logos], who was born, not from blood, nor of the will of the flesh, nor of the will of a man, but of God...

It is quite unlikely that the anti-Gnostic milieu to which Irenaeus belonged could have fabricated it in place of what critical editions (and also all forms of the *textus receptus*) have in the plural:

---

[49] Cf. R. Alan Culpepper, *Anatomy of the Fourth Gospel. A Study in Literary Design* (Philadelphia: Fortress, 1983), 165-169. Irony is particularly frequent when the author is dealing with Jesus' origins (ibid., 171-172).

those [the believers], who were born, not from blood, nor
of the will of the flesh, nor of the will of a man, but of God.

The strongest argument comes from Tertullian, who accuses
the Valentinian Gnostics of having falsified John 1:13 by transpos-
ing what was originally in the singular into plural.[50] A rather powerful proof is found also in 1 John 5:18, a verse in a Johannine writing
in which the idea that we are born of God is inseparably linked to
Jesus' birth of God: "We know that *any one born of God* does not
sin, but *He who was born of God* keeps him, and the evil one does
not touch him."

This quotation from 1 John, which is virtually a comparison
of the two textual variants, sheds light on the meaning of that triple
negation in John 1:13, "not of blood, nor of the will of the flesh, nor of
the will of man." Properly these negations can refer only to Jesus, the
One born from God, the Logos. But in a metaphoric sense it may be
extended to refer also to all Christians as *mirroring in their spiritual
rebirth the virginal conception* of the Logos by Mary. In any case – directly or indirectly – John 1:13 echoes the early Church's faith in the
conception of Jesus by the Virgin. This is, ultimately, not surprising. Even by a most pessimistic estimate John's Gospel was written
around A.D. 100, i.e., at least a couple of decades after Matthew and
Luke and almost as late as the letters of Ignatius of Antioch, who is
quite explicit about the virginal conception.[51]

---

[50] *De carne Christi* 19:1-2 (CCL 2,997). Tertullian provides us with the Valentinian
interpretation: in their understanding that the text refers to a mystical race of spiritual elite (*semen arcanum electorum et spiritualium*) to which they also belong.
Today, most Johannine scholars think that Tertullian was wrong; they argue that
the change of the text took place in the opposite direction, i.e., the plural reading
was replaced by the one in the singular in support of a Christology with a docetic
tinge, by suggesting that, on account of his virginal conception, Jesus' humanity
was of a more spiritual nature. But this method of reconstructing what happened
is hard to accept. It would be strange that Tertullian and Irenaeus would have
fallen into the Gnostic trap by not noticing the alleged docetic "tinge" of the text
in the singular.

[51] One must note that Ignatius' *Letter to the Smyrneans* opens with a phrase resem-
bling Jn 1:13 and often noted as an indicator that Ignatius knew the Fourth Gospel: υἱὸν θεοῦ κατὰ θέλημα καὶ δύναμιν θεοῦ γεγεννημένον ἀληθῶς ἐκ παρθένου.
"Son of God according to God's will and power, actually born of a virgin." The

The singular reading of John 1:13 has its own importance and implications. It inserts the virginal conception fully into the context of Johannine theology. It is quite interesting to see how, for Karl Rahner, the variant of John 1:13 in the singular, together with 1 John 5:18, presents three filiations – the Son's eternal birth from the Father, the Son's birth from the Virgin in time, and that of the Believer at his re-birth by the Spirit – and combines them as extensions of the eternal birth of the Logos. For Rahner this perspective greatly enhances not only the intelligibility of the Johannine Gospel, but also that of the Virgin Birth. He writes:

> The world and its conditions and claim of intrinsic potentialities offer from below no compelling reason why the eternal God himself should descend into history. Since, therefore, in this sense, the Son of God *did not come of the will of man or the will of the flesh*, from the world's forces and energies, he correspondingly willed to become man in such a way that it would be clear from the very manner of his coming that his origin is not of the earth, from the inner forces of human love, but wholly from on high.[52]

Karl Rahner might be right in seeing in John 1:13, understood in the singular and combined with 1 John 5:18, a quasi-technical language about the transcendental character of Jesus' conception, and in linking it to the core of the Fourth Gospel's Logos theology.

2. Mary at Cana and at the Cross: John 2:1-10 and 19:26-27

The story about the Wedding Feast in Cana is one of the few episodes in John which offers in length and structure something quite similar to the pericopes of the Synoptics. Like in the Synoptics,

---

expression "according to God's will and power" is applied here to Jesus' mode of conception as if stating positively the opposite of what Jn 1:13 denies: "not from the will of man."

[52] *Mary Mother of the Lord* (New York: Herder, 1963), 68. I have added the emphasis. It is quite interesting that Rahner quotes Jn 1:13 according to its patristic variant without even noting the main-stream scriptural or patristic references.

the episode begins with a reference to the narrative flow of the Gospel by some casual every-day event (a wedding) linked to a geographic location (Cana in Galilee). But in a surprising way, it is Mary who is mentioned first: she comes to the wedding and that is how the reader is to understand that Jesus has also shown up with his disciples (Jn 2:1-2). Then, in a typical way, the story continues with a crisis in which Jesus' help is sought. The crisis is resolved by Jesus' prophetic and miraculous intervention, which leads him to a pronouncement that sheds light on the nature of his mission and person.

That Mary appears to be present at the wedding independently of Jesus is unparalleled and quite peculiar.[53] The episode opens in a way no Gospel story ever does: at the beginning Jesus is not in the center. Consistent with this feature is the fact that the "crisis" – the lack of wine – is noticed by Mary and it is by her initiative that it is brought to Jesus' attention. But this in itself is not unique. It is similar to what happens at the miraculous feeding of the multitudes: not Jesus, but the disciples notice the crisis (cf. Jn 6:5; Mt 14:15; Lk 10:12). At other occasions, however, it is Jesus who begins speaking about the need for feeding the crowd (Mt 15:32; Mk 3:30; 8:2).

As is typical for John, the rest of the story turns into a dialogue, a feature that has no Synoptic parallel. The assessment of Mary's role and the interpretation of Jesus' words to her have been a matter of intense debate for a long time. A final judgment on the various interpretations depends on the presuppositions with which we approach the text. Most commentators agree, however, that in the Fourth Gospel no episode can be satisfactorily explained in isolation from the work as a whole. Mary's remark, "They have no wine," is not merely a subtle request to help a household in trouble, but an assessment of the status of that *messianic* wedding banquet which Jesus came into the world to celebrate. This is the real "wedding banquet" about which the Evangelist is concerned, as made quite clear in the next

---

[53] Popular preaching regularly tells that Jesus was invited to a wedding and he took along his mother. But the scriptural text says: "On the third day there was a wedding at Cana in Galilee. The mother of Jesus was there, and Jesus and his disciples had also been invited" (Jn 2:1-2).

chapter by John the Baptist's speaking of Jesus as the bridegroom.[54] Therefore, Jesus' reply to Mary must be taken according to the rules of "Johannine irony." Irony shifts a statement about an apparently mundane issue into a symbol of some deeper truth.[55] It turns around the meaning of Mary's report about lack of wine by calling attention to "Jesus' hour" which has not yet come, but is obviously the goal of his ministry. As the theme of his "hour" unfolds in the Gospel, we learn that it means the hour of his self-immolation on the Cross where from his crucified body flow forth "water and blood" and also his Spirit, containing all the gifts of the messianic age, first diffused with his last breath on the Cross and then with his breathing on the disciples at their first encounter after the Resurrection. The arrival of the Spirit should be understood as God's full arrival on earth through Jesus. In this full picture, Mary's role is both historical and symbolic. As a witness, a believer, and a participant, she beholds the torture and death of the Son she bore, but in her association with the Son she symbolizes the Church as the new Eve, the mother of "all the living" in a new order of creation, a new out-pouring of the Spirit of life in the water and blood of the pouring from his body, sacrificed on the Cross.

Most exegetes see some value in the fact that, in his last hour, Jesus entrusts Mary to the Beloved Disciple as an act of filial care, making provisions for her sustenance and support. Yet because of the special characteristics of the Fourth Gospel and the way it reports this story, we must open our ears to hear the connotations which these provisions signify.

Although in the Fourth Gospel Jesus' mother is not called by her proper name, she is obviously a real person, not only a symbol

---

[54] "The one who has the bride is the bridegroom; the best man, who stands and listens for him, rejoices greatly at the bridegroom's voice. So this joy of mine has been made complete" (Jn 3:29).

[55] According to Culpepper, irony and symbolism are closely linked. Misunderstanding, double-entendre, several "levels of meaning" invite the reader to explore hints, implications and suggestions in the text and thus to discover depths beyond the immediate meaning of the words. Cf. R. Alan Culpepper, *Anatomy of the Fourth Gospel. A Study in Literary Design* (Philadelphia: Fortress, 1983), 180-198 with application to Jn 3:29 on p. 193.

for believers. So is also the "Beloved Disciple," although he too goes unnamed. There is, therefore, little doubt that a real person was assigned the task to take Mary under his care and lead her into his home. The identity of the one who became the caretaker of Jesus' mother after the crucifixion would have been public knowledge in the early Church, and a fact important enough to be remembered. With no competing tradition whatsoever about the identity of this person, there can be no reasonable doubt that the Beloved Disciple doing this task was John, the younger son of Zebedee and one of the Twelve.

As early as the 2nd century, the Church Fathers began to comment about Mary's role in this context and the way it is surrounded with symbolism. The Beloved Disciple was also seen as "becoming a son," assimilated to Jesus under the Cross. This means that when John's symbolic sonship is declared by Jesus, a "messianic birth" takes place, fulfilling what Jesus had stated in advance: "When a woman is in travail she has sorrow, because her hour has come; but when she is delivered of the child, she no longer remembers the anguish, for joy that a man[56] has been born into the world" (Jn 16:21).

No doubt the focus is Christological; the central issue is Jesus' death and not his birth. But also a birth is mentioned here, but another birth, a new birth coming about through death, and this would be of no purpose unless, through Jesus' death, all those symbolized by the Beloved Disciple have also been "born" anew. After all, from the third chapter of the Gospel we have been waiting for the fulfillment of Jesus' words about the new birth of the disciples: "Amen, amen, I say to you, no one can enter the kingdom of God without being born of water and Spirit. What is born of flesh is flesh and what is born of spirit is spirit. Do not be amazed that I told you, 'You must be born from above'" (Jn 3:5-7). Under the Cross, then, the disciples' new status is declared. For them, becoming Mary's son

---

[56] The translations have "child" but the Greek text has the word ἄνθρωπος meaning simply "human being." We must be aware of this exact meaning of the word for seeing its link to "Adam," the first man God created. Translating "child" obscures the reference to the Book of Genesis.

means stepping into Jesus' place in the world with not only a new set of chores and responsibilities, but also with a renewed existence. Indeed, there is symmetry between the two sentences of the Gospel: *"He said to his mother,* 'Woman, behold, your *son!'* Then *he said to the disciple,* 'Behold, your *mother!'"* (Jn 19:26-27). This is best understood by seeing Mary's new motherhood as correlative to John's new sonship.

The link that connects Cana with Golgotha is essential for understanding Mary's role in the Fourth Gospel. One of the most important indications of this link is the usage of the word "woman." An exegesis unfriendly or suspicious to symbolism would eagerly point out that Jesus calls "woman" not only his mother, but also the Samaritan woman (Jn 4:21) and Mary Magdalene (Jn 20:13 and 15), and then, on that basis, question any symbolic meaning attached to the word. But the symbolism at hand is not merely philological. "Woman" in John 2:4 and the same word in 16:21 are linked by a "woman and her hour," an hour of anguish at giving birth. Similarly, the word "woman" under the Cross refers to an incipient filial relationship: a birth. This is why we can only approve and admire the early Church Fathers (starting with Justin Martyr),[57] who expanded on this link by pointing out the connection between Mary and Eve, a theme which we will discuss in further detail when we explore patristic Mariology.[58]

Mary in the Book of Revelation: Revelation 12:1-7

The Johannine use of the word "woman" for the mother of the Messiah finds new expression in the Book of Revelation. The birth that this text speaks of is not the birth of Bethlehem, but again the

---

[57] See below, on pp. 66-69.

[58] If we see the symbolism behind the use of the word "woman" by Jesus as he addresses his mother in Jn 2:4 and 19:26, we will not find such language scandalous in the mouth of a son when speaking to his mother. Strange as it may culturally be for people of our age, the word "woman" is used by all evangelists in reference to the female personalities of their stories. In Mt 15:26 ("O woman, great is your faith!") the use of this word goes together with the highest recognition.

"messianic birth": a symbol of pain and anguish turning into joy, as described in John 16:21 (with reference to Isaiah 66:7-8) and ultimately referring back to Genesis 3:16. In Revelation 12 this image becomes much more ample: the childbearing of the Woman means in temporal terms the whole history of the Church. As the Child is separated from his mother and reaches God's glory, the Woman remains in Exile (the Desert) for a time period established by God. The physical and individual mother of Jesus is not directly signified here as a historical person, yet Jesus' mother as a historical person is clearly presupposed. The text focuses on a figurative and collective meaning of the "mother" struggling and suffering while undergoing persecution on earth when her Child is already in heaven's glory, at God's right hand, ruling with an iron rod (cf. Rv 12:5; cf. Ps 2:9). The meaning of this collage of imagery cannot be deciphered unless we retain the symbolism suggested in the Fourth Gospel: Mary bore the Son who has suffered and obtained his glory, and the disciples personified by John are also her sons: their sonship comes about amidst pain and travail. The messianic birth with all its pain is bound to continue in the world. Just like in Cana, where a spiritual wedding feast is signified (by anticipation), so also here Mary's figure overlaps (by extension) with that of the Church. While her first Son reigns from heaven, she remains on earth personified by "the rest of the offspring" who continue to fight the battle against the Dragon. They are those "who keep the commandments and bear witness to Jesus" (Rv 12:17).

In these scriptural verses, Mary is only obliquely implied. What is rather interesting is the way the Messiah is spoken of as the Son of a "cosmic personality," whose individual characteristics are completely veiled by the imagery of the sun, the moon, and the stars. The appearance of precisely twelve stars is noteworthy, since the number elsewhere in this book symbolizes "the twelve Apostles of the Lamb" (21:17). While one finds no direct reference to Mary, the mother who gave birth to Jesus on earth, the symbolic ties with the Church are quite explicit. In this sense, the Book of Revelation draws a clear image of the Church as a cosmic reality encompassing all human existence, but principally by referring to the Church's life-giving and child-bearing function. The Marian meaning of this passage is only indirect. Directly it seems to link the Church more to Eve (the story of the beginnings of the cosmos) as the mother of all human beings, whose battle began in the Garden of Eden and came to a close only with the victory of Mary's Child.

OLD TESTAMENT

Introductory Remarks

Studies about Mary in the Bible deal with this topic in a variety of ways. Those who consider the historical-critical method the one and only ultimately valid method, defining and verifying (or rejecting) all other methods, may find in the Old Testament very few or no texts applicable to Mary, except possibly by analogy, extrapolation, or symbolism, all constituting some sort of *eisegesis*.[59] Accordingly a Marian meaning would not be considered as properly contained in any Old Testament text, but imported from some other scriptural sources, either from the New Testament or from outside of the

---

[59] The "task force" which sponsored *Mary in the New Testament*, Raymond E. Brown, Karl P. Donfried, Joseph A. Fitzmyer, and John Reumann, eds., list four ways of dealing with Mary in the Old Testament. The first three are these: looking for texts which "foreshadow the details of the career of Jesus," or texts of which a "fuller sense" is revealed in the New Testament, or, finally, reproducing the New Testament writer's interpretation of Old Testament texts without worrying if they were valid in the first place. All of these methods are rejected as either "difficult to decide" to be legitimate or just imaginative to the point of becoming *eisegesis* (p. 30). Finally a fourth method, the "canonical reading" of the Scriptures is mentioned, but is also rejected because it is quite difficult to decide whether or not, for example, the Mary/Eve parallel was "in the mind of the Fourth Evangelist" or of the author of the Apocalypse (p. 31). We finally catch here the ultimate problem that separates the historical-critical exegete from other users of the Bible. The historical-critical exegete attempts to reconstruct what the original author "had in mind." Those, however, who assume the unity of the two Testaments assume that the two sets of books belong to one salvation plan and that its unity is not rooted in the mind of any particular human author. If we follow the mind of the Church, we search for what God had in mind to reveal to us for the sake of our salvation through the Scriptures and not assume that the human author's conscious inspection and approval was a necessary condition for any revealed truth to make its way into the Scriptures.

Bible altogether. In fact, the historical-critical approach usually assumes that the meaning of a text must reflect knowledge available
for its author at the time he or she is writing. Thus, unless receiving supernatural knowledge of prophecy in the narrow sense of the
word (prediction of future events), the hagiographer can report only
events and persons belonging to his past or his present but not to
the future. Therefore, the Scriptures written before Mary cannot tell
us anything about her unless by anticipating future events through
divinely obtained knowledge. The historical-critical exegete would
be surprised to learn that he stands in agreement with all the Church
Fathers and the medieval tradition! For, according to a traditional
teaching of dogmatic theology, the Incarnation remained a mystery
(*mysterium stricte dictum*) until it was revealed by Jesus. This implies
that the fact and the significance of Mary's divine motherhood also
had to remain a secret until Jesus' divine sonship was revealed. Thus
only New Testament authors, such as Luke and John, could be regarded as true "biblical sources" for Marian doctrine.

Yet is it still true that all divine revelation, including that of
the *mysteria stricte dicta*, takes place in a temporal process and is
only gradually inserted into history? In view of the Dogmatic Constitution *Dei Verbum* and the tradition it represents, the answer must
be an emphatic yes. Thus it is not only a justifiable but also necessary task for the Christian study of the Old Testament to see how it
prepared and even anticipated the Marian mystery, something that
Christian tradition could not have realized in any other way than by
its retrospective view of the Old Testament. So, as it is with many
other biblical topics, the Old Testament – its history, faith and institutions, including the Scriptures – must be examined also in terms of
presuppositions and preparatory ways (the "foreshadowings"[60]) to-

---

[60] In this matter a full misunderstanding of the Church's tradition is expressed by the
quoted task force as they state in their report: "A theory of foreshadowing of the
NT in the OT reflects, at times, a naïve or precritical understanding of prophecy,
as if the Israelite prophets foresaw in detail the career of Jesus. Most modern
scholars would maintain that the OT prophets dealt with their own time and the
immediate future, not with far distant Christian history" (op. cit., 30). Whether
or not we like the term "foreshadowing," it cannot mean "foreseeing in detail"
and the "career" of Jesus is also an inappropriate term. "Foreshadowing" must

ward the Marian mysteries. Such inquiry not only provides us with an enriched understanding of the explicit texts of the New Testament texts but introduces us to the early Church's tradition about Mary.

The Word Incarnate, and therefore all that concerns his coming in the flesh, was anticipated not only through figures and images functioning as mute antecedents, waiting passively for the moment of the Incarnation, but prophetic events and persons, constituting, for both contemporary witnesses and later generations who reflected upon their testimony, expressions of the experiences of faith which effectively formed God's people in an extended process from Abraham through Moses, the prophets, the scribes and leaders of the exiled people, and the whole People of God awaiting messianic salvation. They were expressed in words through narratives and poetry and as such were verbal forerunners of the Word, preparing the People of God (first Israel and later the Church) for the *fullness of their meaning* in and after the event of the Incarnation.

The most important of these forerunners are the very themes from which the evangelists (Matthew, Luke and John) drew to describe Mary's historical person and her role in the history of our salvation. These appear in both the biblical texts and the earliest tradition of the Church Fathers in a triangular pattern. The three vertices that such scriptural themes, images, and allusions incessantly connect, compare, and combine are the following:

> Mary's virginal motherhood,
> the Church as mother and virgin, and
> the individual believers who participate in this mystery
> reflected and mirrored between Mary and the Church.

Inscribing the Marian mystery within these three themes, both the Gospels and the Church Fathers form concepts and a language

---

mean "foretelling" in some form of communication, not something "in detail" but in some basic and essential way and *without lifting the veil of mystery*. We are dealing here with an epistemological concept that a rationalist understanding of "knowledge in advance" is not capable of conceiving.

for speaking about the female protagonists of salvation history as maternal figures in the chain of the transmission of life (both physical *and* spiritual: Eve, Sarah, Ruth, etc.), and female personifications of God's self-expression (like Wisdom) or of the redeemed collectivity (like Israel, Zion, Jerusalem, the Church). In the context of salvation history each of these figures – on the historical, literary, or symbolic level – refers also to Mary as recipient and transmitter, protagonist and exemplar, believer and leader, as both Mother of the Messiah and Daughter (of) Zion.

The New Eve

Mary appears in the figure of the "new Eve" explicitly only in the 2nd century. We lack documentation about how exactly the comparison of Mary to Eve emerged in the theological world of Justin Martyr (d. 160), but it is hardly thinkable that it was a complete novelty he invented. Reflections on the story of Adam *and Eve* in Genesis 3, comparing and contrasting the new creation brought about by Christ with the first sin of "the Man" (Adam), recur three times in surely authentic Pauline texts[61] and once in the Pastorals.[62] There is also one passage in 2 Corinthians, where Eve is mentioned alone:

> I feel a divine jealousy for you, for I betrothed you to Christ to present you as a pure bride to her one husband. But I am afraid that as the serpent deceived Eve by his cunning, your thoughts will be led astray from a sincere and pure devotion to Christ. (2 Cor 11:2-3)

Although St. Paul makes no reference to Mary, it is in this text that we find quite clearly the triangular interconnection mentioned above, from which ancient Christian literature formed its analogous triangular outline of "Mary/Church/the redeemed individual," a

---

[61] Rm 2:4; 1 Cor 15:22, 45.
[62] 1 Tm 2:13-14, in this place alone are both Adam and Eve mentioned.

theme which deeply inspired the Church Fathers. The Apostle depicts Eve as a virgin for whose seduction Satan disguises himself as "Lucifer," an angel of light. The "virgin" signifies both the first woman and the Church of the Corinthians; the cunning serpent is both Satan and the "pseudo-apostles" posing as heralds of the true Gospel (2 Cor 11:4). The first woman is still in her virginal state just as the Corinthians' faith has not yet been perverted. Paul may refer in this text to an interpretation of Genesis 3 viewing man's first sin with sexual connotations, but that is of secondary interest. In the center of the metaphor we see the virgin-church to be dissuaded from her virginal commitment to Christ, the Bridegroom, by a tempter who claims to excel in eloquence and knowledge over Paul, the authentic messenger. This scene is really some sort of a "counter-annunciation" text, narrating the arrival of a false angel (false apostle) as opposed to Paul, the true apostle who has tried to lead the virgin to her true nuptials with Christ.

In other texts Paul also mentions, if only cursorily, his awareness of the Church's (and even *his* own) maternal function (especially Gal 4:19, but also Gal 4:26; Eph 5:31), as well as the role of Satan as a supernatural seducer or an angel acting in the person of the pseudo-apostles (Gal 1:8). However, it was the Church Fathers' task to integrate it into an antithetic parallelism between the images of the Virginal Spouse and of the childbearing Mother on two levels: (1) that of the historical mother of Jesus and (2) of his super-temporal mother, the Church. They developed this theme with growing attention to the role of Mary as virginal Mother, a concrete symbol of the Church, and a perfect model of the redeemed human being.

We must realize that Christ, called the "new Adam," does not mean only an external and superficial similarity based on the idea of "re-starting" mankind's existence as if from scratch with a new start like it happened in the case of the flood and Noah. In Noah's case man is rescued but history re-starts on an already vitiated basis. Noah's covenant does not signal redemption, only a mysterious tolerance to which God commits himself out of patience and for the sake of an alternative plan which he then keeps hidden for a long time:

> I will never again curse the ground because of man, for
> the imagination of man's heart is evil from his youth;
> neither will I ever again destroy every living creature as I
> have done. (Gn 8:21)

Through Christ, all humanity is regenerated and also recapitulated, i.e., in Christ all mankind is redeemed *with retroactive efficiency*. In this case one can truly speak of a new creation that includes radical novelty. At the same time, however, this new beginning was part of God's original plan designed for his first creation, which is being restored and redeemed: Jesus is born as a child of Adam (cf. Lk 3:38), not only of Abraham and David (Mt 1:1); as he becomes a man "born of a woman" (Gal 4:4) he is a son of Eve, not only the son of Mary. He is a human being who shared the nature of the first couple, Adam and Eve. Christ's birth, life, and passion redeemed and sanctified not only those who lived after him and eventually accepted the Gospel with faith, formally and consciously, but all human beings who, however they were saved, have encountered and accepted God's universal salvific will. In the Incarnation the walls of temporal separation collapse, for, through his divine nature, Christ brought his humanity within reach to all human beings. Jesus Christ is the only-begotten Son, and his unique Incarnation is the universal source of salvation for all people of all times.

As Christ is the first individual of a re-born human race, in Mary, the Mother of Christ, Eve's role is fulfilled: the one who bore Jesus is the "mother of all living." Mary obtains this role through a double linkage. As the mother of Jesus, she receives the Incarnate Word into the family of the first Adam and thus into the whole human race. But since of all human beings she is Jesus' only parent, she also links him all by herself to the whole human race, to both those who temporally preceded his coming and those who were to be born after him. Not only was she the only immediate human ancestor of Jesus but she was also the first to believe in him as the "Son of the Most High" (Lk 1:32). Jesus is linked to the whole human race through her both physically and spiritually since she was also the exemplar of all who were redeemed by her Son for she was the first to hear and accept the Good News announced to her by an Angel. On the one hand, Mary as a human being was born from Eve; on the other hand, in the order of salvation, the whole human race was reborn from Mary's womb.

In this perspective, the Mary/Eve parallelism is neither forced nor off-beat. It is nothing more than an extension of an apostolic exegesis of the Scriptures, reaching back to the first pages of Genesis. Its theological content vindicates the universality of Christ's redemptive work and thus, by the same logic, asserts the universality of Mary's motherhood. All this becomes clear if we realize that the early Church's parallelism between Mary and Eve stands in continuity not only to the Eve/Church parallelism of 2 Corinthians 11:3 but also to the threefold parallelism found in the Book of Revelation (12:1-6). There also, like in Paul, it is the Church and not Mary who suffers before becoming exalted. Yet she is not a purely abstract symbol, but concretely refers to the mother of Jesus who is called "Woman" in the Johannine Gospel (Jn 2:4; 19:26).

The magnificent medieval antiphon,[63] the *Salve Regina*, enshrined this component of Marian tradition, when depicting mankind as "the exiled children of Eve" crying out to Mary for a share in the fruit of her womb. Eve and "the fruit," are references to the first Eden, but the "blessed fruit" of Mary's womb makes reference to the Visitation and also, at least from the 2nd century, to the Annunciation. Countless medieval paintings and sculptures represent Mary, as she holds Jesus *together with a fruit*, emphasizing another aspect of the "antithetical parallelism" that connects Mary and Eve: the fruit forbidden by God but offered by Satan and the blessed fruit of life offered by God in replacement for the first fruit. "The fruit" of Mary's womb is not to be understood as a demonstration or advertisement, but as an act of persuasive enticing and inviting, a call

---

[63] It is again by no oversight that the ultimate perspective of the scriptural text is exposed in reference to its patristic/medieval expansion that helps it reverberate in our faith and spiritual life.

for Adam's posterity to participate in the fruit of the Tree of Life, the remedy of immortality.

Israel: the Lord's Spouse

Beginning with Hosea, the prophetic literature compares Israel's relationship with God to the spousal relationship. The serious weight of this metaphor cannot be grasped within the confines of a merely critical and historically minimalist interpretation. In the prophet's perspective, Israel's God is fully non-physical. Moreover "Israel" means in a canonical context the collectivity of God's people in its trans-historical existence, a chain of generations created from the bodies of Abraham and Sarah over a period of centuries. God's project was falling apart. Yet, as Israel's history passes from the divided monarchy to complete dissolution, there appears new hope, such that a reversal of Israel's fate appears on the horizon: from exile to return and from return to reconstruction. Throughout these two consecutive phases the imagery of Israel's spousal relations to God, rather than losing meaning, becomes ever richer, gaining new substance and importance.

Hosea's passionate presentation of a human drama – seemingly his own – with a hopelessly faithless wife, goes way beyond either a parable or an autobiography, carrying a theological message. Regardless of whether we stick to the historicity of the prophet's experience with Gomer, the whore he married, or we prefer to regard the story as fiction, the text's ultimate impact resides in its connection to the "love story" God narrates to Israel, "the real story" that has truly happened between himself and his faithless people.

This ultimate truth is not about the prophet's bitter-sweet personal tragedy or the tormenting experience of an all-too-human prophet in the throes of jealousy or the humiliations he undergoes in the service of God's word, but the shockingly anthropomorphic inner life of God. It tells about God's "man-like sentiments," which testify to the hopeless distance separating "God from his people" as lovers with irreconcilable differences. While the wife (Israel) cannot give up on her amorous exploits, the prophet (the divine Spouse) re-affirms, on some unspeakable, unfathomable, and yes, irrationally mysterious basis, a love by which, he insists, they belong together and so he makes repeated attempts to restore the covenant between himself (God) and the unfaithful woman (Israel).

This "irrational" dimension stands out already in Hosea and is carried on by the prophetic tradition. The parallelism between idol-atry and harlotry remains as a constant reference to the linkage of their opposites: purity of the monotheistic faith and faithfulness to the Covenant. In the prophet's message the passion with which he, a mere man, lures back to himself his ex-harlot wife, falling back time and again into harlotry, becomes a revelatory tool for teaching about God's undying and inexhaustible mercy for his people.

Regarding the topic Hosea/Gomer, a long and complicated his-torical and literary tradition developed, forming multiple streams of texts from Isaiah to Jeremiah and beyond the exile. For our purpose, it should be enough to quote here a few weighty texts demonstrating how, in prophetic preaching, the spousal imagery is displayed and developed for depicting God's renewed relationships to Israel:

> And I will betroth you to me forever; I will betroth you to me in righteousness and in justice, in steadfast love, and in mercy. I will betroth you to me in faithfulness; and you shall know the LORD. (Ho 2:19-20)

> I have loved you with an everlasting love; therefore I have continued my faithfulness to you. (Jr 31:5)

> For as a young man marries a virgin, so shall your Builder marry you; and as the bridegroom rejoices over the bride, so shall your God rejoice over you. (Is 62:5)

> Sing aloud, O daughter of Zion; shout, O Israel! Rejoice and exult with all your heart, O daughter of Jerusalem! The Lord has taken away the judgments against you, he has cast out your enemies. The King of Israel, the Lord, is in your midst; you shall fear evil no more. (Zp 3:14-15)

It is important that we take time to notice here how the themes of the Old Testament we have named above are linked to the central Mariological texts of the New Testament. In the fullness of time, when the Son of God chose to be "born of a woman" (Gal 4:4), it was against such a background that the Mother of the Messiah was portrayed both in the Annunciation and in the Visitation. Since the publication of an article by Stanislas Lyonnet in 1939,[64] many exegetes have called attention to the Old Testament background of Gabriel's greeting (Lk 1:28). Interestingly, in the case of this Lucan verse, it seemed that it was the text of the Vulgate, translating the Greek χαῖρε by the Latin *ave* that kept on prevailing and obscured the original meaning of Gabriel's greeting. In Hellenistic Greek the word χαῖρε was used idiomatically as a casual "hello," but, of course, it also signified literally the second person singular imperative of the verb meaning "to rejoice." Accordingly, in the Latin text *ave* and the next two words *gratia plena* (translating Χαῖρε, κεχαριτωμένη) began to function as a mixture of a so-called minimalist translation (*"ave"* = "hello") and maximalist interpretation (*"gratia plena"* = "full of grace") of the angelic salutation, each part stretching the text's meaning in opposite directions.

Still today, exegetes of various backgrounds opt either for emphasizing or reducing the literal meaning "rejoice" and rejecting or accepting the Latin *ave* (or the English "hail"). Some point out the many biblical allusions that characterize the first two chapters of Luke, among them χαῖρε as it is found in the LXX, signaling the joyful arrival of redemption to the Virgin Daughter, a figurative image of Zion or Israel (Zp 3:14; Zc 9:9). But other commentators, shying away from a "Mariological" meaning, prefer to follow the judgment of the Latin translators and to see in Gabriel's words a more casual

---

[64] Χαῖρε, κεχαριτωμένη in *Biblica* 20 (1939), 131-141. Since then many Catholic exegetes followed Lyonnet, most decidedly R. Laurentin in his *Luc I-II* (Paris: Gabalda, 1957), 64; McHugh and de la Potterie. Interestingly, the minimalistic translation of χαῖρε by the Latin *ave*, as a Hellenistic salutation with no further depth, is followed by Luke Timothy Johnson ("Greeting!" in English) in his commentary, *The Gospel of Luke, Sacra Pagina* (Collegeville: Liturgical Press, 1991), 37-39, and F. Bovon, *Luke 1, Hermeneia* (Minneapolis: Fortress, 2000), 43-44. Neither of these two authors would elsewhere ever vindicate the Vulgate's text.

(and shallow) greeting, steering clear from the assumption of some need for correspondence with an "original" text in Hebrew. These exegetes even more forcefully reject the translation of κεχαριτωμένη as *gratia plena*. But not so fast! On the one hand, the *ave* of the Vulgate is idiomatic, departing unnecessarily from the literal meaning. It also lacks awareness of the Old Testament background mentioned above, as well as of the fact that, in the Bible, the first word of a heavenly appearance is hardly ever a "casual greeting."[65] Since Luke 1-2 is full of "septuagintal" references to the Old Testament, there is little reason not to follow this lead and restore the Hellenistic literal meaning "rejoice" which also the occurrence of the word χαῖρε signifies in other important messianic texts.

On the other hand, the *gratia plena* ("full of grace") must not be quickly rejected as a Mariological exaggeration. The history of the Latin text of the angelic salutation, which goes back to the 2nd century, is quite rich in theological considerations and must be handled with special care. The Vulgate's solution was the outcome of a linguistic problem. The Latin verb corresponding to κεχαριτωμένη would be *gratiari*, but it is a deponent verb, passive in form but active in meaning, so that it offers no precisely corresponding participle for a literal translation: the form *gratiata* means "gracious" not "recipient of grace." The translator of the Vulgate had no choice but to use several words, of which one had to be *gratia*. The expression *gratia plena* signifies literally a feminine subject who is declared to be the recipient of (divine) grace. Since the grace in question is that of the Incarnation, the Latin expression *gratia plena* (equivalent to the English "full of grace") proved itself not only as "acceptable" but as the correct choice for translation and became quickly rooted in usage. Every *interpretation* of this choice of words is a matter of exegesis and theology and cannot be debated on purely grammatical grounds as a correct or an incorrect rendition. The Mariology

---

[65] The risen Christ appearing to the Apostles says ειρηνη, "peace" or *shalom*, but the greeting is "loaded" with theology and cannot be translated as "Greeting!" (cf. Lk 24:36; Jn 20:19, 21, 26). See also Jg 6:12, where Gideon is greeted by the angel with words to which Lk 1:27 harks back: "The Lord is with you."

connected to *gratia plena* or "full of grace" must be evaluated on theological grounds and not by exegetical criteria.[66] As "text" it allows many possible translations. No translation is ever perfect, because two idioms can hardly ever be mapped onto each other point by point and matched one-to-one.

We can, however, justify an exegesis of the Annunciation according to which the Angel's greeting is not an idle reproduction of a formula in koine Greek, but makes a retrospective hint to certain Old Testament texts and anticipates the message which the Angel is about to deliver. The various exegetes who discussed the meaning of Luke 1:28 should have taken more seriously the direction that Luke himself gives his reader in the verse that follows. For it seems that in Luke 1:29 ("But she was greatly troubled at what was said and pondered what sort of greeting this might be"), we, the readers, are also urged to join Mary in pondering the Angel's words and to assess correctly with what kind of expectation we ought to receive the rest of his message. Ultimately, this is the strongest point, a device built into the text itself that justifies the search and discovery of a deeper meaning. Mary is approached by the angelic messenger according to the prophetic promises as we have them in Zephaniah 3:14, Zechariah 9:9, and Lamentations 4:21, all addressing the Daughter of Zion.

"Behold the Virgin..."

The quotation of Isaiah 7:14 is explicit in Matthew 1:23, but is only implicit in Luke 1:31. Since the 2nd century, Jewish exegetes accused Christians of misinterpreting Isaiah 7:14 when applying it to Jesus. This question has been controversial ever since. It is clear that Matthew (and all Christian sources) quote the Septuagint's (LXX) text in which we find:

---

[66] The New American Bible's "highly favored daughter" was a failed attempt to replace "full of grace" by introducing the word "daughter" and eliminating the Christian concept of grace by replacing it by "favor" with its secular flavor. This choice does reflect earlier English translations, like the King James and Revised Standard Versions, but the fact that it utterly lacks any Mariological, even Christian, resonance is a major problem.

Therefore the Lord himself shall give you a sign; behold,
a *virgin* shall conceive in the womb, and shall bring forth
a son, and thou shalt call his name Emmanuel.

Of course, the LXX represents an understanding of the text by the
Jews of Alexandria in the 2nd century before Christ. Both the Jewish
rabbis of antiquity and modern translators point out that the Hebrew text uses *'almah* meaning a "young girl," not necessarily a virgin. They also opine that this girl originally, that is in Isaiah's mind,
meant King Ahaz' new wife and, therefore, predicted the birth of the
crown prince, Hezekiah, and not the Messiah. So the problem is easily resolved. Most messianic texts refer first to an event in the course
of Jewish history (the paschal Lamb, King Solomon, the return from
the exile) but then to a *further* meaning or a whole chain of further
meanings and an ultimate meaning that eventually come to sight. In
fact, all texts quoted by Matthew are prophetic in such a sense. The
Jews of the 1st century easily understood this since, as the LXX testifies, before the time of Jesus and the evangelists there was already a
Jewish interpretation of Isaiah 7:14 translating the Hebrew *'almah* as
παρθένος, or "virgin." When Christianity began its spread, those of
the Jewish diaspora who did not want to accept the Gospel undertook the task of sponsoring a new Greek translation which widened
the gap between the Hebrew Bible and its interpretation by the Gospels. The best known among them were those produced by Theodo-
tion and Aquila, which, however, are extant today only in fragments.
In Christian tradition Isaiah 7:14 was justifiably read as a text wit-
nessing to the expectation of the Messiah whose very birth will be a
"sign" of God's favor returning to his people. The existence of the
Septuagint's text in itself justifies this reading, the issue is not about
the text in isolation from those who wrote, translated, and used it.
The textual history of Isaiah 7:14 correctly witnesses that it was read
in the last couple of centuries before Christ as a witness to a messianic hope and, in connection with that hope, was taken to be about
a virgin. Those who, in retrospect, did not like the translation of the
Septuagint were free to create a new Greek text, but they could not

alter the history of the text and all the hopes and sentiments that the text has occasioned.

I am fully aware that this short section is just a concise rendition of all Christian thought about Mary nurtured with Old Testament texts. I consider it, however, important for demonstrating that familiarity with historical and critical reading of the Old Testament should not discourage us from investigating the themes and topics of the Old Testament about Mary and, eventually, as we move on to discuss the Church Fathers' Mariology and its scriptural basis, we may grow in appreciation for the presence of further Old Testament themes in their Mariology.

CHAPTER THREE

MARIAN TEACHING IN THE 2ND AND 3RD CENTURIES

Ignatius of Antioch (d. ca. 110)

In Mariology the transition from the canonical books of the New Testament to early patristics is almost imperceptible. About a decade after the Fourth Gospel's composition, Ignatius of Antioch assigns to Mary a modest but important place in the Christology of his seven letters. He mentions Mary by name four times[67] and once refers to her as "the Virgin."[68] Mary's name functions in these texts as an anti-Gnostic device, linking Jesus concretely to the human race through his mother as someone "truly born." The adverb "truly," repeated three times, belongs to Ignatius' anti-docetic vocabulary[69] and remains imprinted as such in the Church's memory.[70] Also in another detail, Ignatius' thought is very quickly accepted as part of Church tradition: he is the first to combine "from the seed of David according to the flesh" (Rm 1:2) with the virginal conception and concludes, or at least makes the reader conclude, that if Jesus' flesh was "truly from David's race" or "David's seed" (*Smyrneans* 1:1; *Romans* 7:3), then Mary herself was a descendant of David.[71]

---

[67] *Ephesians* 7:2; 18:2; 19:1; *Trallians* 9:1.

[68] *Smyrneans* 1:1.

[69] *Trallians* 9:1.

[70] It still resounds in a late medieval Eucharistic poem of the 14th century, at a time when the crisis of Docetism was long past: *Ave verum corpus natum de Maria Virgine, vere passum, immolatum in cruce pro homine.*

[71] It is quite possible that Ignatius refers to a tradition already present – although quite discretely – in Luke's Gospel as he reports the Angel's words: "the Lord God will give him the throne of David *his father*" (Lk 1:32).

In his most important text about Mary, Ignatius refers to her "virginity" (ἡ παρθενία) and her τόκετος (childbearing or "parturition") as two of the three mysteries of salvation history which took place in God's silence, for they were kept hidden from the "prince of this world":

Now the virginity of Mary was hidden from the prince of this world, as was also her offspring (or: parturition, giving birth), and the death of the Lord; three mysteries of proclamation, which had been wrought in silence by God. (*Ephesians* 19:1-2)

Both the thought and the terminology of the passage evoke St. Paul:

We speak God's wisdom, *mysterious*, hidden, which God predetermined before the ages for our glory, which *none of the rulers of this age knew*; for if they had known it, they would not have crucified the Lord of glory. (1 Cor 2:7-8)

In fact, Ignatius names Paul explicitly in this letter as the one who initiated the Ephesians into "the Gospel's mysteries."[72] One would, therefore, think that the Lord's death, the "third mystery" in this text, elaborates Paul's idea: had "the princes of this world (τοῦ αἰῶνος τούτου)" known that Jesus was the Son of God, the crucifixion would not have occurred. But this is not Ignatius' main idea. Using Pauline language, Ignatius pursues his own anti-Gnostic agenda: the triple mystery is about God's true Incarnation, supposing true human conception and birth, and leading to a true death. They remained under the veil of secrecy because the Devil (the prince of this world, in the singular) could not penetrate this mystery and perceive what was hidden behind these events in the flesh (conception, birth, and death): the presence of a Divine Person. The truth of these events was made manifest only after they had happened, and only at the time that God chose to unveil their meaning. So although the

---

[72] *Ephesians* 19:2.

language is Pauline, the theological thought is more Johannine than Pauline, as seen more clearly from the way Ignatius continues his meditation on the triple mystery:

> How, then, was he manifested to the world? A star shone forth in heaven above all the other stars, the light of which was inexpressible, while its novelty struck men with astonishment. And all the rest of the stars, with the sun and moon, formed a chorus to this star, and its light was exceedingly great above them all. And there was agitation felt as to whence this new spectacle came, so unlike to everything else in the heavens.
>
> Hence every kind of magic was destroyed and every bond of wickedness manifested in human form for the renewal of eternal life. And now that took a beginning which had been prepared by God. Henceforth all things were in a state of tumult, because he meditated the abolition of death. (*Ephesians* 19:2-3)

The allusion to Matthew's story of the Magi is more than highly probable: the star (ἀστὴρ: Mt 2:2), the "agitation" (ἐταράχθη Mt 2:3 corresponding to ταραχή in Ignatius' text) and also the word μαγεία corresponding to the "Magi" (μάγοι in Mt 2:1) are no accidental verbal coincidences but closely reproduced keywords, especially if we realize that the martyr bishop is a prisoner without access to his Christian books. Ignatius speaks about the birth of Jesus as a sacred event of cosmic importance and gives a Gentile Christian exegesis of the story. The star signals the appearance of the world's Divine Creator and Ruler, summoning the Magi, who, in fact, come and "do homage" to him (cf. Mt 2:11). The story signifies the abolition of death's regime and the arrival of eternal life. The language and the narrative are here Matthean but the theology is again Johannine: Jesus' birth brings "novelty" (καινότης), i.e., it renews the meaning of human existence as it eliminates the reign of blind destiny.

Mary's unexpectedly "new" kind of motherhood eminently fits

into this theological context as a revelatory tool expressing what *the singular reading* of John 1:13 conveys. For it says that the coming of the Logos in flesh is in discontinuity with "generation for pro-creation," or the practice of human sexual reproduction as a losing battle fought against mortality. When a new generation replaces the previous one, that saves the race but cannot save the person: every individual is born to die. By such birth nothing significantly "new" comes about: everyone who is born is under the law of death. How-ever, through the birth of the Logos "not by man's desire or instinct and not from blood," novelty is sprung from the Word made flesh: death is conquered by life eternal.

Justin Martyr (d. ca. 160)

While Ignatius' *Ephesians* 19:1-3 is little more than a short clip interpreting "the virginal birth," Justin Martyr testifies to a new and original thought in early patristic Mariology. One may even propose that the short text about the parallel between Mary and Eve in his *Dialogue with Trypho* is the most significant patristic thought in the field, from which all subsequent Mariology was suddenly stirred into motion. This is no exaggeration, even if all that Justin seems to do is offer a modest scriptural commentary. At first sight it may appear something of an allegory, with its brief mention of Genesis 3, but at closer examination one sees a concise statement about the emanation of creation and redemption from the single salvific will of the Father that encompasses all mankind, a key concept that unites the two Testaments. We must read this text in full:

> And he is written about as Son of God in the memoirs of his Apostles who also call him "Son"; and we understood as the one proceeding by the Father's will and power be-fore all he made. He is also said to be "Wisdom," and "the Day" and "the Orient" and "Sword" and "Rock" and "Shoot," and Jacob and Israel, called in other and other way in the words of the Prophets.

He became man through the Virgin in order that the disobedience caused by the Serpent might be destroyed in the same manner in which it had originated. For Eve, an undefiled virgin, conceived the word of the Serpent and brought forth disobedience and death. But the Virgin Mary, filled with faith and joy, when the Angel Gabriel announced to her the good tidings that the Spirit of the Lord would come upon her and the power of the Highest would overshadow her, and therefore the Holy One would be the Son of God, answered: "Be it done unto me according to thy word."

And, indeed, she gave birth to him... by whom God destroys both the Serpent and those angels and men who have become like the Serpent, but frees from death those who repent of their sins and believe in Christ.[73]

In the introductory sentence[74] Justin coins a new way of referring to the Gospel books: "the memoirs (or recollections) of the Apostles."[75] In the lines that follow he specifically refers to Luke's story of the virginal conception quoting it *verbatim*. We have here the earliest attestation of Luke's work as an *apostolic* Gospel.

Next, a reference is made to "the words of the Prophets" but it designates specifically the first book of Moses, Genesis. In Christian usage, the Old Testament is called "the Law and the Prophets" (see Rm 3:21) or even simply "the Prophets," especially in contexts such

---

[73] *Dialogue with Trypho* 100 (ed. E.J. Goodspeed, 1915).

[74] The first paragraph of this quotation is usually left out by surveys of Mariology quoting Justin. This is done probably on account of Justin's small but important theological detour, in which he explains that the different "names" of the Divinity in the Scriptures refer to nothing material or corporeal in God but signify a spiritual Being. He takes up this theme in connection with the word "Son," who is generated spiritually, that is, by "will and power." To this he adds a list of metaphors, insisting on the non-physical character of God's eternal Son.

[75] We must notice that Justin asserts here an "apostolic origin" to the Gospel of Luke. This is not a vague idea for enhancing the book's credentials. Justin is a *younger contemporary* to the heretic Marcion, who accepted no other Gospel but Luke's as authentically apostolic, because he accepted Paul as Jesus' only authentic apostle. Thus Justin's verbatim quotation from Luke as written in the "memoirs of the Apostles" asserts the orthodox understanding of the Lucan Gospel's apostolic origins.

as this, in which "Prophets and Apostles" signify the totality of the Scriptures.[76] But it can simply be shortened to "the Prophets."[77]

At the center of the text we find a complex comparison between Eve and Mary. It is mainly a proof of parallelism among several compared terms, enhanced by contrasts closely linked to the parallelism. Both Mary and Eve are virgins and mothers, both received a persuasive visit by an angelic creature (Gabriel and the Serpent, a fallen angel), but with opposite results: Eve disobeyed and Mary obeyed God's will.

This contrast of sin and obedience leads to fundamentally opposite consequences for mankind as a whole: life and death. Justin meanders through several issues to arrive to such a conclusion. He mentions several details about Mary by quoting the story of the Annunciation. We must keep in mind that his interlocutor is assumed to be fully familiar with the third chapter of Genesis. Especially relevant is Genesis 3:16, which brings other parallels and contrasts to light. Justin only alludes to it or assumes it implicitly: such is the "joy" with which Mary brings her child to the world; it must be heard as counterpoint to the "sadness" in Genesis 3:16 (LXX: ἐν λύπαις τέξη τέκνα). Just as importantly, we must look to Genesis 3:20. In this verse, according to the Septuagint, Adam calls the woman "Life" (Ζωή), because she becomes the mother of all the living (ὅτι αὕτη μήτηρ πάντων τῶν ζώντων). Certainly Justin expects his interlocutor to understand the relevance of the parallel between Mary and Eve, because only in Mary does Eve become what she is called, i.e., "life" or "lifegiver," while her act of disobedience led much more immediately to the curse of death pronounced over all children of Adam in the previous verse of Genesis (3:19).

---

[76] See Denis Farkasfalvy, "Prophets and Apostles, the Conjunction of the Two Terms before Irenaeus," in *Texts and Testaments*, edited by E.W. March (San Antonio: Trinity, 1980), 109-134.

[77] It is important to see that Luke's text, since it belongs to the "memoirs of the Apostles," receives from Justin the same respect for normativity that is due to "the Prophets," who also refer to the Son when using various metaphors. Of course, Justin means "Law and Prophets," and eventually begins to refer to Eve and specifically to Gn 3:16, the first book of the Torah, such that our text ends up being an exercise in "opening the meaning of the Scriptures" (cf. Lk 24:44-45).

Reading Justin's text in which Luke's Annunciation story is interpreted in the context of Genesis 3 – a procedure typical for early Christian exegesis – reveals that the Mariology he supposes here is broader and wider than what this snip of the *Dialogue* explicitly says. We are entitled to see this as the tip of an iceberg submerged in the lost Christian writings of the 2nd century, from which, fortunately, some significant further samples protrude to be charted in correspondence with their true context.

Irenaeus (d. ca. 202)

St. Irenaeus, Bishop of Lyons in Gaul (today France)[78] was from Asia Minor, where he knew the Bishop of Smyrna, Polycarp, to whom one of Ignatius' letters had been addressed. Irenaeus also tells that Polycarp at a young age saw and listened to "John, the Disciple of the Lord," whom Irenaeus recognizes as the "Beloved Disciple" and the author of the Fourth Gospel or the person who stands behind its author as the source and key witness.[79] Irenaeus is, therefore, firmly rooted in apostolic tradition. He is also recognized as the first systematic theologian of the Church, a man who explores, by copious quotations from both Testaments and by a systematic exposition of the apostolic faith, the essential elements of the Christian doctrine. His theological edifice is consciously constructed upon the Rule of Faith, the basis that he defends as the truth in opposition to the non-truths and half-truths of a large assortment of Gnostic teachings. At his time these teachings more than all else threatened to transform and essentially alter the Christian message. In the five books of his *Adversus Haereses* Irenaeus presents an overview of the various Gnostic systems of his time and responds to them by a systematic use of the Church's scriptural sources and a serious confrontation of

---

[78] Luigi Gambero, *Mary and the Fathers of the Church*, tr. by Thomas Buffer (San Francisco: Ignatius Press, 1999), 51-58.

[79] In contemporary scholarship this statement of Irenaeus became the subject of heavy debate. I maintain the position that Irenaeus is neither misleading nor misled: he knows that through Polycarp he was personally inserted in a succession of unbroken chain of tradition: Jesus – the Apostle John – Polycarp – Irenaeus.

the philosophical arguments on which his opponents rely.

Irenaeus' importance cannot be overstated in regard to almost any doctrinal issue. On the one hand, he is explicitly aware of the role of tradition in transmitting apostolic doctrine from Jesus' original disciples to the Catholic Christian Church of the 2nd century. On the other hand, he is in firm possession of the Scriptures, both the books that the apostolic generation saw fulfilled in Jesus (Old Testament) and the books that the immediate witnesses of Christ left behind about their teachings and exhortations (the New Testament). In Mariology too he represents a milestone.[80]

Irenaeus is keenly aware of the divine *oikonomia*, a salvation history about which the written sources testify, the Law and the Prophets of the Old Testament as well as the fourfold Gospel and other writings with apostolic authority. In Irenaeus' works we can discern the basic form and function of Christian thought, uniting the two Testaments. His exegesis is consciously canonical: not only does he combine arguments from both Testaments, but compares and sees in unity the four canonical Gospels with their common witness, the Pauline Corpus, and practically the rest of our present-day Canon.[81] In this context it is important to observe that Irenaeus relies also on the doctrinal tradition of the Church Fathers who preceded him, like Justin Martyr and Ignatius of Antioch.

In the third book of *Adversus Haereses*, Irenaeus repeatedly

---

[80] See G. Jouassard, "Marie à travers la patristique": Du Manoir, D'Hubert (ed.), *Maria: Etudes sur la Sainte Vierge*, I (Paris: Beauchesne, 1949), 69-157.

[81] Irenaeus' use of the Scriptures was significantly influenced by a certain "technological" innovation impacting biblical texts, most importantly the Gospels and the Pauline Corpus, during the 2nd century. For reasons not entirely clear, books of the Christian Bible, especially those of the New Testament, began to be copied onto pages of codices while the use of scrolls was abandoned. In the biblical texts written in codices you could page, while in scrolls the text had no random accessibility. In a codex one could easily compare and combine texts by paging and thus had to rely less on memory. Also both parallel texts and variant readings were much more easily traced and compared. Falsifications were more easily controlled by paging from passage to passage in a matter of minutes. From Irenaeus on, a "canonical reading" of the Bible became not only a matter of theory but of practice. Similarly it became easy and practical to inquire into the exactness of a quotation and to raise issues about verbal precision or the use of variant readings that, unconsciously or fraudulently, slipped into the text.

underlines Mary's importance in a holistic vision of Christian teaching, in two ways most explicitly. First, in his short summaries of
Christian orthodox teaching, containing the so-called *regula fidei*,
Mary is always present as the guarantee of a correct Christology
and Soteriology. He refers to Mary as "the Virgin," which regularly
reappears in his texts, often without the proper name "Mary" but
always with a definite article. This usage signals a development that
we already noticed in the letters of Ignatius and reaches in Irenaeus
its completion: Mary is *the* Virgin – κατ' ἐξοχήν[82] – and the reader
is supposed to have become aware of that. Another typical Irenaean
expression – which later disappears from patristic usage – is Christ
as "the Emmanuel, born from the Virgin," what seems a triple reference to Isaiah 7:14, Matthew 1:23, and Luke 1:32.[83] When comparing Mary and Eve, Irenaeus follows in the footsteps of Justin, while
significantly expanding his predecessor's thought. The most important and longest passage regarding that topic is found in chapter 22
of the third book of *Adversus Haereses*:

> In accordance with this design, Mary the Virgin is found
> obedient, saying, "Behold the handmaid of the Lord; be it
> done unto me according to thy word" (Lk 1:38). But Eve
> was disobedient; for she did not obey when as yet she was
> a virgin. Even though Eve had Adam as a husband, she
> was still a virgin. For "they were both naked in paradise
> and they were unashamed" (Gn 2:25) since they were
> created a short time previously to become adults, and
> only then did they begin to multiply. Having become dis-

---

[82] Mary is "the Virgin" in AH III, 5 (211, 104), 19, 1 (211, 372), 19, 2 (211, 376), 20, 3 (211, 393), V, 19, 1 (SC 153, 248). What we translate today as "the Virgin Mary" is in Irenaeus' text Μαρία ἡ παρθένος ("Mary the Virgin"). See III, 22, 4 (211, 445) and also the places quoted in the next note. Irenaeus' usage shows that the des-ignation of Mary as the Virgin developed from quoting Is 7:14 and talking about her child or offspring by keeping in mind this verse of Isaiah as the context. This is the best explanation for the texts of Ignatius, just as well, although Ignatius hardly ever makes explicit references to passages of the Old Testament.

[83] AH III, 4 (211, 47), 5, 1 (211, 53), III, 102 (211, 116), 21, 1 (211, 344), 21, 6 (211, 419), 22, 4 (211, 441).

obedient, she was made the cause of death, both to herself and to the entire human race. So also did Mary, having a man betrothed to her, and being nevertheless a virgin, by yielding obedience, become the cause of salvation, both to herself and the whole human race.

And on this account does the law call a woman betrothed to a man, the wife of him who had betrothed her, although she was as yet a virgin; thus indicating a parallelism in reference back from Mary to Eve. For what was tied together once cannot be loosened except by untying the knot in reverse order so that the second knot be dissolved by untying it first and the first knot be dissolved by untying it second. In this way the former knots become canceled by a latter untying, and the latter ties are set free by the former untying.... In this way the Lord declared that the first will be the last and the last first (cf. Mt 19:30).[84]

At the beginning of this passage we notice the same procedures that Justin used. First, the text of Luke is quoted *verbatim* while the story of Adam and Eve is only presupposed by mentioning the names of the first couple. The reader is expected to know that Eve's transgression caused death – physical and spiritual – for herself and for all mankind. It is also supposed that the reader knows that it was only after the Fall that Adam had relations with Eve and thus, at the Fall, Eve was still a virgin (this is implied in Genesis by the sequence of verses 2:25, 3:21 and 4:1). Quoting Luke's story of the Annunciation, Irenaeus adheres to his "fourfold Gospel canon,"[85] and knows that Mary's betrothal to Joseph (Lk 1:27) counts for being married, as can be concluded from Matthew 1:20. Furthermore, in *Adversus Haereses* Irenaeus uses the Pauline letters. He knows the Pauline metaphor connecting Adam, the first man, with Christ as "the

---

[84] AH III, 22, 4 (SC 211, 439-443).
[85] *quadriforme evangelium* in AH III, 11, 8 (SC 211, 168).

second Adam" (cf. 1 Cor 15:45-47). He also uses the Pauline term "recapitulation" meaning "re-assumption" or "reuniting under one head." In the Pauline letters this word occurs only in its verbal form (ἀνακεφαλαιοῦται in Rm 13:9 and ἀνακεφαλαιώσασθαι in Eph 1:10), while in Irenaeus we find the noun ἀνακεφαλαίωσις[86] and the synonymous noun ἀνακύκλησις (re-circulation).[87] These are used in a particular Irenaean sense, meaning the "reversing" of the Genesis story of human origins through Adam and Eve by a corresponding chain of events through Mary and Christ.

According to the passage quoted above, Irenaeus sees in this "recirculation" of human destiny two parallels, two antitheses, and a reversal in the sequence of the corresponding events. The first parallel is seen in the paradox between "virginity" and yet "having a man" for both virgins are destined to have a husband. Further antithetic attributes are disobedience/obedience, causing death/life respectively. But the reversal of the order is important. At the beginning of human history, Adam was created first; Eve was created out of Adam only afterward. But on the other side of the parallelism, the creation of the Virgin Mary as well as her act of obedience precede the virginal conception of Christ, the second Adam, who is made from the second Eve. Irenaeus explains this reversal of the order by speaking of two knots tied in succession on a string. Untying the second knot must take place before the first can be untied. Irenaeus does not explain the metaphor of the knots; one presumes he thinks that its application is obvious. But the metaphor hides a deeper insight. Not only does it explain why Eve's creation out of Adam's side corresponds, as a reversed parallel, to Jesus' birth from Mary's womb, but also makes us realize that, in this way, Jesus becomes, through Mary, a child of Adam and Eve, but nonetheless Christ truly constitutes a new beginning, a newly created first man, a true "Adam." He is not born like anybody else from the instinct and purpose of procreation but as the result of new creation. We see here also why the singular

---

[86] AH III, 21, 10 (211, 429-431), III, 23, 1 (211, 445).
[87] AH III, 22, 4 (211, 440).

reading of John 1:13, which insists on the novelty and uniqueness of Jesus' birth, is extremely important for Irenaeus. At the same time, he explains at length why in his genealogy Luke goes back all the way to Adam.[88] This happens in order to demonstrate that, born from a woman, Jesus is thoroughly human, although he was generated in a radically different way: not by a man's instinct and will, not by human initiative, but by God (cf. Jn 1:13 in its ancient variant reading).

The antithetic parallelism by which Irenaeus explains the corresponding roles of Adam and Christ with Eve and Mary with their respective functions, is neither as simple nor as forced as some of Irenaeus' commentators make it appear. Irenaeus' views about the virginal beginning of the Incarnation want to solve an otherwise unsolvable dilemma: the birth of all mankind, issued from a couple in a sinful state of rebellion, renders each and every member of the human race incapable of saving the human race from within. But if man is not saved by man, then what is the value or the importance of man's corporal existence? A virgin receiving both the grace to obey and receiving the Son of God in her womb constitutes for Irenaeus the solution of this dilemma. Adam and Eve first joined forces for an act of disobedience, then, after having lost the gift of immortality, became partners of procreation. They populate the earth but they have already lost the gift of eternal life. Man's battle against death is doomed to failure: all human beings are born in order to die. But man is not removed from God's *oikonomia*, because God interrupts the chain of procreated mortality and obtains the Virgin's obedience. She agrees in one single fiat as she receives her call to a virginal motherhood.

Irenaeus sees that, when God becomes flesh in the Virgin, an act of obedience brings about "re-circulation," opening the flow of life from Christ both forward and backward. For Irenaeus insists that being born from Mary, Christ becomes the principle of salvation not only to his contemporaries and those who come to believe in him later, but also to previous generations, all the way back to the first

---

[88] In AH III, 22, 3 and again in III, 23, 4 Irenaeus opens and closes his reflection on "recapitulation" by a reference to Luke's genealogy (3:23-38).

ancestors: *a Maria ad Evam*. So at the end he adds: "This is why the Lord said: 'the first will be the last and the last first' (cf. Mt 19:30 and 20:16)." In fact we must keep on reading through the rest of *Adversus Haereses* 22,4 where he uses bold language: "This is how the Lord received into his bosom the 'ancient fathers' [meaning the Patriarchs and other "saints" of the Old Testament] and regenerated them anew to the life of God, becoming for them the source of new life, just as before Adam became for them the source of death." And he adds again about Mary and Eve: "This is how the knot tied up by Eve's disobedience became untied by Mary's obedience, since what the Virgin Eve tied by her unbelief, has been resolved by Mary's faith."[89]

As we see Irenaeus has a much broader outlook than Justin Martyr. In Irenaeus' mind, in the history of salvation sinful mankind goes through some sort of a "rewinding" as it is re-done by a chain of events that resume identical issues with opposite outcomes. Hence Irenaeus finds a more general principle behind Justin's "contrasted parallels" and applies this principle to many other topics of salvation history. In this way Irenaeus is the first Church Father to work on a Mariology: a set of statements about Mary, integrated into his general theological thinking. It is in his brief work the *Proof of the Apostolic Preaching*[90] that Mary's insertion into his system of "recapitulations" is most clearly manifested:

> Adam had to be recapitulated in Christ, so that death
> might be swallowed up in immortality (cf. 1 Cor 15:54)
> and Eve [had to be recapitulated] in Mary, so that the
> Virgin, having become another Virgin's advocate, might

---

[89] AH III, 22, 4 (SC 211, 440). Here Irenaeus brings us another antithetic element between Mary and Eve in terms of faith and unbelief. This is, of course, fundamental in the scriptural foundations: Eve does not obey God because the Serpent convinces her not to believe what the Lord said about the mortiferous effects of the forbidden fruit (Gn 3:3-4), while Mary's faith is praised by Elizabeth at the Visitation (Lk 1:45).

[90] Usually quoted under the Latin title *Demonstratio praedicationis apostolicae* this is, besides the 5 books *Adversus Haereses*, Irenaeus' only extant work. It was preserved only in Armenian translation so that minute philological questions about the text are answered with difficulty.

destroy and abolish one Virgin's disobedience by the obedience of another Virgin.

The interpretation of the term "advocate" in this text has long been debated. Irenaeus uses it also in the fifth book of his *Adversus Haereses*:

> And if she [Eve] disobeyed God, this one [Mary] was persuaded to obey God, so that the Virgin Mary may become the advocate of the virgin Eve. And as the human race was tossed into death by a virgin, so it may be saved by a Virgin, since the virginal disobedience was balanced out by a virginal obedience. And also the first man's sin was made up for by the First-born [Son] undergoing punishment and the Serpent's cunning was defeated by the Dove's simplicity, untying the chain by which we were linked to death.[91]

The title "advocate" originally might have meant for Irenaeus a "representative" or "substitute," maybe "counterpart."[92] But eventually, in the Middle Ages, it was understood as signifying a "spokesperson." However, almost a thousand years after Irenaeus when the *Salve Regina* was composed by Hermanus Contractus, a monk of the 11th century, we see the medieval meanings closely following Irenaeus' usage:

> Ad te clamamus, exules filii Evae...
> Eia, ergo *ADVOCATA* nostra...
>
> (To you we cry, exiled children of Eve...
> Therefore, our Advocate...)

This text may suggest that Irenaeus is a forerunner, or even the initiator of a tradition in which Mary, once seen in a parallelism with

---

91   AH V, 19, 1 (SC 153, 248-250).

92   The critical edition assumes that Irenaeus used the biblical word παράκλητος (Jn 14:26; 15:6; 16:7), but the text was not preserved.

Eve, is therefore called to be our "advocate" or spokeswoman.[93] In the *Salve Regina*, Mary is directly addressed in the form of a prayer as an "advocate," a person addressed to intercede for us, while in Irenaeus' text she is only descriptively compared in her role to Eve, as of similar importance in the cosmic drama of salvation seen in terms of recapitulation. Mary acts and speaks in a role that is the counterpart of Eve's role and results in a long-expected reversal of man's destiny.

The Proto-evangelium of James (probably 160-170 A.D.)

Handbooks of Mariology present Irenaeus as the peak of the 2ⁿᵈ century's Mariological reflection. In fact, nobody before Irenaeus outlined with such theological clarity and emphasis the important role of Mary in the history of salvation. Even if Jesus' birth from Mary by the Holy Spirit is explicitly present as a pillar of anti-Gnostic orthodoxy in the letters of Ignatius, only in the writings of Irenaeus do we find a theological system for which the virginal birth is foundational: the mystery provides a doctrinal guarantee of the true birth of a true man who is truly God. In Irenaeus, Mariology obtains growing importance due to its new and rapidly developing theological context: the theology of the Incarnation.

In the 2ⁿᵈ century, however, we find a similarly influential work which had similar impact on the promotion of the Church's Marian devotion, even if it leaves much to be desired in theological depth and acumen. In spite of the controversial assessment that it has received in theology, Catholic and otherwise, as a primary source it reflects the Church's growing interest in Mary and the force which mariological devotion obtained in the 2ⁿᵈ century. We are speaking about a work called today *Proto-evangelium Jacobi*, or the *Proto-evangelium of James*. Although a complete, ancient Latin translation has not survived, it exercised immense influence in both East and

---

[93] In Irenaeus' use Mary speaks on behalf of Eve and thus reverses her disobedience. In the medieval text of the *Salve Regina* Mary speaks on *our behalf* both when she welcomes the Incarnate Word to "dwell among us," and when speaking on behalf as an intercessor, defending our cause.

West in liturgical texts and sermons, feasts, devotions, and eventually the theological tradition.

A large number of scholarly works classify it as an "apocryphal infancy Gospel," but it is no Gospel, nor does it narrate, beyond the birth alone, anything about Jesus' infancy. It is certainly an apocryphal work for a double reason: the work as a whole is attributed to James as a half-brother of Jesus thus qualifying to be "James, the brother of the Lord," mentioned in Pauline letters and the Acts of the Apostles.[94] Furthermore some part of the text about Jesus' birth is written in first person singular in the name of Joseph, Mary's husband. The work, however, hardly reflects the knowledge of a Jewish milieu in the early 1st century. Therefore, serious claims to authenticity cannot be supported. But it certainly reflects a surprisingly high degree of interest in Mary's life and person. As most scholars admit today, its original title was not *euangelion*. Rather the traditional title, Γένεσις Μαρίας (Genesis of Mary) suits it well: a book about Mary's origins, birth, and early life up to the point where she gave birth to Jesus in Bethlehem.

The current title *Proto-evangelium Jacobi* comes from Postel, its 16th century editor who for the first time prepared a printed edition of a Latin translation and re-introduced the knowledge of this text in the West. Postel believed in its authenticity. Although this opinion soon lost credibility, the text, apparently very ancient, drew the attention of many scholars. Such luminaries as Griesbach, Tischendorf, and Harnack studied it. Tischendorf attempted a critical reconstruction of the original text, but could not achieve his goal. For decades Adolf von Harnack's opinions were followed by most scholars, claiming multiple ancient sources from which a secondary compilation was achieved at a relatively late date in the 4th or 5th century.

New light was thrown on the *Proto-evangelium* in 1952 when one of 22 papyrus codices, found in Egypt and purchased by Martin Bodmer, Bodmer papyrus 5, turned out to contain the complete text of the *Proto-evangelium*. A printed edition of the codex quickly followed in 1959 by Michael Testuz, and with the claim of recov-

---

94   Gal 1:9. Cf. 1 Cor 15:5; Ac 12:2, 17; 15:13, 18.

ering its most ancient textual form, a critical edition was promptly published in 1962 by a Belgian Bollandist, a Jesuit named Émile de Strycker.[95] Strycker established that Bodmer papyrus 5 originally formed the first forty-nine pages of a 168-page codex, from which the whole codex was reconstructed in its entirety from various other parts of the Bodmer papyri, some already published independently in previous years. The codex is neither a liturgical book nor a book of biblical texts, but a loosely connected collection of texts, including parts of both Testaments, like First and Second Peter, some Psalms (Ps 33 and 34) and even some homilies.[96] It is best described as a devotional book. Whatever purposes such books might have served, it was certainly not created for public liturgical use, but for private reading by individuals or small communities.

Studies about Bodmer papyrus 5 proved that the various redactional hypotheses, like those of Tischendorf and Harnack, were incorrect. Strycker came to the conclusion that the unity of the work is original. The whole composition belonged together: even the last parts, an account by Joseph about Jesus' birth and the "martyrdom of Zechariah," come from this single original author. Moreover, the publication of the critical text has advanced the debate about the *Proto-evangelium*'s dating, literary genre, and social and ecclesial milieu, and helped in the assessment of the theological meaning of the text. Of course, many critical issues have not been resolved. For example,

---

[95] Emile de Strycker, *La forme la plus ancienne du Protoévangile de Jacques* (Bruxelles: Société des Bollandistes, 1961). A bilingual (Greek/English) text is published in Bart Ehrman and Zlatko Pleše, *The Apocryphal Gospels* (Oxford: University Press, 2011), 31-71. It follows de Strycker's edition of the Greek text with only a few changes. As a major addition, it includes chapter 18 which is missing from Bodmer 5. Unless indicated otherwise, Ehrman's edition is used here for all English quotations and references.

[96] The pages of the codex are numbered, so that its table of content is now known:
- 1. "The Nativity of Mary" (*Proto-evangelium Jacobi*)
- 2. Two apocryphal letters of Paul to the Corinthians
- 3. The 11ᵗʰ Ode of Solomon
- 4. The Epistle of Jude
- 5. Homilies of Melito of Sardis
- 6. Fragments of Christian hymns
- 7. The Apology of Phileas
- 8. Psalms 33 and 34
- 9. 1ˢᵗ and 2ⁿᵈ Epistles of Peter

the *Proto-evangelium*'s possible dependence on Justin Martyr is under continued debate. But Strycker's arguments convincingly indicate that the work is safely dated to the second half of the 2nd century.[97]

What is truly noteworthy in this new critical evaluation of the *Proto-evangelium* can be summarized in a few points.

First, the *Proto-evangelium* is not an apocryphal Gospel, but in many ways it uses and quotes the canonical Gospels. It certainly depends on both Matthew 1-2 and Luke 1-2, which are quoted frequently and *verbatim*. It contains a substantial narrative about Zechariah, the father of John the Baptist, which the *Proto-evangelium* identifies with the martyred prophet mentioned by Matthew 23:35 as "murdered between the sanctuary and the altar." It handles with remarkable freedom the Infancy Narratives of Matthew and Luke, altering rather than harmonizing them for the sake of its own version of Jesus' birth. This amazing sense of freedom and creativity with regard to two Gospels that were already regarded as canonical in the late 2nd century may be the best evidence for its very early origin.

Second, the *Proto-evangelium* is not a Gnostic work, not even in the broadest sense of the term. In fact, it can be characterized as anti-Gnostic because of its insistence on the true corporal nature of Jesus at his birth.

Third, despite the fact that modern exegetes, both Catholic and Protestant, have long shown distaste for the *Proto-evangelium*, it is an excellent source for historical-critical research in 2nd century mariological interests and beliefs. Although the story it narrates deserves no historical credibility, it contains abundant information about the early reception of the first chapters of Matthew and Luke. It shows how the incipient Gospel canon co-existed side by side with divergent non-canonical books representing a larger stream of traditions.

The *Proto-evangelium* constructs a hybrid narrative not only by switching back and forth between Matthew and Luke but also by freely suppressing one or another detail of the canonical narratives in order to make room for its own story line. For example, the *Proto-*

---

[97] Op. cit., p. 421.

evangelium omits all references to Galilee and Nazareth in order to link Mary's entire childhood to the Temple of Jerusalem, leading up to her wedding to Joseph in Jerusalem, which is immediately followed by the story of the Annunciation, the Visitation, the birth in Bethlehem and the visit of the Magi and finally concludes with the rescue of the infant John the Baptist from Herod's persecution and with the martyrdom of his father Zechariah.[98]

---

[98] Most puzzling is the following detail, which has so far defied all explanation. According to *Protoev* 13, 2, when Joseph finds Mary pregnant and asks of her an explanation, Mary swears that she does not know how her pregnancy came about. Even earlier, as she is visiting Elizabeth, we are told that she did not understand why Elizabeth called her "the mother of the Lord," since "she forgot the mysteries that the archangel Gabriel spoke to her" (12, 2). Strycker adds here a note suggesting that with this the author attempts to harmonize his narrative with Lk 2:50. This explanation is not convincing. Only a modern exegete would think that, in the story of the twelve-year old Jesus in the Temple, the parents' "incomprehension" of their child's words would mean that they were unaware of the virginal conception. In fact, already when meeting Elizabeth and when confronting Joseph, Mary fails to recall what happened to her at the Annunciation, so that Mary's "non-remembrance" of her virginal conception is not an afterthought, but an integral part of the *Proto-evangelium*'s story line. There must be a better explanation for Mary's "forgetting." It seems to me that it reveals some linkage with a concept of revelation whereby the mystery is not revealed and divulged automatically, but only after additional divine intervention. Without further divine acts not even Mary can tell anyone what happened to her or what she learned from an angel. For Elizabeth John the Baptist's "leaping for joy" in her womb is awaited for the transmission of the mystery of Mary's conception, while for Joseph, in agreement with Mt 1:20, an angel must appear and explain how Mary's pregnancy had its origin from the Holy Spirit. The *Proto-evangelium* aims at showing how John the Baptist is the only human herald of the mystery of the Incarnation. Harmonization with the verse 2:50 in Luke's story of finding Jesus in the Temple is hardly an issue here, for the latter episode is not even mentioned in the *Proto-evangelium*.

But there might be something else which helps even further to explain the strange forgetfulness of Mary in the *Proto-evangelium*. The exact wording of the text (XII, 2) is important:

«Πόθεν μοι <τοῦτο> ἵνα ἡ μήτηρ τοῦ Κυρίου <μου> ἔλθη πρὸς ἐμέ; Ἰδοὺ γὰρ τὸ ἐν ἐμοὶ ἐσκίρτησεν καὶ εὐλόγησέν σε.» Ἡ δὲ Μαρία ἐπελάθετο τῶν μυστηρίων ὧν ἐλάλησεν Γαβριὴλ ὁ ἄγγελος.

("How is it that the mother of my Lord should come to me? For see the child in me leaped and blessed you." But Mary forgot the mysteries that the angel Gabriel spoke.)

The first sentence quotes verbatim Lk 1:43. The second line switches to a narrative mode as the particle δὲ indicates, rendered by the French translation's "or" in Strycker's critical edition. The third line names the object of Mary's "forgetfulness" as "mysteria." This is the word that Ignatius of Antioch also used when noting that three "mysteries," completed in God's silence, remained hidden from the "Prince of this Age":

Fourth, in spite of lacking heretical tendencies (either of Gnosticism or Marcionism), the *Proto-evangelium* was always handled with suspicion by the Church Fathers, such that it has never even been tentatively introduced into the canon. Its text practically disappeared from use in the West, although the feast of Mary's Presentation in the Temple "survived" both Trent and Vatican II. It is included in the Roman liturgical calendar up to this day. Some considered this fiction-based apocryphal work dangerous to the faith, since it was certainly endangering the privileged status of the four canonical Gospels by introducing further variation and patently fictitious elements into the Birth Narratives. At the end of the 5th century Pope Gelasius (492-496) went as far as to prohibit its reading even in private.[99] By then, however, Mary's perpetual virginity was firmly taught by the Church and became, by the influence of St. Ambrose and St. Epiphanius, even a touchstone of orthodoxy.[100] The decree of Gelasius did not stop the general reception of the tradition about Mary's childhood, but explains why early Latin translations had poor chances of surviving.[101]

Finally, I mention as a fifth issue the ecclesial background against which the *Proto-evangelium* was written. Articles in patrol-

Καὶ ἔλαθεν τὸν ἄρχοντα τοῦ αἰῶνος τούτου ἡ παρθενία Μαρίας καὶ ὁ τοκετὸς αὐτῆς, ὁμοίως καὶ ὁ θάνατος τοῦ κυρίου· τρία μυστήρια κραυγῆς, ἅτινα ἐν ἡσυχίᾳ θεοῦ ἐπράχθη.
"And Mary's virginity and her childbearing escaped the notice of the Prince of this age, similarly also the Lord's death. These are three mysteries of proclamation, which had been accomplished in God's silence." (*Ephesians* 19:1).
The first two of the "mysteries" are Mary's virginity and her "childbearing," meaning Mary's virginity *ante partum* and *in partu*. As it seems the *Proto-evangelium* applies to the story in a simplified and possibly crude way the same theology of revelation: what happened at Mary's virginal conception (and later at her miraculous childbearing) belongs to the divine mysteries originating in silence and becoming "proclamation" (κραυγὴ) only by divine intervention. The crucial words are close to identical: ἔλαθεν ... μυστήρια in Ignatius and Μαρία ἐπελάθετο τῶν μυστηρίων in the *Proto-evangelium*.

99 Also Pope Innocent I already in a letter from the year 405 to Exsuperius, bishop of Toulouse, about the canon of Scripture mentions a book attributed to "James the Minor," telling that it must be rejected (Denzinger-Schönmetzer, 213).

100 Cf. Charles W. Neumann, *The Virgin Mary in the Works of St. Ambrose* (Fribourg: University Press, 1962), 142-146.

101 Strycker published Latin fragments found in late medieval codices originating from lectionaries or other secondary sources.

ogy textbooks and lexicons usually say that this work was produced and promoted for the sake of providing tangible historical witness to Mary's perpetual virginity. This is not quite correct. After Jesus' birth, this document describes how, indeed, one of the midwives attempted to verify Mary's physical virginity. But the proof is anything but "tangible." At best it is indirect: her hand is burned off as she attempts to touch the private parts of the Virgin. The *Proto-evangelium* is not as pre-occupied with empirical proofs for Mary's enduring virginity, as demonstrating the sacred character of Mary's virginity and childbearing. We see here the continuity with Ignatius of Antioch, who called the virginal conception and birth a "mystery," lying beyond human reach.[102] Thus, even when pointing out Mary's virginity *in partu*, the focus of the *Proto-evangelium* rests on Mary's virginal motherhood as something sacred, consecrated by the God who chooses to be born from a Virgin. Therefore, the readers for whom the *Proto-evangelium* was written (and copied into the devotional book preserved by Bodmer papyrus 5) were quite probably groups of ascetics, both men and women, who, around the beginning of the 2nd century, launched the early monastic movements in the Church. Specifically, I refer to the so-called *virgines subintroductae*, unmarried women, dedicated to prayer and ascetic practices and living under the tutelage of ascetic men, whose authority provided them patronage and legal existence in a society otherwise obliging women to marry and to live under the authority of their husbands. In the *Proto-evangelium*, Mary is represented as a virgin entrusted to a respectable elderly man of proven virtue who guaranteed her virgin-

---

[102] I think that we have here in this scene of the *Proto-evangelium* the best explanation of the ancient antiphon used since patristic times: *Rubum quem viderat Moyses incombustum, tuam agnovimus virginitatem, Dei Genitrix...* ("In the bush that Moses saw burning but not consumed by the fire, we recognize your virginity, holy Mother of God...") Translated from Greek, this antiphon was used at "the most ancient Marian feast in Rome, January 1st." See B. Capelle, "La liturgie mariale en Occident" in D. du Manoir, *Maria*, I, 221. This antiphon remained in the Roman Breviary until the reforms after Vatican II. It closely compares God's self-disclosure to Moses with his appearance in the flesh at his birth from Mary. Justin Martyr's Logos theory is transparent: in the burning bush the Incarnation of the Logos is pre-figured.

ity and supervised her behavior. This framework is the *Sitz im Leben* in which the author applies and expands, with fictional re-interpretation, the data of the Infancy Narratives in Matthew and Luke.

Tertullian (ca. 160-220)

It would be quite tempting to treat Tertullian after Origen, but chronologically Tertullian's works antedate Origen and, if there was dependency between them, only Origen could have depended on Tertullian, not the other way around. Moreover, Carthage in Latin Africa, where Tertullian lived, was under the influence of Rome rather than Alexandria, so that Tertullian, who wrote all of his works in Latin, is rightly considered the first major theologian of the Latin Church of the West and is inserted only with some difficulty into the developmental family tree of Eastern, Greek theology. This we must keep in mind in order not to stretch the truth about the development of Mariology by either favoring or discrediting Tertullian.

In many respects Tertullian is a worthy successor to both Justin Martyr and Irenaeus, both of whom wrote in Greek but lived in the West. Tertullian takes over from them the Mary/Eve parallelism and in *De carne Christi* 17 builds strict parallelism between the first Adam and Eve, created from a virginal earth, and the second Adam born from the Virgin. Then, in a separate paragraph he compares the two Eves by antithesis: the first Eve disobeys by listening to the Serpent; Mary obeys by believing in the Angel. The first Eve leads to perdition, by introducing death; the second Eve allows the life-giving Word to enter the world and thus erases the fault that the first Eve had introduced. The text is more logically crafted than that of Irenaeus, but the idea of recapitulation disappears. Nor does Tertullian mention that the order between Eve and Adam (the woman formed from the man's body) is reversed when the second Adam's body is born from Mary, the second Eve: Tertullian's text is apparently more logical, but lacks the same depth.

Similarly powerful is Tertullian's insistent apologetics on behalf of Jesus' virginal conception by Mary: an anti-Gnostic barrage.

He does not just attack and ridicule Marcion and the Valentinian Gnostics, but literally demolishes them by his wit and sarcasm. His best publication on this matter is *De carne Christi*, a book that kept Tertullian on the reading list of Western Christology and Mariology. In this book he defends the doctrine of the Incarnation against the Ebionites (Jewish Christians who did not believe in Jesus' divinity), different Hellenistic groups of Gnosticism, and Tertullian's chief enemy, Marcion. For Tertullian is best known through his five books *Adversus Marcionem*, which also managed to preserve most of our present-day information about Marcion. From this book we know how, at the end of the 2ⁿᵈ century, the exact form of biblical texts and their exegesis, sometimes down to the minute details, became important for both sides of the disputes. In any case, Tertullian offered a lasting portrait (or caricature) of Marcion. It was partly through the debate he was leading against Marcion that Pauline exegesis and theology obtained new motivation and importance.

With respect to Jesus' virginal conception by Mary, Tertullian seemingly says nothing new. Yet he might have been the first of the Church Fathers for whom Jesus' virginal origin is explicitly linked to two particularly important issues. On the one hand, against the Gnostics and especially Marcion, it demonstrates Jesus' true human nature; on the other hand it shows that Jesus' origin was not tainted by a man's passion or carnal impulse. For proving the latter, Tertullian uses the western text of John 1:13 and reads it in the singular, passionately arguing that the plural reading is a falsification initiated by some Gnostic editors of the Fourth Gospel.[103] He offers

---

[103] "Quid est ergo, Non ex sanguine nec ex voluntate carnis nec ex voluntate viri sed ex deo natus est? Hoc quidem capitulo ego potius utar, cum adulteratores eius obduxero: sic enim scriptum esse contendunt, Non ex sanguine nec ex carnis voluntate nec ex voluntate viri sed ex deo nati sunt, quasi supradictos credentes in nomine eius designet, ut ostendant esse semen illud arcanum electorum et spiritalium quod sibi imbuunt." *De carne Christi* XIX: E. Evans (ed.), SPCK, 64. ("What is it then: 'He was born neither of blood, nor of the will of the flesh nor a man's will, but of God'? This text I prefer to use rather than quoting those who bastardized it by demanding that it was thus written: 'Neither of blood, nor of the will of the flesh, nor of the will of man were we born but from God,' as it designated the believers. This they did in order to demonstrate that seed of the elect and spiritual which they drink into themselves.") About this see more above pp. 40-42.

another interesting textual remark regarding the Pauline text about Jesus' human origins "from a woman" (Gal 4:4): he asserts that the word "woman" (*mulier*) can be applied to the Virgin Mary, since she was called by this word even by the Angel Gabriel in his greeting: "Blessed are you among women (*in mulieribus*)."[104] The issue is seemingly relevant only to the Latin translation of the Bible, because in Latin, by normal usage, *mulier* means a married woman. Tertullian is obviously well informed about all textual details of Scripture, at least of the Old Latin text.

Often it is said that his care about the precise meaning of the biblical text adduced him to deny Mary's perpetual virginity. The issue is certainly not so simple. His position on Mary remaining a virgin at Jesus' birth was quite acceptable in the context of the Church at his time: Mary conceived as a virgin and until Jesus' birth remained a virgin so that her womb was opened not by a man in sexual intercourse but by her child. For Tertullian this is "the sign" to which Isaiah refers when he says that "the virgin conceives and bears a son" (Is 7:14). In his *De carne Christi* 23, Tertullian finds a formula which is certainly new in its language, but *per se* does not state that Mary lost her virginity at Jesus' birth: *virgo quantum a viro, non virgo quantum a partu.*[105] Afterwards, however, Tertullian tells us, Mary had marital relations with Joseph and bore several other children, all brothers and sisters of Jesus, and so she is a role model for both virgins and married women.

---

[104] Of course, here also, Tertullian uses a Western variant of Lk 1:28 which present-day critical editions (Nestle-Aland and Metzger in particular) do not admit, but it is found in the vast majority of the manuscripts. See below pp. 98-103.

[105] The phrase is hard to translate in its laconic compactness, and needs a careful paraphrase: "virgin as having no relations with any man, but not virgin as on account of bearing children." This in itself does not state that Mary's parturition was like any other. In fact, in chapter 17 of the same work, when contrasting Eve to Mary, Tertullian states that after the sin Eve "conceived, for she gave birth as one rejected, and in fact she gave birth in pains": *concepit nam exinde ut abiecta pareret et in doloribus pareret.* The repetition of *pareret* connects with emphasis the words *abiecta* and *in doloribus* (sinful and painful) which is the traditional exegesis of Gn 3:15. Eve's conception and parturition took place after her sin and hence the latter was painful. The contrast drawn in this passage would indicate that, according to Tertullian, Mary did not give birth in pain as Eve did.

Does Tertullian refer here to some "tradition" which represents original facts and earlier views about Jesus' family and only later was changed under the influence of the *Proto-evangelium* as well as the ascetics, male and female, who favored and spread the use of the *Proto-evangelium*? Tertullian's most explicit summary on this issue and the context into which it is inserted provides a rather clear answer:

> She was a virgin who gave birth to Christ, but after giving birth she was married to one man so that both ideals of holiness might be exemplified in the parentage of Christ in the person of a mother who was both virgin and married to one husband only.[106]

Tertullian has custom-tailored his opinion about Mary's "other children" for one of his particular theological positions: he condemns the practice of remarrying. In his book *De monogamia*, which comes from his Montanist period, we find this thesis explicitly proposed and in harsh terms, condemning all Christians who disagree. This book followed suit with several others, all characterized by moral rigorism, banning several features of daily life that characterized the Hellenistic cities of his age: public shows of entertainment (*De spectaculis*), elaborate female hairdo (*De cultu feminarum*), and proper and improper fashion for unmarried Christian women (*De virginibus velandis*). In his *De monogamia* he argues for the immorality of getting married a second time even after a spouse's death. Disapproving second marriages was so important for Tertullian that it led

---

[106] *Et Christum quidem virgo enixa est, semel nuptura post partum, ut uterque sanctitatis titulus in Christi censu dispungeretur per matrem et virginem et univiram.* De monogamia 8.2. The added word *univiram* shows that Tertullian even makes a point that after the birth of Jesus Mary entered marriage, but only one, so that both Joseph and Mary were each other's spouses and thus on both accounts (virginity and living in one single marriage) title to sanctity would be warranted for Jesus' records. We see here the influence of Roman Law according to which one is not validly married until the marriage is consummated. This concept of marriage influenced also Ambrose but in an opposite direction: Mary is espoused, but not married in full sense even after moving in with Joseph. But then, after Jesus' birth, according to Ambrose, for the same reason Mary and Joseph live in separate households. See below pp. 127-132.

him to become an innovator in Mariology. Specifically it meant for him that he could not accept the so-called "Epiphanian view" about the brothers of Jesus (Joseph having children from an earlier marriage) because it implied that, if Joseph had been a widower, Mary's betrothal to Joseph would thus have been morally unacceptable. Living with Joseph and his children from a previous marriage would have meant for Mary to live in a morally objectionable arrangement. Also, Joseph's intention to marry the Virgin Mary would have meant aiming at an illegal union. If Joseph was married (at least in the eyes of the public[107]) a second time that would have meant that at his birth from Mary Jesus would have become part of a family linked by an illegitimate marriage bond.

We must not forget that Tertullian as a Montanist embraced a number of rigorist positions. Most important of these was his claim that the Church cannot grant absolution more than once to the three "capital sins" of murder, apostasy, and adultery. In any case, his denial of Mary's perpetual virginity *quantum a viro* (in terms of marital relations) was part of a moral code that he wanted the Church to impose on all faithful, and thus put an end to the process of moral erosion and assimilation in which he saw signs of decay in the Church. While Tertullian's teaching on the sacrament of penance caused much confusion and debate for centuries, his work *De monogamia*, by being chronologically one of his last works, had less impact on the Church. But in the long run, Tertullian's thinking about Mary's virginity *post partum* had a great influence and provided ammunition to those who in the 4th century stepped up the controversies about Mary's perpetual virginity. Among others, it was probably Tertullian's authority and influence that ultimately caused the obliteration of the "Epiphanian view" in the West, and probably also prompted Jerome to superimpose on St. Joseph an ascetic ideal of virginity and to develop the theory that Jesus' brothers and sisters were his "cousins."

---

[107] But such a distinction was also unacceptable for Tertullian, since in agreement with Roman Law "marriage" implied not only a consent or a contract but also the consummation of marriage.

It is often observed that Tertullian had an unfavorable view of the 2ⁿᵈ century's Marian piety.[108] The clearest example for this alleged "severity" appears in one of Tertullian's best known works, *Adversus Marcionem*. Here he interprets Matthew 12:37 (par. Lk 8:21) as if, together with his brothers, Jesus had rebuked and disowned also his mother, contrasting them to those who, without ties to him according to the flesh, listen to his word and obey it.[109] But the real reason for Tertullian's insistence that Jesus and his brothers were born of the same mother might lie elsewhere. Against Marcion and other Gnostics, Tertullian insisted that Jesus was a true "flesh-and-blood" human being, taking real flesh not from the stars or some "stellar" phantom-like substance, but from Mary, who bore other children. At least in his *De carne Christi*[110] this is the reason he cites for denying Mary's continued virginity. Finally, on account of its apocryphal credentials, Tertullian must have had negative views about the *Proto-evangelium*, and thus readily rejected any miraculous birth story.

Origen (184/5-253/4)

While Irenaeus is the first theologian of the Church, Origen is the first man whom we can call a "full-time" theologian. While living in Alexandria, he was not ordained to serve as a presbyter; yet he was fully engaged in a catechetical school, undertook immense text-critical studies (six columns, comparing various versions of the Old Testament, called *Hexapla*), wrote ambitious and detailed biblical

---

[108] Gambero, discussing Tertullian, entitles a section "Tertullian's Severity on the Blessed Virgin." See Luigi Gambero, *Mary and the Fathers of the Church*, tr. by Thomas Buffer (San Francisco: Ignatius Press, 1999), 62-63.

[109] *Adversus Marcionem* IV, 19, 11 (SC 456,247-8). Such texts, patronized by the 4ᵗʰ century Marian heresies and by most Protestants of today, were regarded in modern apologetics as the so-called "anti-Mariological" texts of the Bible. Here as elsewhere, Tertullian makes his point that the brothers of Jesus were, in fact, full brothers, for otherwise the irony in Jesus' question, "Who are my brothers?" would not make its point.

[110] Chapters 4 and 5.

commentaries, and, in his most important systematic work of theology, the *Peri Archon* (*About the First Principles*), presented a broad theological compendium.

In the context of his theological reflection, Mary obtains a remarkably important place, and he often gives meticulous explanations for it. Since most of Origen's work were lost and some survive only in fragments and in Latin translation, we must not forget that generalizations about his theology must be made with much caution, for his extant works constitute not much more than ten percent of what he wrote. After the critical edition of Origen's works, only one major, modern study has been written about his Mariology, by the Italian Benedictine Cipriano Vagaggini. This book, written about seventy years ago, has not yet been matched by any other either in precision or in depth.[111] In its appendix, the author carefully collected all passages of Origen's extant works in which Mary is mentioned. These form eighty-eight passages, which Vagaggini named Origen's *Corpus Mariologicum*. By extrapolation, one may conclude that, had Origen's works not been mostly destroyed, he would have left behind hundreds of similar passages dealing with the Virgin Mary.

About Origen's Mariology I will try to generalize those aspects that mark a development of thought on Mary in relation to Irenaeus and the 2nd century in general.

The anti-Gnostic character of Origen's Mariology may not be its most important feature, but it makes us understand how this apologetic concern still kept pushing the figure of Mary to the forefront, especially in function of Christology. Origen is aware of the fundamental importance of the *Regula fidei*, in which Jesus' true human birth from a specific historical person signifies and guarantees that Christian faith can never compromise on Jesus' full humanity. On the other hand, the virginal character of his conception and birth is equally important. Origen takes it over from tradition as a mat-

---

[111] *Maria nelle Opere di Origene* (Rome: Pontificio Istituto Orientale, 1942). Written during World War II and in Italian, this excellent book has hardly ever been used extensively, not even by authors as well documented as René Laurentin.

ter on which the Church's faith has been expressed and settled. It is very important to notice here that Origen claims no knowledge of extraordinary or miraculous details about the birth of Jesus in Bethlehem. He is acquainted with the *Proto-evangelium*, known already to his teacher, Clement of Alexandria, but he does not use it as a historically reliable source regarding the mode of Jesus' birth. He quotes the *Proto-evangelium* for what it claims to say: even the midwives summoned to Jesus' birth could not check on Mary retaining her corporal integrity during the birth, because they were miraculously prevented from touching Mary's private parts. However, it seems that Origen gave credence to the mistaken notion of the *Proto-evangelium*, assuming that Zechariah, John the Baptist's father, is the one mentioned in Matthew 23:35, and suffered martyrdom between "the sanctuary and the altar."[112] In this way Origen, whose works were widely read, copied, and translated, greatly influenced the reception of the *Proto-evangelium*. This was especially important for the West, where no Latin text of the *Proto-evangelium* survived, but Origen's *Homilies on Luke* were widely read in Latin translation and Ambrose, a most popular source for Western Christianity, incorporated their content into his own *Commentary on Luke*. Similarly, either from the *Proto-evangelium* but more probably from a more widely circulating early tradition of the 2nd century, Origen adhered to the position that Jesus was Mary's only son because his brothers and sisters were half-siblings born from an earlier marriage of Joseph. Origen knows that some of the faithful support this view and names two apocryphal works as possible sources, the Gospel of Peter and the "Book of James" (i.e. the *Proto-evangelium*). Without approving these apocryphal sources, he states that, nonetheless, such a view "is in harmony with reason":

---

[112] Remarkable is the detail that, according to the *Proto-evangelium*, Zechariah, at that time the High Priest, allowed Mary to retain her place in the Temple among the virgins and thus recognized Mary's virginity *post partum*. This Origen does not quote, quite possibly because he does not consider it historically reliable.

But some say, basing it on a tradition in the Gospel according to Peter,[113] as it is entitled, or in "The Book of James," that the brethren of Jesus were sons of Joseph by a former wife, whom he married before Mary. Now those who say so wish to preserve the honor of Mary in virginity to the end, so that that body of hers which was appointed to minister to the Word which said, "The Holy Spirit shall come upon thee, and the power of the Most High shall overshadow thee," might not know intercourse with a man after that the Holy Spirit came into her and the power from on high overshadowed her (cf. Lk 1:35). And I think it in harmony with reason that Jesus was the first-fruit among men of the purity which consists in chastity, and Mary among women;[114] for it were not pious to ascribe to any other than to her the first-fruit of virginity.[115]

Origen's comment about the apocryphal nature of the sources which some people in the Church use to prove that Mary never entered into sexual relations with any man is also methodologically most interesting and important. He does not even attempt to support these two books, because he knows that the Church attributes no authority to them. However, he tells that he agrees with their position about Jesus' brothers and sisters as something "in harmony with reason." I do not think I am mistaken when stating that for Mariology this text by Origen is the oldest document in which a Marian teaching is said to be a theological conclusion obtained by reason and reflection, even if it is narrated in a source which is otherwise not accepted by the Church in the way the Gospels are. To obtain

---

[113] Of the Gospel of Peter only fragments are extant, which do not contain references to James, the brother of the Lord. About these fragments see Paul Forster (ed.), *The Non-Canonical Gospels* (New York/London: T & T Clark, 2008), 30-42.

[114] Origen is the first who explicitly makes a parallel: Jesus is the first exemplar of consecrated virginity for men and Mary is the exemplar for women.

[115] *Commentary on the Gospel of Matthew* X, 17 (GCS 21, 19). Translation by John Patrick, first published by T & T Clark in Edinburgh in 1867. See also C. Vagaggini, op. cit., 120-121; in the Appendix no. 172.

this conclusion from an authoritative source and then conclude "in harmony with reason," Origen immediately quotes Luke's account of the Annunciation. But he does not stop there. He indicates the context and spiritual milieu in which this "theological conclusion" is formed: Jesus is the ideal of virginal life for men and Mary is similarly such an ideal for women. In fact, as we pointed out above, the *Proto-evangelium*'s original readers (including those who must have sponsored its 4ᵗʰ century copy found in the Egyptian sand)[116] belonged quite probably to such ascetic-monastic groups of the 2ⁿᵈ century, who were inclined to reflect on the full message of the virginal conception from Mary's point of view.

Here we touch upon an important point for Mariology. All studies about Origen's Mariology say that Origen was unclear or hesitant about Mary's virginity *in partu*, while he was fully convinced about her ongoing virginity *post partum*. We must sense right away that we are dealing here with a problem of terminology. How could he remain convinced that Mary preserved her virginity after Jesus' birth and be doubtful, at the same time, whether she retained it at his birth? In fact, in Origen we do not encounter a threefold division of Mary's virginal status which eventually entered parlance only much later (*ante partum, in partu, post partum*), nor do we find a claim that virginity would be equivalent to some physical attribute of bodily integrity. Origen seems to be concerned about quite different issues. For example, he has difficulty with Exodus 34:9, quoted by Luke about Mary's purification in the Temple: "Every male that opens the womb shall be consecrated to the Lord" (Lk 2:23).[117] He actually thinks that this scriptural verse was fulfilled *only* in Mary. No woman's womb was ever opened the first time *from within* by the birth of her first child, male or female, but only from without, namely at her first intercourse, which precedes conception and birth. Only with a birth following a virginal conception would the womb

---

[116] As we said above and must be mentioned again: Bodmer papyrus no. 5 is a "devotional book." Its sponsor and users must be identified as a private readers or a group of people listening to its communal reading. See above p. 79.

[117] *Homilies on Luke* 14 (GCS IX, 100).

be opened "from within." Thus, for Origen Exodus 34:9 is a prophetic text obtaining its fulfillment *only* in Mary's virginal motherhood.[118] Therefore, Origen calls Mary both *virgin and mother* also after Jesus' birth.[119] He is apparently unconcerned with tying Mary's virginity to the physical consequences of giving birth and simply assumes that after the opening of her womb (in Latin translation: *reseratio vulvae*) her virginal status is retained.

There is another short text of Origen's, in which he again shows his familiarity with the *Proto-evangelium of James*, although again he does not attribute authenticity to the apocryphal book. Commenting on Matthew 23:35, he refers to a "tradition" according to which Zechariah, the father of John the Baptist, defended Mary against the accusation that, "after giving birth to the Savior" (*postquam genuit Salvatorem*), she lost her right to stand in the Temple "in the place reserved for virgins." For in spite of having given birth to Jesus, "she still was entitled to be at the place of the virgins since she was still a virgin (ἔτι παρθένος)."[120] This is, in any case, a bold statement. It suggests that, according to Origen, the last martyr of the Old Testament died for defending Mary's perpetual virginity. That the identification of Zechariah in Matthew 23:35 and in Luke 1:5 is historically mistaken is beside the point. More important is the linkage Origen saw in this legend between virginity and martyrdom.

Origen is not only a man of immense erudition, thoroughly

---

[118] This very same scriptural text (Ex 34:9 as quoted by Lk 2:23) is treated earlier in a similar way also by Tertullian yet he denies Mary's perpetual virginity. *De carne Christi*, 23. Tertullian admits that for Jesus' birth the first opening of the womb (*reseratio vulvae*) occurred in a miraculous way "from within." But that happened for the first child, only. After Jesus' birth Mary and Joseph began marital relations and thus Mary ceased to be a virgin also *quoad virum*.

[119] This is clearly stated in the seventeenth Homily on Luke: *Virgo mater est, signum cui contradicitur* (GCS IX, 115). Cf. Vagaggini, op. cit., 93.

[120] This passage is found in his *Commentary on Matthew* 25 (GCS IX, 42). The phrase "ἔτι παρθένος" became programmatic for Helmut Koch's once famous book *Adhuc Virgo, Mariens Jungfrauschaft und Ehe in der altkirchlichen Überlieferung bis zum Ende des 4. Jahrhunderts* (Tübingen: P. Siebeck, 1929), [*The Virginity and Marriage of Mary in Early Church Tradition until the end of the 4ᵗʰ Century*] in which he tried to reconstruct the origins of Marian doctrine and cult with the tools of the history of religion (*Religionsgeschichte*), as based on pagan antecedents in the cult of Isis in ancient Egypt.

acquainted with all matters biblical. He resonates with inner conviction and personal devotion to the texts on which he comments.
While the "spirit and fire" which permeate his exegetical writings
have often been indicated,[121] it is also important for us to see that he
was one of the first ecclesiastical writers with enthusiastic and tender
feelings toward Mary. In the introductory chapter of his *Commentary on John* he speaks about the Fourth Gospel as the "first fruit" of
the four Gospels and even of all Scriptures, "whose profound meaning nobody can receive unless he rested his head on Jesus' breast and
also received Mary to be his mother."[122] This passage then continues by stating as a known fact, that Mary had no other son besides
Jesus. Finally he adds that neither did Jesus on the Cross indicate
that Mary bore John as an additional son: he only wanted to convey
that John now remains with Mary as another Jesus, and, in fact, all
those who reach that degree of perfection by which they do not live
but Christ lives in them (cf. Gal 2:20) are meant here by Jesus to be
Mary's sons.

We are dealing here with substantial portions, although preserved only in fragments, of true Marian piety, which Origen did not
merely develop as an idiosyncratic and personal attribute but appropriated from the milieu of the Alexandrian Church where this kind
of devotion, as well as the earliest traces of organized monasticism,
flourished and left behind some important documents, recovered
only recently, in the 20ᵗʰ century's papyrus findings.

Praying to Mary: The Ancient Text of the *Sub Tuum* (before 300)

Still in 1917, well before Bodmer papyrus 5 was reconstructed,
a small papyrus leaf was found in the Egyptian sand. Because the
First World War was still raging, and thereafter Europe was for decades in turmoil, its publication had to wait until 1938. As it turned

---

[121] See this characterization of Origen's writings in *Origen: Spirit and Fire, An Anthol-
ogy of His Writings*, edited by Hans Urs von Balthasar (Washington, DC: Catholic
University of America Press, 1984).
[122] *Commentary on John* I, 4 (GCS IV, 8).

out, it contained the Greek text of a famous prayer, known for centuries in many ancient languages, whose origin had never been exactly identified. It is still habitual to refer to it to by the first two words of its Latin translation, and thus it is called the *Sub Tuum*.[123] It is still widely used with some variants both by Catholics and by all Eastern Orthodox Churches. Although the dating of the papyrus was never fully settled, it is today usually called an "antiphon," a short prayer to be chanted. It soon became regarded as "the earliest known Marian prayer." The text of the papyrus is reconstructed as follows:

Ὑπὸ τὴν σὴν εὐσπλαγχνίαν
καταφεύγομεν, Θεοτόκε.
Τὰς ἡμῶν ἱκεσίας
μὴ παρίδῃς ἐμ περιστάσει,
ἀλλ᾽ ἐκ κινδύνου ῥῦσαι ἡμᾶς,
μόνη Ἁγνή, μόνη εὐλογημένη.

[Under your mercy
we take refuge, O Mother of God.
Our petitions
do not disregard in necessity,
but deliver us from dangers,
you alone pure, alone blessed.]

By paleographical evidence, the papyrus text was first dated to the 3rd century, yet, because of "the discomfort of many experts" with an alleged "anachronism" of such an early dating, authors began to speak of it as coming from the 4th century. Today, theological dictionaries assign it to "about 300 A.D."

Three elements of the text are remarkable: First, it directly addresses Mary in prayer; second, the title ΘΕΟΤΟΚΟΣ appears in it as a

---

[123] Still used in the Latin liturgy in the following form: *Sub tuum praesidium confugimus, sancta Dei Genitrix. Nostras deprecationes ne despicias in necessitatibus nostris, sed a periculis cunctis libera nos semper, Virgo gloriosa et benedicta.* A literal English translation would be: "Under your protection we run, Holy Mother of God (=Theotokos). Do not ignore our petitions amidst our needs. But from all dangers deliver us, holy Virgin, glorious and blessed."

matter of course. Third, the last line "you alone pure, alone blessed" describes Mary as "standing alone" (μόνη) or "the only one," most probably with reference to her purity, meaning her *virginal mother-hood*. The adjective "pure" (ἁγνή), following the first μόνη, requires a complementary noun, probably παρθένος. In this way the expression obtains a quasi-technical meaning, παρθένος ἁγνή, or an "undefiled virgin." This is certainly very close to the variant reading of the Latin text: *Virgo gloriosa et benedicta*.

The literary structure is loosely chiastic, going back and forth between "you" and "us":

A Under *your* mercy we take refuge, *O Theotokos*.
B Do not disregard *our* petition in necessity
B' but deliver *us* from dangers,
A' [*you*] alone *pure*, alone *blessed*.

The first and last lines address Mary, first as *Theotokos*, then at the end as "alone pure, alone blessed." The second and third lines, each in a different way, refer, to "us."

The opening words about "fleeing for refuge" to the Virgin certainly constitute a remarkable phrase, especially if we think of what the gravest issue was in the persecution-filled 3ʳᵈ century: the dilemma of fleeing or not fleeing (and if yes: when and to where), a theme so well known from the life story of St. Cyprian, Bishop of Carthage. In such a context its early dating might be dramatically vindicated.

The last line of the Latin version of the text has been punctuated in two ways:

a) *libera nos semper*, Virgo gloriosa et benedicta, OR
b) "libera nos, [o] *semper Virgo*, gloriosa et benedicta"

By dating the *Proto-evangelium* to the second half of the 2ⁿᵈ century, this issue became less significant. Its readers were certainly contemporaries or the immediate forerunners of those who first prayed the *Sub Tuum*. More significant, of course, is the appearance of Mary's title *Theotokos*, but that is not considered anymore as an innovation of the 4th century, for it had won general acceptance well before the Council of Ephesus (431). But if around the year 300 Mary is addressed as *Theotokos*, and around 170-190 the *Proto-evangelium* regarded Mary's role at the birth of Jesus as a sacred event, then the word "mystery" applied to Mary's *toketos* (childbearing) by Ignatius of Antioch also obtains its full meaning and all these details are lined up in a probable sequence of development. By being the physical source of the humanity of the divine Savior, both Son of God and son of Mary (cf. Ignatius, *Ephesians* 7,2) the virginal birth is not a mere "nature miracle," but a revelatory event, meaningful only for the eyes of faith.

A 2nd Century Variant Reading of Luke 1:28

An impressive set of manuscripts[124] has for the angelic salutation in Luke 1:28 a longer variant reading:

καὶ εἰσελθὼν πρὸς αὐτὴν [ὁ ἄγγελος] εἶπεν·
χαῖρε, κεχαριτωμένη, ὁ κύριος μετὰ σοῦ.
[εὐλογημένη σὺ ἐν γυναιξὶν].
(and entering unto her, the angel said:
Hail, full of grace, the Lord is with you.
Blessed are you among women.)

According to contemporary scholarship's understanding this is a secondary, variant reading, adding the words that appear here in brackets. It is usually said that it "obviously" expands the Angel's greeting in the original text by a phrase borrowed from Elizabeth's greeting at the Visitation (Lk 1:42).[125] Moreover, most but not all the

---

[124] Among them the most important are A (Codex Alexandrinus), C (Codex Ephraemi Syri Rescriptus), D (Codex Bezae), most minuscules, all ancient translations (*Vetus Latina*, Vulgate, the Peshitta, Gothic, Georgian, Ethiopian), the *Diatessaron*, Tertullian and other patristic witnesses.

[125] Most commentators do not mention this variant reading. François Bovon suggests that it originates with "a few scribes" who have taken it from Tatian's *Diatessaron*. This suggestion came from August Strobel "Der Gruss an Maria (Lc 1,28)"

manuscripts that carry this variant also insert ὁ ἄγγελος as if to indicate that, indeed, all this has been uttered by the Angel Gabriel.

In his *Textual Commentary* Bruce Metzger[126] classifies the inserted words with the *siglum* {B}.[127] He adds that "copyists inserted them here from verse 42 where they are clearly attested." However, it is not at all clear how by a copyist's mistake a phrase can be inserted *from* 1:42 *into* 1:28 by anticipation. To do this, inadvertently, he would have had to skip ahead thirteen verses and come back where he left off. This is not an acceptable explanation. A more plausible scenario would be that the copyist knew both the Angel's and Elizabeth's greeting *as already fused together* into one single greeting and so the mistake occurs because he or the one who dictates to the copyist follows, instead of what is before his eyes, a text he has in his memory.

But even in this case we are left with two questions in need of explanation. First, how did it happen that several different textual types began carrying this mistake? It must have entered the text at a very early point in time. Furthermore, how is it explained that practically all textual witnesses which have the variant reading of the Angel's greeting reinforce the mistake by inserting also an additional ὁ ἄγγελος, as if calling to the reader's attention that all that follows are, indeed, the words of the Angel, and not just Elizabeth's words,

---

in *Zeitschrift für neutestamentliche Wissenschaft* 55 (1962) 86-116. See François Bovon, *Luke 1* (Minneapolis: Fortress, 2002), 50, n. 67. In fact, the *Diatessaron* and the *Proto-evangelium* are the oldest known patristic witnesses of the variant reading. It is not known which one was written earlier. The same variant occurring in both these documents points to an earlier source. The *Proto-evangelium* is nowhere based on the text of the *Diatessaron*. Moreover the exact wording of Lk 1:28 in the *Diatessaron* is not so clear, because St. Ephrem, whose commentary is our only source for the original text of the *Diatessaron*, quotes Lk 1:28 in isolation, independently from the Annunciation. Therefore, we can say, that the *Diatessaron*'s textual variant for Lk 1:28 is not sure at all. Ephrem quoting the Angel's greeting may not be quoting the *Diatessaron*. (Cf. Louis Leloir's edition of the Commentary to the *Diatessaron* in *Sources chrétiennes* 121, Paris: Cerf, 1966, p. 102.) But, in any case, the question remains: how did this strange combination of Gabriel's and Elizabeth's reading originally come about?

[126] Bruce M. Metzger, *A Textual Commentary on the New Testament* (London/New York: United Bible Societies, 1970), 129.

[127] "{B} indicates that there is some degree of doubt concerning the reading selected for the text." Ibid., XXVIII.

inserted here by mistake? For the list of those which Metzger calls "fairly good witnesses," those that contain ὁ ἄγγελος in Luke 1:28, are practically identical with those that carry the expanded angelic greeting.[128] From this insistence, as it were, of so many early manuscripts on the validity of the variant, there resulted a rather strange combination of facts: not only the *textus receptus* accepted it, but it is contained even today in all the well-known translations, old and new alike, Catholic and Protestant, such as the *Vetus Latina* (quoted by Tertullian), the Vulgate, the Peshitta, the King James Version, and Luther's Bible even in two of its most modern editions. Regardless, therefore, how the variant text came about, it was consciously accepted at a very early point in the history of the text, and we have every right to suspect that what has happened by accident was perpetuated for a theological reason.[129]

I think that new light was shed on this matter by the critical text of the *Proto-evangelium*, which uses the Infancy Narratives of Luke extensively but with remarkable freedom. It not only includes the words "blessed are you among women" within the Angel's greeting, but entirely omits the same phrase from its original place in the greeting of Elizabeth. More exactly, in the *Proto-evangelium* the Annunciation consists of two scenes. In the first scene, Mary is at a well and receives a greeting from a "voice" by an invisible speaker: "Hail, full of grace, the Lord is with you, blessed are you among women." Then in the next scene, after Mary enters the house, puts down the water jar, and sits down to her work, "an Angel" appears to her announcing, mostly in the words of Luke 1:30-38 but also Matthew 1:21, that she will conceive and bear the Divine Child.

The chief witness of the variant's early provenance is Tertul-

---

[128] This detail is entirely missing from the less documented apparatus of the American Bible Society's critical Greek text.

[129] There exists, to my knowledge, no study how the expanded textual variant was questioned, accepted but also at times rejected through the centuries. I know only that St. Bernard of Clairvaux considered the variant of the Vulgate spurious, for he comments on the Angel's words: "'Benedicta tu in mulieribus' Libet adjungere quod Elisabeth cuius haec verba sunt, prosecute coniunxit: Et benedictus fructus ventris tui," in *Laudibus Virginis Matris, Sancti Bernard, Opera Omnia* (Leclecrqu-Rochais) IV (Rome: Editiones Cistercienses, 1966), 38.

lian. Not only does he know the variant reading from the early Latin version, but uses it for a theological point: both the Angel Gabriel and the Apostle Paul spoke of Jesus' mother as "woman" (cf. Gal 4:4). He writes: "I also acknowledge that the Angel was sent to the Virgin and when he declares her blessed he locates her among women and not among virgins: 'Blessed are you among women.' The Angel, therefore, knew that a virgin can be called also 'woman'" (*De virginibus velandis* 6,1). We have seen earlier that Tertullian, who denied Mary's perpetual virginity *post partum*, was rather ambiguous about her virginity *quantum a partu*, namely her integrity being preserved at giving birth. However here he quotes the Angel, so he must be speaking about Mary's virginity before Jesus' birth (*ante partum*). Of course, it is rather strange that, according to Tertullian, the Angel Gabriel and St. Paul are in agreement, but we are in the 2ⁿᵈ century, at a time when correct biblical language and usage just begin to be argued about and cross-references from book to book are used for deciding the correct interpretation. (Neither Tertullian nor his readers would be bothered that the Angel, Mary, and the Apostle Paul did not speak Latin.) In any case, Tertullian thinks that by calling Jesus' mother *mulier* St. Paul does not question her virginity because that is what the Angel Gabriel called her at the Annunciation.

From the mosaic of the text-critical facts regarding Luke 1:28 and 1:42 a few important conclusions can be made.

First, its presence in the *Proto-evangelium* shows that around the middle of the 2ⁿᵈ century Elizabeth's words ("blessed are you among women") in Luke 1:42 were duplicated in Luke 1:28. The insertion of ὁ ἄγγελος in the same manuscripts demonstrates that this insertion was either consciously made or, once it entered into the manuscript tradition, consciously preserved. Why? There are small, yet important signs suggesting that early readers of Luke's story might have wanted to see the two greetings harmonized. Ignatius of Antioch already says that the mystery of the virginal birth was first kept in "God's silence" then communicated by proclamation. Ignatius uses the Greek word κραυγὴ meaning a loud cry, the same word which in the Gospel text describes Elizabeth's "crying out in a loud voice" (κραυγῇ μεγάλῃ καὶ εἶπεν· εὐλογημένη σὺ ἐν γυναιξὶν). Thus, the heavenly messenger and the infant prophet in the womb made the same proclamation,[130] and what Elizabeth utters Mary hears now a *second time*: "Blessed are you among women."

Second, the early origins of the *Sub Tuum* suggest that the connection of the two greetings (Lk 1:28 and 42) and the composition of a prayer *addressing Mary* are likely come from the same milieu. The presence of the variant in the *Proto-evangelium* further validates this hypothesis. In view of the "heavenly Jerusalem" described in Hebrews (12:22-23) and the Book of Revelation (22:10-12) we might say that such an understanding of the realm of the saints of the Old and New Testaments as contemporaneous to the earthly life of the Church, especially when assembled in liturgical prayer, is a notion expressed in these books of the New Testament. The only difference is that while Hebrews and the Book of Revelation speak of the Prophets, Apostles (Rv 18:20.24) and the Martyrs (Heb 12:1, 17:6) as members of the heavenly assembly, the *Sub Tuum* indicates that the Virgin Mary, the *Theotokos*, is also to be thought of as included among the "the righteous made perfect" presented in Hebrews:

> You have come to Mount Zion and to the city of the living God, the heavenly Jerusalem, and to innumerable angels in festal gathering, and to the assembly of the firstborn who are enrolled in heaven, and to God the judge of all, and to the spirits of the righteous made perfect. (Heb 12:22-23)

Third, the last line of the papyrus where the *Sub Tuum* addresses Mary as the one "alone pure" "alone blessed," i.e., "singularly blessed," is especially relevant. It sounds like an explanation of the meaning of Elizabeth's words: "You are *singularly* blessed among all

---

[130] It is hard to exclude the possibility that the original Lucan text had "blessed are you among women" at both places. In that case the ancient "text critics" of the Gospel texts in the 3rd and 4th centuries who tried to clean them from unwarranted repetitions, caught the repetition and eliminated this variant of Lk 1:28 from many manuscripts.

women." Of course, we heard from Tertullian that "woman" may stand for "virgin."

Furthermore, the word εὐλογημένη eventually becomes a key word for rooting Mary's role into the beginnings of salvation history in two important ways. First, it recalls by contrast, in the fashion Justin and Irenaeus handled the Mary/Eve parallel, the curses uttered after the first sin – Mary is *benedicta* in contrast to all that is *maledictus* or *maledicta*: the cursed condition of the Serpent, the soil, Adam's work struggling with thorns and thistles, and Eve's childbearing in pain. Second, Abraham's story is recalled on account of the promise: "All tribes of the earth will be blessed in you."[131]

General Conclusions about Ante-Nicene Mariology

We have seen in this chapter a short summary of the main theological developments in Mariology before the Council of Nicaea (325), which also marked the cessation of persecutions and opened the door to a massive, Empire-wide conversion and eventually led to the Christianization of all Europe.

In the first decades of the 20th century, many historians believed that most of what happened in the 4th century could be described as "hellenization" of Christianity, a basic transformation of the original message of Jesus and the apostolic Church into a system of doctrines with a Hellenistic philosophical foundation. Writing in the 1920's and 1930's about early Mariology, Hugo Koch[132] popularized the notion that the 2nd century's interest in Mary came about as part of this process. He was convinced that the exaltation of Mary's virginity came about in the early Church as a transposition of the

---

[131] For understanding early Christians we should read the Septuagint: ἐνευλογηθήσονται ἐν σοὶ πᾶσαι αἱ φυλαὶ τῆς γῆς (Gn 12:3). This short sentence contains three of the crucial words concerning the future blessing promised to redeem man's sinfulness: "will be blessed," "all," and "earth."

[132] *Adhuc virgo. Mariens Jungfrauschaft und Ehe in der altkirchlichen Überlieferung bis zum Ende des 4. Jahrhunderts* (Tübingen: Mohr, 1929); *Virgo Maria - Virgo Eva. Neue Untersuchungen über die Lehre der Jungfrauschaft und der Ehe Mariens in der ältesten Kirche* (Berlin-Leipzig: Walter de Gruyte, 1937).

cult of pagan female deities into this new religion as it inserted itself into the syncretistic religious culture of the Roman Empire. Certainly, there is ample evidence about mankind's age-old addiction to fertility cults, which is ultimately rooted in every human civilization's indebtedness to the origins of agriculture. Up to the threshold of modern times, man experienced deep fascination with the apparently mysterious regular changes of dry and rainy seasons, and their relationships with the moon and the constellations – all unexplained phenomena on which the fertility of the soil and the survival of all physical life depended for man and beast alike.[133] Consequently, there are innumerable examples in both the primitive religions and various documents of cultural history that illustrate the perception that both virginity and motherhood belong to the realm of the sacred. Of course, the dispute over the reduction of Judeo-Christian revelation to *Religionsgeschichte* – the general religious history of mankind – is not so much an issue to be treated in Mariology, but a more fundamental question to be discussed in the interpretation of the New Testament, including, in particular, the two independent narratives of Matthew and Luke about the virginal conception of Jesus. If these Gospel narratives reflect historical revelations, essential for Christian origins, then we must expect that in the 2nd century, together with Christology, Mary's role in salvation history would naturally have also begun to attract attention and start to appear as topics important for Christian reflection and piety.[134]

What our rather cursory survey of early patristic Mariology demonstrates is not so much a display of newly obtained apologetic tools, but rather new and increased evidence that what René Laurentin calls "a silent growth" and "quiet development"[135] was neither

---

[133] See for example Mircea Eliade, *Patterns in Comparative Religion*, tr. by R. Sheed (London: Sheed and Ward, 1958).

[134] I find significant the appearance of new approaches to the historical roots of Mariology in contemporary scholarship outside of the Catholic community as exemplified in John McGuckin, "The Early Cult of Mary and Inter-religious Contexts in the 5th Century Church" in Chris Maunder (ed.), *The Origins of the Cult of the Virgin Mary* (London/New York: Burns and Oates, 2008), 1-22.

[135] *A Short Treatise on the Virgin Mary*, tr. by Charles Neumann (Washington, NJ: AMI Press, 1991), 52-53.

as slow nor as silent as the scarcity of documental evidence made the researchers believe in the first half of the 20th century.

Present-day evidence about the critical text of the *Proto-evangelium* and the *Sub Tuum* shows that these are tips of an iceberg pointing to a much larger context submerged in history. In the 2nd century, Christianity was certainly still in its initial period; yet the theological importance of Mary's role for the Incarnation and a fast-developing popular devotion to her in a numerically small but empire-wide and rapidly growing Church were indisputable. Mary's importance in theological thought is most evident from her firmly established place in the *regula fidei*, a 2nd century anti-Gnostic formula summarizing the essential elements of orthodox Catholic Christian faith. Starting with Ignatius of Antioch all the way down to Origen, Mary's name is quite often evoked not so much as an instance of theological reasoning but as a reference to the historical, carnal, and visible reality of Jesus Christ, which cannot be reduced to a mere mental or spiritual entity.

Another insight, which only more recent research has proved, concerns the word *Theotokos*, the term which textbooks still tend to date as late as the Council of Ephesus. The actual papyrus fragment dated to around 300 A.D., with the *Sub Tuum* and the word *Theotokos* on it, antedates by more than a hundred years the Council of Ephesus (431 A.D.). But of course, the text on the papyrus fragment is a prayer with a terminology that must have been in use for some time, so the term *Theotokos* must be dated to the 3rd century. Moreover the use of this word, which appeared with dubious authenticity in the extant texts of Origen, has received an independent confirmation from this fragment. Thus we must conclude that, according to independent evidences, this ancient moving force of Mariological thought – the realization of Mary's divine motherhood – goes back almost certainly to the time of Origen, i.e. to the opening decades of the 3rd century.

The theme of the Mary/Eve parallel, recognized for a long time as the most ancient element of constructive Mariological thought, has also gained a new intelligibility in modern research. For many theologians the parallel seemed an interesting but ultimately arbitrary comparison between two biblical figures. However, a more recent and still growing knowledge of early Christian reading of the Old Testament and the role it played for Christian beginnings brought new insights. The central issue here is not an external similarity between Mary's and Eve's virginity and motherhood, but its contribution to the Christian exegesis of human origins as described in Genesis 3. The Christological mystery is penetrated down to its very roots with the Pauline keywords "first and second Adams" (cf. 1 Cor 15:45-47; 1 Tm 12:13-14; Rm 5:14) and "new creation" (Gal 6:15; 2 Cor 5:17). They point to that true new birth which is both "like and unlike" the natural birth of every human being. While the conception and birth of Jesus stand apart from every other instance of human reproduction, it is a human event fully inserted into mankind's family tree so that Jesus becomes a blood relative to all mankind. Thus our redemption happened in both a carnal and spiritual way. Mary's virginal motherhood means the unity of these two parallel yet antithetical aspects.

Beginning with Ignatius of Antioch, Mary is called *the Virgin*. Thus when studying the Church Fathers the point of departure for elucidating Mary's virginity is not *virginitas ante partum*, as the primary datum but *"the Virgin* who conceives and bears a Son" (Is 7:14, with Mt 1:23 and Lk 1:29), both completing and disrupting the reproductive chain beginning with Eve and leading to Jesus. The second Adam marks the beginning of a "new man" who is nonetheless a human being – a descendant of Adam – and renews mankind to perfection on an unexpected and unsurpassable divine scale. That this is essential for understanding the Old Testament was clearly seen by the early Church Fathers and is only half-way understood by modern exegesis. The issue is the following. If all redemption is given through Jesus and the first and fully perfect fruit of this new humanity is already achieved right at the beginning in the Incarnation, then the genetic link which inserts Jesus into the human family must be also seen as salvific: a link that is both carnal and spiritual. Redemption is not merely putative and meritorious by some heavenly bookkeeping of forgiveness, merit, gracious will, and eventual ultimate outcome of acquittal at the last judgment. Redemption is real, participatory, and comprehensive as it provides a new genesis and birth to all mankind. The Church Fathers said many times that all patriarchs and prophets, all the righteous of the first Testament were saved through Christ, so that not only Adam but also Christ establishes unity for mankind through both physical and spiritual oneness. Not only Abraham's physical descendants but all human families are blessed in "Abraham's seed" (who is, however, according to Paul, one individual member of mankind[136]), and correspondingly all generations of all time should also call Mary "blessed" (Lk 1:48), she who is the physical link (the only immediate and direct link) between Christ and the rest of all previous and future generations.

When Mary is called "the Virgin," this title only implicitly regards her remaining a virgin in and after giving birth. For this title could not be retained if it was only applied to the way she conceived her first child and then lived afterward in marital relations. But Origen correctly sees that this title applies to Mary in a full and broad sense as the exemplar of virgins. Tradition, starting with the Apostolic Fathers, does not regard her as a "retired" virgin, or somebody who once, while she was still a virgin, conceived and bore a son. The meaning of the expression "still" (ἔτι) a virgin means rather the opposite: a virgin in spite of her parturition. As Origen sees it, the curse pronounced over "the woman" in Genesis 3:16 will not apply to her. But there is a further implication: she remains consecrated by her virginal conception to a way of life so that after giving birth her status as a virgin continues, a status which she described when speaking to the Angel: "I do not know man" (Lk 1:34). These words may not express an intention and even a vow about which the evangelist possessed historical information, or some evidence obtained from a confidential oral or written source (like the *Proto-evangelium*), but it stands in the inspired text as the apostolic Church's preaching about

---

[136] Gal 3:16.

the origins of the Incarnate Word in the sense it was already suggested by the pre-Christian version of Isaiah 7:14 in the text of the Septuagint and confirmed by the *sensus fidelium* in the Church. Even many modern exegetes who cannot or do not want to see in Luke 1:34 the expression of a "vow of virginity," admit that the phrase, and especially the context, cannot be explained away by dismissing the possibility that they indicate an intention and/or desire to retain the status of virginity, which God does not "nix" in response to her question but brings to unexpected fulfillment in her virginal motherhood. Mary is not described by either Luke or the Church Fathers as a virgin only "for a while" or "temporarily."[137] As in the *Sub Tuum*, she is addressed in prayer, in the context of a lasting and ongoing eschatological presence as "the Virgin."

Another important conclusion leads us to our next chapter. It is the point we observed about Tertullian. Tertullian must not be mistaken as a sober married man, who, as an exegete reacts to the

---

[137] A survey of recent Catholic exegetes wrestling with this text is judged in harsh words by Joseph Fitzmyer, *The Gospel According to Luke I-IX, Anchor Bible* 28 (Garden City, NY: Doubleday, 1981), 348-51. That Catholics *do not have to* follow the tradition, which interprets Mary's response in this way, is beside the point. Fitzmyer's comments about his own translation of the verse are as follows: "In my translation I have left Mary's words as vague as they are in the Greek text." He may not realize that he implies to know what the text means in its strict sense so that he can make it *as vague as* its grammar allows to. In fact, he isolates Mary's question from the context of the story as a whole and does not admit any other tool of interpretation than grammar. A little more logical is Raymond Brown when he states that he could not find any other satisfactory explanation than that of a mere literary device: Luke wants to create a dialogue between Mary and the Angel in which he wanted to call attention to the mode of conception by framing it in a response to a question formulated by Mary.

I find it more than just curious that such highly skilled contemporary authors with their allegedly "modern" sensitivity about women so easily assume that God would simply impose his will and overpower a virgin's womb without seeking free consent to covenantal relationship with the girl who becomes pregnant and the mother of God's Son, something she could not have intended when espousing Joseph. Therefore, Luke and the tradition he transmitted *must imply* by their reference to each Person of the Holy Trinity as acting personal subjects, that Mary's question, the Angel's reply and Mary's final answer as a statement of acceptance about the mode of conception *are more than* a mere literary dialogue: the Virgin encounters God, she learns about his will as a call, grace, and challenge, which, by its nature, cannot be imposed, but can only be freely accepted. See also above pp. 26-32.

"hellenization" or "paganization" of Christian doctrine and, therefore, raises objections against unwarranted exaggerations of popular devotion to unmask the hidden influences of paganism in popular piety. Tertullian has his own agenda, which makes him embrace his own exaggerated devotions and doctrinal trends as he promotes the "new prophecy" of Montanism. This movement opted for elitism by its practice of denying forgiveness for penitents falling back into major sins, demanded a stricter moral code to be imposed on the faithful against the easy-going lifestyle of Hellenistic cities and loosening standards of sexual and social mores among Christians. This is how he came to the program of his *De monogamia*, denigrating the practice of re-marrying altogether. By doing so he pushed for further restrictions than those found in the Pastoral Letters, which forbad remarriage only from bishops (1 Tm 3:2), deacons (1 Tm 3:12), consecrated widows (1 Tm 5:9), and presbyters (Tt 1:6). It goes without saying that in a society where life expectancy is relatively low, demanding all widows and widowers to remain celibate makes the rules of sexual morality quite harsh and unrealistic. Tertullian had certainly no qualms about the continence practiced by those in a virginal state, but was nonetheless suspicious of apocryphal works like the *Proto-evangelium*. Certainly in the writings of both Tertullian and Origen we can anticipate that there remained unfinished theological issues about Mary's virginity. Indeed, as soon as the Christological debates began to move into the center of ecclesial attention, mariological debates had to flare up unavoidably on both the theoretical and the practical level, lining up both support and criticism as soon as the monastic movements of the 4ᵗʰ century began to make their influence felt.

CHAPTER FOUR

MARIOLOGY BETWEEN NICAEA AND EPHESUS

Introductory Remarks

It is well known that the Church's freedom from persecution, obtained under Constantine the Great, opened the way to the crisis of Arianism, for which no easy and quick solution was forthcoming. The problem of Arius' heresy was not and could not have been solved by a single Empire-wide gathering of bishops: later called the First Ecumenical Council (Nicaea, 325). As it has often turned out to be the case afterwards, the Emperor's personal backing of one side or another introduced more new problems than it solved. We cannot describe and examine here the Christology emerging after the Council of Nicaea. However, we will attempt to assess how the orthodox concept of Christ's being *homoousion* ("of one substance") with the Father and the contrary efforts of the Arians and semi-Arians impacted the Church's Marian doctrine and devotion. This in itself could have been expected and is easy to see. However, it is much less clear how a *pre-Nicene* concept of the divine motherhood – Mary the "God-bearer," professed as early as Origen and as popularly rooted as the *Sub Tuum* fragment demonstrates – contributed to the victory of the Nicene faith and played an important role in helping the faithful persevere in it.

In practical terms, we see Marian reflections move forward in a rather peculiar way. In the 2nd and 3rd centuries Mariology appears to be an "unregulated" field; it first develops with spontaneity. While inspiring fervor it has only secondary importance for controversies and for a while it did not serve as a litmus test for Nicene orthodoxy. Yet, by the end of the 4th century, it obtains an importance and the controversies about it increase. Titles and biblical key texts multiply, charges and countercharges of heresy are made, and ecclesiastical authorities become involved so much that regional synods must be called to decide the issues. Eventually, the promoters of Marian orthodoxy end up being regarded as the heroes of the faith and the leaders of the opponents are condemned as heresiarchs.

We need to keep in mind that all this appears to be closely connected with the sudden emergence of the monastic movement, which first gained a spectacular success in Egypt, and then was gradually spread, promoted greatly through St. Athanasius' repeated exiles to different regions of the West. The ascetic and monastic links of Marian orthodoxy are quite clear in the case of its most influential leaders, St. Ambrose and St. Jerome in the West and the Cappadocian Fathers in the East. This period closes with the rich doctrine of St. Augustine, whose writings contain and transmit to the Latin Church practically every doctrinal element of early patristic Mariology. These were then retained in a long and undisturbed constancy in medieval Mariology throughout the following millennium.

Athanasius (ca. 298-376)

Athanasius, the central figure of the first post-Nicene decades, led the anti-Arian forces to a decisive victory in the Church, yet his mariological thought remained in obscurity for a long time. Discoveries in the 20th century revealed the importance of his immediate predecessor, bishop Alexander of Alexandria, whom he accompanied as deacon and secretary to the Council of Nicaea, to whom he succeeded in 337 as bishop of Alexandria, and whom he followed as role model during a long and eventful career. From sermons found on papyrus fragments in Egypt we know that Athanasius quoted his predecessor, preaching to groups of consecrated virgins about Mary as the model of ascetic life.[138] This topic, which appears also later in the writings of Athanasius, was one of the most important components of Marian teaching and devotion even in the pre-Nicene era. It is a natural extension and continuation of what we said above about Origen's Mariology and its congenial audience among those who had previously sponsored the copying and translating of the *Proto-evangelium* and adhered to the practice of addressing Mary in prayer as we saw it exemplified in the *Sub Tuum*.

There is solid evidence of the importance Athanasius attributed to the Marian title of *Theotokos*, as an expression of the correct doctrine about the Incarnation: "Christ being God became man for our sake and was born of Mary, Mother of God, to free us from the devil's power."[139] But we find in Athanasius a new feature, which obtained increasing importance in the post-Nicene period and powerfully inspired later preaching and devotional literature: the paradox of Christ's two natures and their unity in one person, the second person of the Trinity. Mary is admired, praised, and exalted as the locus of the Christological paradox. Athanasius marks the beginning of a new tone:

> O noble Virgin, truly you are greater than any other greatness. For who is your equal in greatness, O dwelling place of God the Word? To whom among all creatures shall I compare you, O Virgin? You are greater than all of them. O [Ark of the New] Covenant, in which is found the gold vessel, containing the true manna, that is the flesh in which the Divinity resides. Should I compare you to the fertile earth and its fruits? You surpass them for it is written: "The earth is my footstool" (Is 66:1). But you

---

[138] Athanasius' influence on the development of asceticism in Alexandria is described in a well documented and fascinating narrative by David Brakke, *Athanasius and the Politics of Asceticism* (Oxford: Clarendon, 1995).

[139] *On Virginity* 3 (PG 28,56)

carry in yourself the foot and the head and the entire body of the perfect God.[140]

The text is not a haphazard pile of superlatives. Its logical core is the Trinitarian truth of Nicaea, allowing the *communicatio idiomatum*: Mary's womb contains the "body parts" of the divine person: feet, head, and all the rest. This understanding of the incarnate "carnality of God" allows not only the application of such scriptural verses as Isaiah 66:1, but many other images and themes as well. One may, of course, insist that ultimately there is nothing new in this kind of exegesis: such a method of reading Scripture comes from the Apostolic Age. The golden vessel with manna, deposited in the Ark is quoted in the Epistle to the Hebrews: "In it were the gold jar containing the manna, the staff of Aaron that had sprouted, and the tablets of the covenant" (9:4). And the "manna," identified with the Incarnate Son, who came down from heaven to be distributed to mankind in the Eucharist, refers to John 6:49-50.

But with regard to its style, not only as a matter of words but as a new rhetoric, carrying true novelty of thought, Athanasius' sermon further expands on the term "greatest of all creatures" by explaining why Mary exceeds all angels:

> I say that heaven is exalted, but it does not equal you [Mary] for it is written 'Heaven is my throne,' while you are God's place of repose. If I say that the angels and the archangels are great but [I must add that] you are greater than them all, for the angels and archangels serve with trembling the One who dwells in your womb and they dare not speak in his presence, while you speak to him freely.[141]

As we see, Mary's greatness above the angels, later a staple in medieval and modern Mariology, is already formulated here from

---

[140] Homily of the Papyrus of Turin, edited by T. Lefort in *Le Muséon* 71 (1958), 216-7 quoted by Luigi Gambero, *Mary and the Fathers of the Church* (San Francisco: Ignatius Press, 1999), 107.

[141] Ibid.

scriptural verses interpreted in the light of the Nicene dogma. Although our sources are fragmentary, we find a list of ideas and arguments that became popular only through later authors but are all, nonetheless, rooted in Athanasius' preaching and writings. For example, the portrayal of Mary as a model of consecrated virgins, pictured with concrete details of behavior, which are to be elaborated later by St. Ambrose, originated with Athanasius.[142] Athanasius argues for Mary's *virginitas post partum* from the fact that on the Cross Jesus entrusted her to the Beloved Disciple. With the allowance that her womb was "opened from within" Athanasius asserts Mary's perpetual virginity much in the way that Origen did. Of course, Nicene orthodoxy also requires a strong defense of Christ's true humanity against Manicheans and Gnostics. About this point, Athanasius, as many of his contemporaries and successors, realized that he had to fight on a double front. On the one hand, the virginal conception suggests that Jesus' origins differ from ours; on the other hand, orthodox faith also requires confessing that Jesus' body was like our own.

> If the Son of God had wanted merely to appear, he could certainly have any kind of body, even a body better than our own. Instead it was our kind of body that he took and not just in any way. He took it from a pure and unstained Virgin who had not known man. This body was pure and not corrupted by any union with man. For since he is the All-powerful and the Craftsman of all things, he made for himself a Temple within the Virgin; that is to say a body.[143]

Here we probably find that element in the doctrinal tradition about Mary for which Athanasius' contribution was the most important. The virginal conception appears as a matter of free choice

---

[142] Hilda Graef calls this idea of Christian perfection for virgins an "imitation of Mary," quoting several passages from Athanasius' *Letters to the Virgins*. *Mary: A History of Doctrine and Devotion*, vol. I (New York: Sheed and Ward, 1963), 53.

[143] *De Incarnatione Verbi* 8, PG 25, 109.

by God, not of necessity. But that does not mean he could have fashioned for himself a body just in any imaginable way. In the concrete way in which God chose to assume a body, he proved himself to be "All-powerful and the Craftsman of all," i.e., the One who initiates his Incarnation and makes it happen in a way that is most fitting and eloquent for revealing God's inner life and the chosen path of the economy of salvation. The virginal conception is planned and executed as a sovereign divine act, designed with no constraints yet in a most dignified and wise manner.[144] The second thought in this text may be more difficult for our present-day thinking and we can here only touch on it briefly. The idea of "incorruptibility" is ultimately a divine attribute linked with immortality. *Per se* only God is immortal and "incorruptible" (not exposed to decay) but, according to biblical and patristic thought, a creature, and even the human being, for whom the body is an essential component, can participate in divine immortality in various ways and degrees. For a materialistic culture, this is implausible and sounds even mythical, but the primary Christian sources consider it as divinely revealed truth. It is used in the Pauline letters to explain the condition of the glorious risen body of Christ as well as of us who are saved when we reach the age to come (1 Cor 15:38-52; cf. 1 Tm 1:17). They call the condition of the body after the resurrection a spiritual body in opposition to a natural body (1 Cor 15:44). Both the word and the concept reached Jewish thought through Hellenistic influences before the time of Christ, as the Septuagint testifies. We can find it in the Book of Wisdom (1:16-18) with a strong moral connotation: to be corruptible means not only to be mortal and thus exposed to decay, but to be contaminated morally. Thus, in contrast to what is holy, what is corruptible is incapable of union with the divine so that it cannot receive, transmit and mediate it.

For the Church Fathers the condition called ἀφθαρσία or incorruptibility is that of the redeemed flesh, lifted above its natural

---

[144] "Wisdom has built her house" (Proverbs 9:1) is a biblical verse applied to the Incarnation in such a sense: the Logos is the *architect* and the one *dwelling* in the house, while Mary is the house which God had built for himself to dwell in.

limits by unmerited grace in the Incarnation, by the holiness conveyed in the sacraments and at every instance of sanctification, a condition obtainable only by participation in the divine nature. The connections between incorruptibility and virginity also need to be further explained especially in today's culture which sees "virginity" only negatively, as a merely bodily condition of being left untouched or unused: simply not engaged in those actions for which human reproductive capabilities were created.

Indeed, why would Athanasius say that when a woman's body is being used for its natural reproductive purpose, it becomes "corruptible" as if stained at the loss of its virginity? Why does it become "used" in a pejorative sense, as if making its first steps, or simply slipping, "down" on the road of decay? For a reply, we must remember here the tradition in which Athanasius is rooted, which evolved from earliest Christian times. Justin Martyr already compared Mary to Eve before the fall as to the "virginal soil" of the first creation. The human drama starts linking sin and death at the very first instant of human history. The two components of the first man and woman, their body and soul, are left to the forces of nature as procreation follows the Fall. While man and woman were created sinless and put to the test of learning that both the "Tree of Knowledge" and the "Tree of Life" could be given them only as an additional gift, after their failure they begin a journey marked by sinfulness and punishment that permeates their relationships and the destiny of their offspring. Now every birth produces another being destined to live out a mortal life, and every mortal being is born into the inevitable fate of death. They transmit life in a perspective of "reproduction" as their offspring also extend and reproduce their lives, but cannot save their children from death. Moreover, birth, decay, mortality, and death begin to flow in succession under the relentless current of suffering and pain. For Eve and all her daughters, giving birth implies immersion in pain and initiating an offspring into mortal life: the propagation of ongoing suffering. This link connecting birth and death and both being encompassed by suffering are part of the patristic concept of "corruptibility." On the other hand, divine life is "incorruptible" – not engaged in the act (or desire or instinct) of natural reproduction. Such a concept of immortality as opposed to sexual reproduction is found in the well-known synoptic pericope about the Sadducees who challenged Jesus about the resurrection of the body. In his response the Lord states that risen bodies of the age to come – after the close of human history – will be like the angels in their spiritual state. For they do not engage in sexual union, i.e., as the old Latin text says in imitation of the Greek phrase: *neque nubent neque nubentur* (Mt 22:30; Mk 12:25): "neither will they marry nor be taken in marriage." Quite correctly, the members of the nascent monastic movement identified this statement as a description of the "angelic life" that they wanted to lead in anticipation through celibate and virginal continence. They intended to anticipate the life of heaven by a life that by-passes human reproduction. This is an important part of the context for the patristic esteem of Mary's virginity. Without it the Church Fathers' teaching about Mary's virginity collapses into a Manichean condemnation of sex and marriage as if essentially linked to sinfulness.

More specifically, the virginal conception and birth of Jesus take place as an eschatological sign: it points to an offspring who is not merely human, because not a result of human reproduction. The unanimous testimony of the Church Fathers is that the virginal birth is an unmistakable sign of Jesus' divinity. In contrast to a rather broad skepticism in modern Christology, in patristic thought (including even those few who denied virginity *in partu*, like Tertullian) the child's birth from a Virgin without an earthly father indicates without a doubt that in her womb the Eternal Father's Son – God's Son in a non-metaphorical sense – has taken a human body. This is explicit, they say, in the text of the Annunciation: "The Holy Spirit will come upon you, and the power of the Most High will overshadow you; therefore *the holy Offspring to be born*[145] will be called the Son of God" (Lk 1:35).

---

[145] The phrase τὸ γεννώμενον ἅγιον κληθήσεται υἱὸς θεοῦ (Lk 1:35) is, in my opinion, simply mistranslated in most English versions used today. For example, the New American Bible imitates the Revised Standard Version: "Therefore the child

118

We needed such a long elaboration of the concept of ἀφθαρσία also to render intelligible that the virginal conception and birth signified for the Church Fathers with natural ease Mary's sinlessness. Modern Mariology made valiant efforts to track down and enumerate one by one the Church Fathers who held the thesis of Mary's strict and absolute sinlessness, and those who found in her a smaller or larger amount of "culpability" by commenting about the trials that her faith had to endure or the possible doubts and hesitation she might have had about her Son's eventual Resurrection, final victory, entrance to heaven, etc. Few of the studies – although almost always done with the critical method of modern history – notice that this inquiry is highly anachronistic and theologically (maybe only psychologically) naïve. If Christ is tempted in the desert and utters words about being abandoned by adopting the text of Psalm 22:2 on the Cross, what is the point in guessing the psychological content of Mary's pondering all that her experience as "Virgin and Mother" brings her to? How can one reconstruct "critically" the consciousness of one whom we believe to be both Virgin and Mother, who nonetheless lives in history and a human time frame, interacting with events to be perceived as acts of self-definition, encounters with God and the self, all located in a process of gradual revelation, but acts of both human freedom and limitation which must remain real as long as she is *in via* – a traveler on earth, just as her son, the Son of God, was? Therefore, while the application of the principle in reconstructing Mary's life was different from author to author, patristic witnesses lined themselves up with amazing unanimity behind Athanasius who, probably in a surprisingly short time, formulated the principle of Mary's complete sinlessness when he defined her to be the model of consecrated life in the Church, especially consecrated virginal life.[146]

---

to be born will be called holy, the Son of God." The Church Fathers who read it in Greek or Latin (or Syriac) all saw that the subject of the sentence is τὸ γεννώμενον ἅγιον.

[146] We possess such texts from Athanasius thanks to discoveries in the 20th century, when some Coptic texts from his writings and preaching about virginity were discovered.

Athanasius also made it clear that he was not trying to "re-construct" Mary's way of life empirically, by extrapolating from bits and pieces of scriptural witnesses, but tried to apply a fundamental principle that he trusted enough to use it deductively and elucidate its implications: "You have to consider the conduct of Mary, who is the type and model of that life which belongs to heaven." Speaking of Mary's life as a "heavenly lifestyle" (called *vita angelica* later in the Latin West in reference to Mk 12:25), he tried to describe it in detail:

> Mary is like a wise virgin.... She did not eat to give plea-sure to the body but only according to the demands of na-ture. ... She sat always with her face turned to the East because she prayed continually.... Her brothers came to visit her and speak with her but she did not want to receive them. Since the angels visited her at different times, they could observe her exemplary way of life and admire it.[147]

Athanasius transmits here a traditional thought, which, of course, needed further elaboration. The 4th century's patristic authors took over the tradition about Mary's virginity in such a context. So we have in the leading authorities of both the East and the West a clear and unanimous outlook embracing the tradition trying to express that the events of the Incarnation – Mary's way of conceiving, giving birth, and continued virginal life *post partum* – must not be inserted into the patterns that a mortal life normally entails.

We see, therefore, that for Athanasius and those following him, "uncorrupted virginity" is effectively holiness in "spirit and body," a Pauline phrase which later becomes a staple for spiritual writers when speaking about either Mary or consecrated virgins, or, as we will see, a third entity analogous to Mary as Mother and Virgin: the Church. Rather than meaning a merely corporal attribute, it served to emphasize the linkage of virginal purity and divine motherhood, in terms of holiness and moral sanctity.

---

[147] Quoted from various editions of Coptic manuscripts in Gambero, op. cit., 100-1.

Ambrose (ca. 340-397)

Ambrose's whole life falls into the post-Nicene part of the 4th century.[148] As opposed to Origen and Athanasius, he spent his whole life in one place, Milan, and almost all his works were preserved in Latin, the language in which they had been written. But also in many other ways he represents the peak of patristic Mariology.

An educated layman of exemplary life and high culture, Ambrose was elected bishop by popular acclamation. He accepted this unexpected election only with reluctance, for he had planned to remain a layman and a public official. But once made a bishop, he quickly plunged into studies to complete his knowledge of Church doctrine. By diligent reading of the Scriptures and of the early Church Fathers, among whom Origen influenced him the most, he became a competent theologian, although he never refrained from borrowing the thoughts of his predecessors and role models. His preaching deeply impressed the young rhetorician Augustine, who had just recently moved to Milan in 384 from a short stay in Rome after leaving his native Latin Africa in 383. Under Ambrose's influence, Augustine finally asked for baptism in 387 and became, in a true sense of the word, Ambrose's most important heir and spiritual son.

Four main characteristics of Ambrose's Mariology must be kept in mind.

First, it is deeply *scriptural*. Of course, this attribute applies to all the Church Fathers. But in the case of Ambrose, Mariology specifically depends on the first two chapters of Luke connected with his *Commentary on Luke*, a work in close theological dependency on Origen's scriptural commentaries, especially those on Matthew and Luke. Thus with Ambrose a systematic, verse by verse exegesis of Luke 1-2 entered western Mariology and remained its firm basis.

Second, in his teaching about Mary, Ambrose is deeply influenced by his time's *monastic movements*. In other words, Ambrose

---

[148] The best book on the subject of his Mariology is by an American author, Charles W. Neumann, *The Virgin Mary in the Works of St. Ambrose* (Fribourg: University Press, 1962).

consciously continued responding to the spiritual needs of early ascetics, consecrated virgins and monks whose spiritual care he considered one of his main pastoral duties. His older sister, Marcellina, lived in a community of nuns in Rome and thus provided him a living link with the needs and problems of his times' religious women.

Third, in developing his Mariology Ambrose was deeply involved in *controversies*. As the bishop of Milan, at that time one of the most important cities of the Western half of the Roman Empire, whose previous bishop, Auxentius, had been one of the last strong Arians in Italy, Ambrose fought to defend and promote, in conjunction with the dogma of Nicaea, the Church's doctrinal norms about Mary. With a new vigor he brought the questions of Marian doctrine before the public and confronted all doubts or denials. It is in this way that Ambrose's teaching on Mary's perpetual virginity became an issue of capital importance not only because of its anti-Arian relevance, but also because of its significance for the monastic movements which for awhile had encountered an unfriendly response from certain intellectual circles but, at the same time, experienced sudden and spectacular increase across the Empire. The rising influence of monks and consecrated women in church communities was observable everywhere, especially in the community of Rome. This meant an increase in popularity and also in power. No wonder, therefore, that, after various doctrinal controversies, negative reactions also sprang up, and that some leaders began to challenge the new concepts of Christian perfection focused on celibacy and virginity. Ambrose, and after him Jerome, stood up to the challenge and vigorously defended both the lifestyle of the consecrated virgins and Mary's image as their ideal. As a result, for the first time, Christians denying Mary's perpetual virginity were explictly treated as heretics.

A fourth and final point of Ambrose's special merits in Mariology is based on a somewhat unexpected aspect. Ambrose was not only a literary genius, but a *poet* of exceptional originality. It is no exaggeration to state that Ambrose single-handedly invented a new form of poetry: the Latin Christian hymn. For centuries, a church hymn consisting of four-line iambic stanzas with eight syllables in each line was named simply an *Ambrosianum*.

The combination of the four aspects enumerated above made Ambrose's impact on the Church's Marian teaching and devotion not only special, but extraordinary. In terms of doctrinal content, his thought about Mary is centered on her *virginal divine motherhood*. Although this element of Church teaching belonged to the core of the Church's tradition for centuries, it was under Ambrose's influence that Church teaching focused on the virginal motherhood and made it explicitly an essential part of Christian orthodoxy. Ambrose is clear and explicit about the connection of Mary's virginity with the truth of the Incarnation. Yet he does not state it in the way of a strict or *a priori* necessity, as if God could have been born in no other way. The virginal birth is not a matter to be deduced by reasoning but is a fact revealed first to Mary, then to Joseph, and through the apostolic preaching to the entire world. We hear Ambrose time and again reasoning about the "fittingness" or dignity of the virginal conception and not a logical necessity to which our reason concludes. But he also says that, in the way we can see it, to be born of a Virgin is the *only fitting* mode for God to enter into the world: he enters the virginal womb as a temple, a "shrine" or *sacrarium*, which has not been contaminated by a non-sacred use of human procreation. One of Ambrose's best written poetic couplets expresses the link between the Incarnation and the virginal birth in terms of "fittingness" with as much force as charm:

> Miretur omne saeculum:
> Talis partus decet Deum.[149]

The virginal birth is "fitting" not only because it befits the holiness of the Offspring, but also because it serves as a tool of revelation. It provides a sign not only to prove the Child's divinity, but to

---

[149] "Let every age in wonder fall: / Such birth befits the God of all." These lines belong to one of Ambrose's rather few authentically preserved hymns, *Intende qui regis Israel*. With some adjustments it was restored to the new Roman Breviary after Vatican II and is used in the last week of Advent for the Office of Readings.

reflect and mirror the eternal generation of the Word from God the Father. The latter argument is a most telling "post-Nicene" feature of Ambrose's thought. It expresses the explicit awareness that in Jesus two natures are united in one person. Hence Christ is born not as someone different from the Son born from the Father, but he is the same one born in both cases but each time in another way: *non alter ex Patre, alter ex Virgine, sed idem aliter ex Patre et aliter ex Virgine.*[150]

In particular, the virginal conception must not be regarded in function of a physical notion of original sin as if sinlessness of the offspring would necessarily require non-sexual reproduction or, conversely, the sexual act would imply sinfulness, and thus we could again logically conclude to the necessity of the virginal conception. Even if such thought may appear in some writings of Tertullian or Origen,[151] this was certainly not Ambrose's teaching.[152] However, in spite of the lack of historical clarity about the two synods, one in Rome and one in Milan, that condemned Jovinian, there is no doubt that at both places the status of consecrated virgins in the Church and Mary's perpetual virginity were closely connected.[153]

---

[150] "Not another one is born from the Father, and another one from the Virgin, but the same one is born another way from the Father and another way from the Virgin" (*De Incarnatione* 3:5, PL 16:827c). This is quoted without much dogmatic commentary by C.W. Neumann, op. cit., 74. Indeed, the depth of the statement might be easily overlooked by the technicality of its Nicene language. But Ambrose expresses here the fundamental mystery of Mariology: the Trinitarian dogma revealed by the birth in Bethlehem not merely as symbol – not only by external similarity, but through an analogy brought about by the identity of the Person who is born in an eternal Nativity from the Father and in the course of time (the fullness of time) from the Virgin. This contemplation of the Trinitarian procession in the birth of Bethlehem comes back in more and more explicit ways in later developments of Mariological thought.

[151] Origen admits that without virginal conception, the physical origins of the Son of God would "not have been worthy" of him, but he does not say that the Incarnation had to happen in the way it did. See C. Vagaggini, *Maria nelle Opere di Origene* (Rome: Pontificio Istituto Orientale, 1942), 64.

[152] Neumann's interpretation of Ambrose's comments on Ps 37 (op. cit., 78) is misleading in this regard. The text he quotes does not say that in order to avoid being born in sin (*in iniquitatibus et in delictis*) Christ *necessarily* had to be born by virginal conception.

[153] St. Jerome reports among Jovinian's errors condemned at this synod in Rome in his *Adversus Jovinianum* I, 3 (PL 23,214c): "*Dicit [Jovinianus] 'virgines, viduas*

That after being condemned in Rome, Jovinian chose to move to Milan may sound strange, but it only indicates that he intended to seek an open confrontation with Ambrose, whose teaching about Mary's perpetual virginity was best known. However, Ambrose received formidable support from other bishops in Northern Italy, like Zeno of Verona and Gaudentius of Brescia, so that Jovinian stood no chance to win approval. We will briefly return to this topic when speaking of St. Jerome. But now we should first mention some additional aspects of Ambrose's Marian teaching.

Ambrose's works provided an explanation of practically all important scriptural passages about Mary. This does not regard only her virginity. In the footsteps of the Alexandrians (mostly Origen, Alexander, and Athanasius) Ambrose presents Mary as "the model of Virgins." What he describes in such texts is a quasi-monastic ideal of a girl vowed to virginity and cultivating a life of moral virtues in a contemplative environment. Ambrose built this image of Mary's virginal life mostly from elements received from previous patristic generations. He might have directly copied much of it from Pope Liberius and St. Athanasius. But we should see Ambrose in a broader context. Following Nicaea the praise of virginity and virginal life became a literary *topos* – a subject fashionable in Church literature – with roots that go back all the way to the 2nd and 3rd centuries. Ultimately we reach there the same background from which the *Protoevangelium* took its inspiration. But we should not think only of apocryphal writings expanding the Gospel reports about the virginal conception, or exegetical and homiletic exercises based on Luke's account of the Annunciation by adding legendary narratives. The lifestyle of consecrated women established in the 2nd century constituted a real experience of Christian life, which began to motivate reflection

---

et maritatas quae semel in Christo lotae sunt, si non discrepent caeteris operibus, ejusdem esse meriti.'" ["(Jovinian) says that virgins, widows and married women, once they are washed in Christ, and live the same way, are of equal merit."] See C. Neumann, op. cit. 144. This condemnation of Jovinian began a controversy about the status of virginity (and celibacy) which, renewed at the Reformation, prompted the Council of Trent to take a stand. A balanced authoritative statement appeared in John Paul II's teaching. See on pp. 239-240.

and prayer life as they were built around scriptural themes with a particular focus on Jesus' virginal origins. In this context Mary is described as living a life dedicated to prayer and work, vowed to celibate chastity and spent in withdrawal from the world. Origen's enthusiasm for celibacy and virginity would be hard to explain without such a milieu. But there is more: as the 4th century comes to an end, a whole literary genre emerges. It is all "de virginitate": sermons, letters, and treatises focusing on this topic. They include, besides Ambrose's *De virginibus* and *De institutione virginum*, other texts we should mention at least by title: from the 3rd century, Cyprian's *De habitu virginum*, then from the 4th century, Athanasius' *Letter to Virgins* and *De virginibus*, Methodius' *Banquet*, Jerome's various letters and his *Adversus Helvidium*, Epiphanius' *Panarion*, Ephrem's sermons on the topic, then *De lapsu virginis* by Nicetas of Rheims, *In laudem virginitatis* by Gregory of Nazianzus, the more lengthy and substantial *De Virginitate* by Gregory of Nyssa, *De vera virginitatis integritate*, earlier attributed to Basil the Great, but probably written by Basil of Ancyra, various sermons by John Chrysostom, Cyril of Jerusalem, Zeno of Verona, and, of course, a great deal of the literary output of St. Augustine. This widening stream of literature about virginity not only shows the growing importance of the topic in the late 4th and early 5th centuries, but demonstrates how strongly at that time the development of Mariology was stimulated from the quickly increasing movements of consecrated life.[154]

The passages by Ambrose describing Mary's "virginal life" must not be harshly judged as products of mere fantasy. Rather, Ambrose undertakes the task of presenting her in a picture of feminine perfection as he learned it from Scripture and tradition, and deepened his understanding by reading the classical, mostly Stoic, sources about morality, with their descriptions of the ethical life in very concrete images of behavior, internal and external.[155] Although

---

[154] Charles Neumann included in his book on Ambrose a very valuable chapter under the title "Historical Survey of the Idea, Mary the Model of Virgins."

[155] See in particular Cicero's *De officiis*, extensively used by Ambrose in his *De officiis ministrorum*.

Ambrose does not directly depend on the *Proto-evangelium*, he still depicts the Virgin as a "holy shrine" whom God prepared in the most fitting way for the Incarnation of his Son. So Ambrose is one of many Christian authors who use both biblical and philosophical tools to complete and concretize what the revealed doctrine, especially the story of the virginal conception and its implications, tells about Mary. In this way he formulates a Marian ideal of the religious life: a way of life led by all Christians but especially those called to Christian perfection. In his understanding of Christian life as a continuation of the Incarnation of the Word into history, the Marian ideal of Christian perfection is not a blind or fortuitous choice. In every age this kind of lifestyle is called to extend God's coming to man through Christ and his saints into all spheres of human life and every culture. That this process must be in continuity with the one and only *ensarkosis* (enfleshing or incarnation) of God into the texture of human history means that for both the Church as a whole and the individuals called to perfection, a connection with Mary is predetermined by the call Mary received. We are talking of her, of course, not only as "the historical Mary" but as she appears in a supra-temporal vision of the virginal motherhood and becomes the source of the continuous divine presence – Immanu-El – renewed in every age and period of Christian history.[156]

By no means does this imply that Ambrose or his contemporaries lost interest in the Mary of history. On the contrary, besides expanding a "Marian ideal of religious life," Ambrose confronted most issues previously raised about the literal meaning of the biblical texts, and probably with most attention to those which concerned her perpetual virginity. One such issue was her betrothal to Joseph. In this regard the Gospel reports are ambiguous. Both Matthew and Luke clearly state that Mary and Joseph had no marital relations *ante partum*, and pretty clearly suggest that they began to live together but without sexual relations soon after the virginal con-

---

[156] This is why the blossoming of Mariology in the 4th century brings about a steady growth of the awareness of the relationship between Mary and the Church, which we shall discuss further below.

ception. Following long-standing tradition that we can trace all the way to Ignatius of Antioch, Ambrose also held the view that for the world (and thus for Satan, "the Prince of the world") Jesus seemed to be Joseph's son. Therefore, Mary's non-sexual, yet marital relationship with Joseph remained under the cloak of secrecy. In this connection, by using Origen as his source, Ambrose made a statement that echoed through centuries: God preferred to risk that some would raise doubts about his true origins as a man than about his mother's reputation.[157] To harmonize this tradition of "concealment" and the disturbing impression that this marriage was bordering on a lie, Ambrose used the definition of marriage by Roman Law, which was current by his time: essentially marriage is a contract by consent (*pactio coniugalis*) not by its consummation as a carnal union.[158]

Mary's virginity *post partum*, a theme which Ambrose only treats in his early *De Virginibus*, became a major subject of controversy when the dispute against it began (382). Helvidius claimed that "the brothers of Jesus" were born from the consummated marriage of Joseph and Mary. However, at this time Ambrose kept silent and allowed Jerome, who by then had returned from the Holy Land and, settling in Rome, became a close associate to Pope Damasus, to respond and develop his counterattack against Helvidius. Chances are that Ambrose was hesitant about some of Jerome's arguments, especially those which assumed that the "brothers of Jesus" were not Joseph's but his brother's children and thus only cousins to Jesus rather than, as an earlier tradition held it, half-brothers and sisters through Joseph's earlier marriage. The thesis that Joseph was espoused to Mary as a widower (called today the "Epiphanian solution") was certainly known in the West. Hilary of Poitiers states it in

---

[157] *Maluit autem Dominus aliquos de suo ortu quam de matris pudore dubitare. Expositio in Lucam* (PL 15, 1551d). Ambrose must have liked this sentence, because he repeated it later in *De institutione virginum* 5:37 (PL 19, 315b).

[158] See the discussion of this question in C. Neumann's book quoted above, pp. 85-87. The adage of Roman Law formulated by Ulpian was retained by the Latin Church: *Nuptias consensus, non concubitus facit* (Marriage comes about by consent, not by sexual intercourse).

his *Commentary on Matthew*[159] and Ambrose also remarks about it as an explanation which, he says, a "more careful explanation" would recommend.[160] But Ambrose eventually developed also another view about Joseph, a view which makes him stand apart among his contemporaries. As we said before, he held that Mary was in fact legally married, but only by a marriage contract (*pactio coniugalis*), which, if not consummated, was dissolvable. He, therefore, seems to have excluded for the time following Jesus' birth even a non-sexual cohabitation between Mary with Joseph. He also seems to assume that at Jesus' crucifixion Joseph was still alive but not living with Mary. It was for this reason he thought that Jesus selected John as a substitute to himself for Mary's support to be her companion for the rest of her life. This view is clearly expressed in Ambrose's last work on virginity, *De institutione virginum*. We see here an ancient tradition resurface: its roots go back at least as far as the 2nd century, the time when the apocryphal *Acts of John* were written (c. 160 A.D.). This book already reflects the belief that John, the Apostle and Beloved Disciple, never married and became a model of virginal life for men. Ambrose might have received this idea by the mediation of Origen. The assignment of Mary to John's care by her dying Son is for Ambrose not only an apologetic proof that Mary had no other sons besides Jesus, but also an act by which Mary received in John, a virginal – and therefore congenial – guardian. Ambrose also states that John's deeper penetration of the mystery of the Incarnation is due to his closeness to Mary, whose life he shared and from whom he directly learned about her virginal motherhood.[161]

---

[159] *In Matthaeum* 1, 4 (*Patrologia Latina* 9, 922). See L. Gambero, *Mary and the Fathers of the Church* (San Francisco: Ignatius Press, 1999), 184-5.

[160] *De institutione virginum* 6:43 (*Patrologia Latina* 19, 203) See a detailed discussion in C. Neumann, op. cit., 252-257.

[161] When commenting about Jn 19:26, Origen says that John as a virgin could better grasp the mystery of the Incarnation and had a deeper intuitive understanding of Mary's virginal motherhood than the other evangelists. Thus, on the one hand John's virginal life makes him more congenial as a companion and supporter of Mary; on the other hand living with her, John learns to understand with more authenticity the virginal conception as the mode of the Incarnation. On these see C. Neumann, op. cit., 194-197; 261-263.

The threefold categorization of Mary's virginity, *ante partum*, *in partu*, and *post partum*, does not come from Ambrose, nor does it really appear in such a textbook formula for several more centuries. Yet it is in the 4th century that the polemics against those who denied Mary's virginity began to drive the formulation of the dogma in this direction. Polemics against Jews, Ebionites, and pagans who denied the virginal conception (*ante partum*) were long known, but now, Helvidius, Jovinian, and Bonosus, following Tertullian's understanding of certain scriptural texts, attracted more attention to the specific issue of Mary's virginity *in partu* and forced the question about Jesus' brothers and thus the virginity *post partum* into the foreground. We find a triple statement about Mary's virginity in Zeno of Verona as a forerunner for the triple classification of Mary's virginity:

> Maria virgo incorrupta concepit,
> post conceptum virgo peperit,
> post partum virgo permansit.[162]

Ambrose and his contemporaries saw three time periods of Mary's "virginities" as if rooted in one single intention of living her life expressed in Mary's reply to the Angel: "I do not know man" (Lk 1:34).[163] This means that in Ambrose's view Mary's virginal status came from one definite, stable and unchanging act of consecration preceding the Annunciation. Such an exegesis might be debated in various ways, but it is essential to acknowledge that the Church Fathers' approach to this issue was based on an exegesis founded on the Christian experience of consecrated virginity and not on a historical reconstruction of 1st century Jewish spirituality in Palestine. In any case, Ambrose saw Mary's life *ante partum* as open to a call to consecrated life. This life is approved of and accepted by God through the Angel's message and it is not compromised but rather comes to

---

[162] "Mary conceived as an undefiled virgin, after conception she gave birth as a virgin, after birth she remained a virgin" *Tractatus* 2:8:2 (PL 11:451b).

[163] Cf. Neumann, op. cit., 100-102.

full fruition in the way Mary receives God's Son in her womb. At the birth of Jesus, in the holy and extraordinary event of her parturition, she is even further introduced to an exclusive intimacy with God who joins her daily existence on earth as her divine Son. Ambrose connects two views: the view of a woman's consecrated life and the way he sees John the Apostle as the virginal "Beloved Disciple," chosen to be Mary's caretaker after Jesus' death and as such becoming more capable to explore and express in his Gospel, especially in its Prologue, the mystery of the Incarnate Word. Even if he did not read the apocryphal *Acts of John*, Ambrose shared and promoted a view held in the Church almost unanimously and expressed up to recent days in traditional liturgical texts: on the cross Jesus entrusted the Virgin to a virgin – *Virginem virgini commendavit.*[164]

It seems correct to say that Ambrose underrated Joseph's role in Mary's life. Of course, he follows the tradition emphasizing that Joseph was a faithful witness, guarantor, and protector of Mary's virginity. However, by assuming that Joseph was still alive at Jesus' death and yet emphasizing that it was John the Apostle to whose care Mary was entrusted, we get an unclear picture of the relationship between Mary and Joseph during Jesus' adult life.[165] This question might need further scrutiny. In any case, it seems that, beginning with Tertullian and continuing in the Western Church for centuries, the definition of marriage in Roman Law as a *pactio* was accepted, so that a *matrimonium ratum sed non consummatum* (a marriage valid yet non consummated) was dissolvable. This blurred the image of what we describe in more idyllic terms as "the Holy Family," a community of three persons united by a common call and destiny in the house of Nazareth, a social setting created by the Incarnation. This gave rise in the past two centuries to a spirituality with valuable insights and experiences, but the Western tradition remained isolated from some of its roots. Understanding how the home of Nazareth functioned as that cell of society where the Incarnate Word took

---

[164] Until the liturgical changes which followed Vatican II, in the Roman liturgy this antiphon was part of the texts for the feast of St. John, December 27.

[165] Neumann, op. cit., 192-197.

flesh, lived and "grew in wisdom, in stature, and in favor with God and with people" (Lk 2:52) is grounded in biblical truth, which some patristic sources simply might not have tried to exploit or, at least, do not seem to have spoken about in unison.

Jerome (ca. 347-420)

Jerome was a younger contemporary of Ambrose, but older than Augustine. He stands in many respects at the "intersection" of East and West. As an advisor and friend to Pope Damasus I, he was the main leader in the battle against Helvidius – a dispute in which Ambrose preferred not to involve himself. As a man who enjoyed controversies and used his talent for satirical prose to the utmost, he later supported Ambrose's struggle against Jovinian and Bonosus. He took a major role in the way Catholic teaching about Mary's perpetual virginity was effectively and officially defended and declared. Although both Jerome and Ambrose received papal endorsements, the actions undertaken against those groups who denied Mary's perpetual virginity took place in local synods and did not receive full publicity in the Church; hence the synodal conclusions cannot be considered as acts of the extraordinary Magisterium. However, their teaching was widely accepted as representing the whole Church, with its doctrine unanimously taught by East and West. For this reason we can say that, by the 5th century, Mary's perpetual virginity must be regarded as part of the Church's defined dogmas in virtue of its *ordinary* Magisterium, uniformly taught throughout the whole *oikoumene* – i.e. by all the Churches of the Roman Empire.[166]

In several ways Jerome's contribution to the development of Mariology was unique. Born in Dalmatia (today Croatia), he soon went to Rome to obtain an education. But in Rome, where he began a promising career under Pope Damasus, he became acquainted with

---

[166] The Lateran Council of 649, considered ecumenical by Catholics but not by most Orthodox Christians, eventually stated Mary's perpetual virginity as a dogma. Cf. Denzinger-Schönmetzer, *Enchiridion Symbolorum*, 36th ed. (Freiburg in Br.: Herder, 1976), n. 504.

the monastic movement and moved to the East, traveling through Egypt and Palestine, seeking and finding first-hand exposure to eremitical and cenobitical life. As a linguist and biblicist he obtained a high reputation in the Western Church by re-working and re-editing the whole Bible. The Latin text which he championed as translated from the original text (the Old Testament from Hebrew) became known as the Vulgate and was in fact the Latin Church's official Bible for the next fifteen hundred years.[167]

His most important contribution to Mariology was an apologetic work directed against Helvidius, a layman who had denied Mary's perpetual virginity in a published work. Jerome's response was the book *De perpetua virginitate adversus Helvidium* (PL 23, 183-206), which remained highly influential in Western Christianity.

Yet Jerome's influence on Mariology in the Western Church is difficult to evaluate. Besides his vitriolic style aiming at overkill when fighting his opponents, his well-motivated caution against apocryphal sources and philosophical errors made him change his views repeatedly while quickly adopting new positions without sufficient prudence. For a while he was an enthusiastic supporter of Origen's legacy, translating several of his works into Latin; later he became one of the most passionate anti-Origenists of the time. While consistently defending Mary's perpetual virginity, he was hesitant to endorse the tradition about Mary's miraculous parturition because he rejected – quite correctly – the authenticity of the *Proto-evangelium*.

When Jovinian's heresy brought up specifically the question of Mary's virginity *in partu*, Jerome retained an ambiguous position. It seems that he was hesitant to attach any specific physical attribute to Mary's continuing state of virginity, but he spoke of Mary as the Virgin both "before" and "after" giving birth. Jerome's anti-docetic emphasis (Jesus was *truly* born) gave him occasions to make statements that seemingly ascribe to Jesus a "fully natural" birth. Nonetheless, Jerome is explicit about Mary's perpetual virginity. He thinks of this

---

[167] Presently the Latin Church uses the so-called Neo-Vulgate, an improved edition of the Vulgate.

as an attribute that carries both a bodily and a spiritual meaning. He refrained from speaking of Jesus' "miraculous birth," which other Church Fathers, especially Ambrose, had clearly emphasized.

After Tertullian, and the controversies that Ambrose and Jerome had to sustain, the threefold distinction of Mary's virginity (*ante* and *post partum* and *in partu*) become more separable topics, but obviously virginity *post partum*, in a strict logical sense presupposes virginity *in partu*. However, Jerome's reticence to speak about Jesus' miraculous birth (and a virginal parturition) reveals a real issue. The rejection of the *Proto-evangelium* as an apocryphal writing makes such persons as Jerome unwilling to defend or support any of its claims about the miraculous birth or to use the testimony of a midwife who witnessed its extraordinary character. Consequently the perpetual virginity of Mary became centered on the relations of Mary and Joseph after Jesus' birth and, specifically on the scriptural quotations about "the brothers of Jesus." On this question, Jerome introduced a new position. He proposed the different meanings of the word "brother" in the Bible and suggests that Jesus and his "brothers" were cousins, according to his identification of Mary of Cleophas as Jesus' aunt. This interpretation gained growing popularity in the Latin Church and remained the *opinio communis* until modern times. However, due to the influence of the *Proto-evangelium* and later of Epiphanius of Salamis, the tradition of the East preferred to see Joseph as an aging widower to whom Mary was betrothed for a marriage not meant to be consummated. It is quite probable that Jerome chose his exegesis about Jesus' brothers and sisters mostly on account of Tertullian's continued influence. For throughout Latin patristics, Tertullian continued to be regarded, in spite of his Montanist record, as a very important authority on biblical issues. Thus, although the perpetual virginity of Mary was equally retained as normative, East and West started diverse traditions on the specific description and historicization of the marriage of Mary and Joseph down to small, non-biblical details, through the centuries.

In distorted and simplified terms, in theological handbooks of recent centuries, the record about Jerome and Tertullian has also significantly changed: Tertullian was said to have clearly rejected virginity "during" and "after" birth, Ambrose championed all the three "virginities" and Jerome remained ambiguous in his endorsement of the virginity "during" birth. However in both Catholic and Orthodox liturgy and theological teaching, up to recent times, Mary's perpetual virginity was professed as a truth unambiguously taught and an article of faith admitting no compromise. Due to lack of specific details about Mary's parturition in the universally accepted scriptural record, the specific physical meaning of Mary's virginity *in partu* remained in the realm of the unknown and suffered from a lack of precision, especially for those who tended to reduce it to a corporal attribute and a miracle of nature. But, in some sense, this was quite rightly so. Asserting the dogma of Mary's perpetual virginity on the basis of credence to apocrypha with clinical details and describing individuals invading the privacy of Mary's body and of the sacred events she experienced would have been not only sheer untruth but a distortion of the faith, as well as the role of eye witnesses. Even Jerome, with his aggressive apologetic zeal, understood this better than most people. He refers only to discreet, indirect hints in the scriptural description of Jesus' birth. He sees an allusion to Mary's painless birth in the biblical detail that she takes care of the newborn and she wraps him in swaddling clothes:

> There is no midwife, no busy little women trying to take care of things. She wraps the infant; she is both mother and midwife. "And she put him in a manger," it is said, "because there was no place for him in the inn" (Lk 2:7). This sentence alone is more convincing than the crazy stories of the apocrypha, as Mary herself envelops the child in swaddling clothes. No chance is offered to Helvidius' suggestion of pleasure, for no nuptials are taking place in an inn.[168]

---

[168] Nulla ibi obstetrix: nulla muliercularum sedulitas intercessit. Ipsa pannis involvit infantem, ipsa et mater et obstetrix fuit. *Et collocavit eum*, inquit, *in praesepio, quia non erat ei locus in diversorio* (Lk 2:7). Quae sententia et apocryphorum deliramenta convincit, dum Maria ipsa pannis involvit infantem; et Helvidii expleri

As with many other exegetical proposals, Jerome can hardly win modern approval for his conclusion, for it is clear that he is only looking for indirect clues about a painless birth and provides no more detail on the birth in Bethlehem. But, of course, we may add, we have a lack of specific details about many other dogmatic propositions, like the resurrection of the body or the specifics of original sin, for the Church often does not go beyond the core of a doctrinal statement and imposes no specific understanding of further details.

The Road to Ephesus

We could go a long way into reading and writing about the abundant material coming from the late 4th century and see in many more details the special importance Mary had in the theology of the "Golden Age of Patristics." One may certainly question if the texts analyzed above duly represent the treasures of this age. What we said above about Ambrose applies also to Jerome, the Cappadocian Fathers (Gregory Thaumaturgos, Basil, Gregory of Nazianzus, and Gregory of Nyssa), John Chrysostom, and Augustine: they see Marian devotion in the context of both the Incarnation and consecrated virginity, and so they write and preach about her as the primary model of the Christian and, especially, of "consecrated" life. However, by the end of the 4th century an additional motivation takes the lead in the development of Mariology. As the Christological controversies after Nicaea increasingly influenced the Christian doctrine about Mary, her title as *Theotokos* or *Dei Genitrix* ends up becoming the symbol of orthodoxy at the Council of Ephesus. Although monastic communities and leaders became involved in large number, now the issue was less importantly the value or dignity of ascetic life, but the correct understanding of Christ's one, single divine person in two natures, which justifies Mary's exceptional place in the order of salvation. We will mention only a few important names and facts.

Gregory Thaumaturgos ("the Wonderworker") is the first per-

---

non patitur voluptatem, dum in diversorio locus non fuit nuptiarum. *Adversus Helvidium* 8 (PL 23, 192A).

son reported to have witnessed a Marian apparition. The event is described by Gregory of Nyssa in his *Life of Gregory the Wonderworker*. According to his report, Mary, "the Mother of God," commands John the Evangelist to explain to Gregory Thaumaturgos the truth of the faith. The record is, therefore, not only the first mention of an apparition of Mary but the first representation of Mary as a guarantor of orthodoxy, a forerunner of the famous phrase frequently mentioned in later times: *Cunctas haereses sola interemisti, Dei Genitrix,* "You, God-Bearer, single-handedly destroyed every heresy."

Following closely in the footsteps of Origen, the Cappadocians fully appropriated the scriptural heritage of the great Alexandrian and spread it abroad in the East. But while at about the same time, in the West Ambrose and Jerome had to face contradictions and controversies, the Fathers of the East, and the Cappadocians in particular, speak of Mary's virginity as a doctrine in the peaceful possession of the Church. A good example may be taken from a sermon of St. Basil explaining that Matthew 1:25 is consistent with the doctrine of perpetual virginity:

> For "he did not know her," it says "until she gave birth to a son, her firstborn." But this could make one suppose that Mary, after having offered in all purity her own service of giving birth to the Lord by the intervention of the Holy Spirit, did not subsequently refrain from normal conjugal relations.
>
> But that would not have affected the teaching of our religion at all, because Mary's virginity was necessary until the service of the Incarnation and what happened afterward does not need to be investigated as to its impact on the doctrine of the mystery. However, since the lovers of Christ [i.e., the faithful] do not allow themselves to hear that the Mother of God (*Theotokos*) ceased at a given moment to be a virgin, we consider their testimony to be sufficient.[169]

---

[169] *On the Holy Generation of Christ* 3, PG 13, 1464bc.

Characteristically, Basil appears to be in no need of exegetical arguments or of analyzing Greek grammar and biblical usage – as did Ambrose and Jerome – to show that Matthew's statement would not necessarily imply sexual relations between Mary and Joseph after Jesus' birth. He simply appeals to the *sensus fidelium*. He states that the faithful are unwilling to hear about any "normal conjugal relation" between Mary and Joseph and that alone closes the issue.

Gregory of Nyssa, Basil's younger brother, handles Mary's virginity with similar ease. Since he wrote a treatise about consecrated virginity and is clearly familiar with the *Proto-evangelium*, it may be of little surprise that he interprets the Annunciation by assuming Mary's lifelong vow of virginity.[170]

In a Christmas sermon,[171] Gregory includes a remarkable passage interpreting the "burning bush" of Moses (Ex 3:1) as a manifestation of the mystery of Christ's birth from a virgin:

> As on the mountain the bush was burning but was not consumed, so the Virgin was giving birth to the light and was not corrupted. Nor should you consider the comparison to the bush embarrassing for it pre-figures the God-bearing body of the Virgin.[172]

This patristic gem, losing its shining appeal only in the 20th century, is all the more precious because it incorporates a principle already developed by Justin Martyr and Irenaeus: God revealed himself

---

[170] "Mary's own words confirm certain apocryphal traditions. For if Joseph had taken her to be his wife for the purpose of having children, why would she have wondered at the announcement of maternity, since she herself would have accepted becoming a mother according to the law of nature?" *On the Holy Generation of Christ* 5 (PG 31,1140C-1469A); see Luigi Gambero, op. cit., 157. Of course, the earliest witness about Mary's vow of virginity is the anonymous author of the *Proto-evangelium*.

[171] *On the Birth of Christ* (PG 46, 1133-46).

[172] Cf. Gambero, op. cit., 155. This comparison was taken up in the liturgy. The Roman Breviary preserved it until Vatican II in the form: *Rubum quem viderat Moyses incombustum, tuam agnovimus laudabilem virginitatem: Dei Genitrix, intercede pro nobis.* ("In the burning bush not consumed, that Moses has seen, we recognize your virginity, worthy of our praise: O Mother of God, intercede for us.")

from the beginning and throughout salvation through the Logos. Thus, by appearing to Moses, it was the Logos who revealed God the Father, anticipating "by a foreshadowing" the one and only bodily appearance of God on earth, the birth of Christ from the Virgin. Similarly, according to Theophilus of Antioch, also of the 2nd century, it was the Logos who sought Adam in the Garden of Eden and addressed him.

Gregory's thought, free of any defensiveness about Mary's perpetual virginity, soars aloft as he speaks of the birth in Bethlehem, happening with no pain and in a way that Mary herself does not notice physical details. Gregory goes as far as to say that this event is fully unique and, properly speaking, cannot be called "parturition." Gregory clearly depends also here on the *Proto-evangelium*, which – we may discern it from Gregory's uninhibited language – the Latin tradition in its strict anti-Marcionite and anti-Gnostic language was unwilling to follow. Gregory, however, although his Christology is certainly devoid of any trace of Gnosticism, has no problem with such rhetoric. In his *Commentary on the Song of Songs*, he described the "unpolluted" and "incorrupt" conception and birth of the Lord by the Virgin to a bridal union between God and man: the Power of the Most High covering Mary with its cloud is the bridal chamber and the splendor of the Holy Spirit shining upon her is like a bridal torch.[173]

Gregory of Nazianzus, a close friend and school companion of St. Basil, left behind relatively few texts about Mary. They are, however, important, for they apply with sharp clarity the truths of the Christological dogmas formulated in the 4th century.[174] He explains how the two natures and one person in Christ justify the term *Theotokos* for Mary and, at the same time, demand that both her true

---

[173] *On the Song of Songs* 13, PG 44,1052D-1053B. We must anticipate here to commend the re-appearance of this image of bridal symbolism in Scheeben's theology in the middle of the 19th century. See below p. 219.

[174] Gregory of Nazianzus also reflects the highly developed Marian piety of his Church as he recounts the story of a virgin, who when strongly tempted by satanic forces, turned to Mary by addressing her in prayer: *Oration* 24, 9-11, PG 35 1177C-1181A. See L. Gambero, op. cit., 166-7.

motherhood and virginal way of giving birth be affirmed. He speaks the language of the ecumenical councils with sharp distinctions and use of *anathemas*:

> If anybody does not admit that holy Mary is the Mother of God (*Theotokos*) he is cut off from the Godhead. If anyone claims that Christ merely passed through Mary as if passing through a channel, but denies that he was formed within her both in a divine way (because there was no intervention of a man) and in a human way (because according to the laws of conception) he is also godless.[175]

This short passage convincingly brings us to the Council of Ephesus, at which the title *Theotokos* became the touchstone of orthodoxy and was remembered as such for the rest of Christian history.

In this listing of the reaffirmation of the tradition about Mary, we have postponed until this point the name of St. Augustine of Hippo (353-430), who died not even a full year before the Council of Ephesus. Of course, Augustine left his fingerprints on almost all theological topics of the patristic era; yet his role in the development of Mariology is difficult to evaluate. At first sight it seems that, as to doctrine, he said or wrote little that would appear new in the context of his time. But as is generally recognized, Augustine channeled much of the patristic legacy to the Latin West in an excellent rhetorical style, borrowed and imitated widely in the Middle Ages. Especially his sermons, preached to simple people yet marked for their style and clarity, made much impact. His statement on Mary's perpetual virginity reflects the qualities of a well delivered sermon:

> Concipiens virgo, pariens virgo, virgo gravida, virgo feta, virgo perpetua.[176]
>
> (Conceiving as a virgin, giving birth as a virgin, pregnant as a virgin, delivering as a virgin, always a virgin.)

---

[175] Letter 101, PG 37 (177C-180A).
[176] *Sermo* 86, 1 (PL, 38, 999).

Another compact statement, preached in a long sermon to the people of Hippo, entered the language both of theology and of the liturgy:

Illa enim virgo concepit, virgo peperit, virgo permansit.[177]

(She conceived as a virgin, gave birth as a virgin, and remained virgin thereafter.)

Augustine's Marian teaching is genuinely pastoral: it was developed mainly in the context of his sermons. The sermon quoted last is indeed full of questions and issues touching "the common man's" interest and answering his questions: what specific roles men and women have in salvation history, how Mary and Joseph are linked for life through the common gift and task they received in the child, how a virginal conception does not obscure and reduce familial authority (due to a father in the Roman family), but is preserved in the Holy Family on account of the virtues of the parents. One may say, exactly because of his closeness to the simple parishioner of his town, a tiny place in comparison to Ambrose's Milan, Augustine contributed more than his own spiritual role model, Ambrose, did, by bringing the mystery of a virginally conceived child close to the simple believer, a mystery in which both Mary and Joseph participated – a mystery that gave unsuspected gifts and depths to their marriage. Another way Augustine enriched the Marian doctrine of the Church came to full appreciation when his teaching about "Mary and the Church" was resumed and exposed with full appreciation in the Second Vatican Council's Dogmatic Constitution on the Church. We will return to this topic at the end of the book.

In mariological matters Augustine never had to fight heresy, so we can consider his Marian piety undisturbed by turbulent events or hostilities within the Church. Unfortunately, however, in the last years of his life, the Pelagian controversies carried him in unforeseen ways into a dispute about Mary's sinlessness at birth. While he was

---

[177] *Sermo* 72, 12 (PL 38,342).

prevented by death from fully answering the charges, his last stance in the matter became an obstacle to the doctrine of the Immaculate Conception and, in that respect, he was remembered for centuries as objecting to it. Regarding this, too, we will have to return to St. Augustine, but in a different context.[178]

Cyril of Alexandria and the Council of Ephesus

In some sense the Council of Ephesus is a worthy conclusion of a long journey the Church traveled from apostolic times, a journey concluded with the affirmation of her Christological faith in statements exalting the Mother of God. But in another sense this Council, with its complicated and disturbing historical and political developments, shows quite well in advance how, more than a thousand years later, Marian doctrine and devotion were able to split the Western Church with unexpected suddenness through the Protestant Reformation, in spite of the unfailing unity of the East and the West through their shared faith in Mary for more than a thousand years.

The story usually associated with the names of Nestorius of Constantinople and Cyril of Alexandria, which led to the debacle of Ephesus, was rooted in the Christological controversies of the 4th century. Cultural and political alienation between East and West and the growing rivalries within a "world-wide" and powerful Church with five patriarchal sees (Rome, Constantinople, Alexandria, Antioch, and Jerusalem) represent the basis and the ultimate causes of these many violent clashes in a declining Empire. The prelude to Ephesus is constituted by the skirmishes caused by the afterlife of Arianism and the misunderstandings surrounding the concept of the "two natures," human and divine, united in one divine "person." It was a turbulent process in which East and West and various groups and Church leaders used their different understandings of Christological orthodoxy with the result of widening their multiple

---

[178] See below, pp. 147-150, 199, 283.

cultural and linguistic alienations. The Greek word *hypostasis* understood as "subject" or "essential constituent" or even "person" and the word *ousia* (being) as well as *prosopon* ("person" or just "face" or "appearance") were combined with *physis* ("nature") in an abstract or concrete sense in numerous attempts of resolving the clashes and conflicts. The emperors, worried about the unity of the Church and of their people, freely and at times arrogantly intervened by promoting, demoting, arresting, or exiling Church leaders. Since most of the emperors claimed authority and some of them even expertise in matters of the faith, but none was trained in theology, they worsened the state of the Church even when they meant to help it.

The story of the Council of Ephesus starts with the activities of Nestorius, patriarch of Constantinople, criticizing the famous orator Proclus (later himself a patriarch of Constantinople) for his use of the appellation *Theotokos* or God-bearer for Mary. Nestorius' criticism was based on the principle that God cannot be "born" as he is uncaused, thus Mary is Mother of Christ or *Christotokos*, but not Mother of God. In retrospect, we see that Nestorius' position might have been more of a misunderstanding or lack of understanding than a heresy. He did not understand the Christological truth of what is called in theology the *communicatio idiomatum* in Christ. Since the ultimate subject in Christ is the divine person, all his actions in the flesh apply to the Son of God: the second divine person was born, suffered, died, rose, and was glorified. None of these actions is to be restricted only to his human nature without being predicated also of the Son of God – the Divine Being who became flesh. Nestorius was contradicted most forcefully by Cyril, the patriarch of Alexandria. Both Nestorius and Cyril appealed to the Pope, who took Cyril's side from the beginning. The Emperor Theodosius II, siding with Nestorius, the patriarch of his capital city, intervened and so, at his request, a Council was convened to Ephesus in Asia Minor. For reasons not quite clear, Cyril of Alexandria opened the first session of the Council before all the bishops had arrived, among the absent also the papal delegates. At this session, on the evening of June 22, in anxious defense of the traditional faith, a great throng of local faithful, began shouting "be praised the *Theotokos*," and demanded the condemnation of Nestorius. This indeed happened with Cyril presiding. On June 26, John, the patriarch of Antioch, a traditional rival of Alexandria, arrived to the Council with the bishops of Syria and held a separate session, excommunicating Cyril and supporting Nestorius. On July 10, when the papal delegates arrived, the second session was officially opened, approving the position of the first session and excommunicating both Nestorius and John of Antioch. With the eventual arrival of the imperial representatives, the Council reached a tragic end: both Nestorius and Cyril were arrested and the Council disbanded. Only in September could Cyril return to Alexandria, while Nestorius withdrew to a monastery. The mutual excommunications were lifted only in 433 when, under Pope Sixtus III, an Edict of Union with a profession of faith (the "Symbol of Ephesus") was promulgated and accepted by all bishops of the East, including John of Antioch. But the damage was never undone: even today there are still "Nestorians," Eastern schismatic Churches, unwilling to accept the Council of Ephesus, just as there are also "Monophysites," Churches which refused to accept the Council of Chalcedon (451) twenty years after the "Edict of Union," because of their interpretation of Cyril's position at Ephesus, which they taught to have brought an unfair victory to the Antiochian Church. Sadly enough all these Churches fail to recognize their unity while adhering to an essentially identical Marian faith. For all of them, as well as the rest of the Catholic and Orthodox communities, recognize Mary as *Theotokos* and cultivate deep piety and unfailing devotion toward the Mother of God.

St. Cyril's Mariology is deeply embedded in the Alexandrian tradition. It is important to mention that his sermons reflect the tradition of praying to Mary as they address the Virgin in forceful and intimate terms that reflect prayer to her personally not just as a rhetorical custom of addressing the subject of the sermon. Since the discovery of the *Sub Tuum* in the Egyptian soil, this observation is of great importance for seeing how Mary was thought of as a reality with continuous presence in the Church's experience of heaven, just as heaven was also anticipated in prayer and spiritual life. Cyril's invocations of Mary surpass the rhetoric of flowery texts or exegetical periphrases of the words of Gabriel and Elizabeth, as we can see from the following texts:

> Hail Mary, Theotokos, Virgin Mother, lightbearer, uncorrupt vessel. Hail, O Virgin Mary, mother and handmaid, virgin, for the sake of him who was born virginally from you, mother, for the sake of him whom you carried in your arms and nursed with your milk; handmaid for the sake of him who took the form of a slave. For the king entered into your city, or rather into your womb, and he came forth from it as he wished while your gate remained shut. For you conceived without seed and gave birth divinely.[179]

> Hail, you who contained the one that cannot be contained, in your holy and virginal womb. Through you the Holy Trinity is glorified, the precious Cross is celebrated and adored throughout the world.... Through you the holy baptism and the oil of gladness are administered to the faithful, Churches are established throughout the world; the peoples are brought to conversion.[180]

These brief excerpts demonstrate Cyril's enthusiasm, but also the suggestive power by which he engaged the faithful and brought the crowds of Ephesus to passionate defense of the title *Theotokos.* One might also understand from these texts why rationalist scholarship, anxious to explain the sudden outburst of a boisterous popular piety at the Council of Ephesus, claimed that this was nothing less than a revival of the worship of the goddess Artemis, a cult that turned against the preaching of Paul almost four hundred years earlier (Ac 19:28-34). Of course, connecting the two events as expres-

---

[179] Homily 11, PG 77,1032 C.
[180] Homily 4 in Ephesus against Nestorius, PG 77, 992-6.

sions of devotion identical in origin would lead us to an unsolvable dilemma. If one claims historical continuity between the two riots[181] one must postulate that this "cult of Mary" in Ephesus goes back to apostolic times in which it eventually replaced the cult of Artemis, but remained connected with the city's cultural identity. How can that be without contradiction: both replace and preserve the same cult of a feminine deity? However, Mary's exaltation in Ephesus in 431 A.D. is a new development having nothing to do with idolatry or the silversmiths' booming business of idol-making. In the latter case the Marian devotion has nothing to do with the cult of Artemis, which, in fact, could have hardly survived the sharp cultural shifts that took place much later than Paul's preaching: at the time of the Christianization of the Empire.

For both the memory of the Church at large and the future of Marian cult, the Council of Ephesus marks an important point in history. This was not a mere victory won by Cyril against Nestorius, by Alexandria against Antioch, or by the Pope against the Emperor. The Church at large was on Cyril's side from the beginning. Not even his sometime impetuous behavior, nor his hasty and imprudent actions, were able to turn the tide. Those who on a newly obtained theological ground began to question the title of *Theotokos* were the ones proposing a novelty against established tradition. The title and cult of the "Mother of God" was no Alexandrian idiosyncrasy. For a long time, at least one and a half centuries before Nestorius found fault with it, this title was used not only in Egypt but also in Rome and several Eastern Churches, as Athanasius and the Cappadocian Fathers eloquently testify. However, what happened in Ephesus signaled that the Marian theology and devotion of the Church had grown powerful, capable of eliciting contrary sentiments and affecting the masses of the faithful.

---

[181] Even those who see the Marian cult of late antiquity as a return to the cult of goddesses do not attempt to prove continuity. An openly conducted public demonstration in honor of Mary cannot be even projected any earlier than after Constantine the Great, almost three hundred years after Paul's arrival to Ephesus.

The Sanctity of Mary: Augustine (ca. 353-430) and Pelagius (354-418)

As we mentioned above, Augustine's Mariology stands out, in retrospect, as significant for its practical success, but is not a true milestone, especially in comparison to what we see in his Trinitarian theology or theological thought on grace and free will. However, the question about Mary emerged in the course of the fight against Pelagius and so Augustine's name and fame marked Mariology for more than a thousand years. His thought produced lasting consequences, even though his death had prevented him from further clarifying his position.

Mary's personal holiness became a well-rehearsed and often repeated topic of Mariology as early as Origen, but then it passed into a widely and broadly confessed part of Church teaching through the legacy of Alexander, bishop of Alexandria, and his very influential successor Athanasius. It was most successfully and eloquently communicated in the Western Church by the writings of St. Ambrose. The reason that this topic was obvious in antiquity and difficult to research today lies in the precise meaning of the term "purity" applied to a virgin "in both body and soul" – the Pauline ideal of 1 Corinthians 7:34, consistently applied in the parlance of the Church Fathers to the Virgin Mary, or to the Church, both as "mother and virgin," or to the ideal of consecrated individuals, especially those dedicated to lifelong virginity in the Church. Certainly, Augustine states with special insistence that Mary's virginity was not a mere bodily condition but represents the integrity of her faith and that in this quality she was prepared by God to be the Mother worthy of her divine Son in both body and soul.

When the Pelagian controversy broke out, no issue of Mariology seemed to be involved. The fight against Jovinian was well remembered, and especially monks and consecrated virgins eagerly accepted the position of Jerome and Ambrose, which, after all, put in relief the dignity of their vocation.

However, when responding to Augustine, Pelagius, himself a

monk, came to the realization that Mariology had offered him an obvious example supporting his position. He focused his attention on Augustine's sweeping statement that, besides Jesus, no human being was born into the world in a state of sinlessness, a statement, of course, that was patently false. The Virgin Mary, born naturally from two parents, came to Pelagius' mind as an obvious counter-example, for she was believed to be sinless through her entire life although, obviously, she was born and grew into adulthood before her Son's redemptive death. Pelagius' text in which he explained his thought has not survived, but the gist of it is contained in one sentence turned into a dependent clause by Augustine quoting him: *ipsam etiam Domini ac Salvatoris nostri Matrem quam dicit [Pelagius] non peccato confiteri necesse est pietati*.[182] In English and by contemporary interpretation this says, "Pelagius mentioned [besides other examples] also our Lord and Savior's Mother, about whom one owes it to the faith not to admit any sin." This seems to be what Pelagius said, because, in fact, the term *pietas* in the Christian usage of the 4th century involves faith not just "devotion."[183] Mary's sinlessness is quite clearly expressed by both Ambrose and his model Athanasius, but before Pelagius nobody had made a statement as sweeping and absolute about Mary as he did, and we, in fact, must catch our breath to see how Augustine took up this challenge. In his response, Augustine neither reduced nor limited his opponent's claim about Mary's sinlessness in any way. He joins Pelagius in affirming what he says about Mary when he responds:

> The Virgin Mary is an exception about whom, for the sake of our Lord's honor I do not want to make mention of any sin: to her more grace has been granted for gaining complete victory over sin (*vincere ex omni parte peccatum*). For she was worthy to conceive and to give birth to

---

[182] *De natura et gratia* 42, PL 44, 267.

[183] Cf. G. Jouassard, "Marie à travers la patristique," in d'Hubert du Manoir (ed.) *Marie, Études sur la Sainte Vierge* (Paris: Beuchesne, 1949) I, 115.

the one in whom there has been absolutely no sin (*nullum habuisse peccatum*).[184]

When Augustine speaks of an exception, he makes it clear, that while agreeing on Mary's sinlessness he does not admit Pelagius' argument. He adds under the same heading that if we gathered all the saints of the past, men and women, and asked them if they had been sinless, they would answer in unison with the Apostle John, "If we say, 'We have not sinned,' we make him a liar, and his word is not in us" (1 Jn 1:10).

In this fascinating exchange well before the Council of Ephesus, Augustine and Pelagius agree on the one single point that interests us here: Mary is sinless, and this is believed, it seems, in the universal Church's faith and thus neither side can raise any doubt about it.

As the Pelagian controversy continued, a follower of Pelagius, Julian, the deposed bishop of Eclanum in Italy, pushed a bit further and expanded Pelagius' Marian argument. In great style but bad taste, he accused Augustine of being a heretic worse than Jovinian. He attacked the old bishop of Hippo, suggesting that while Jovinian "dissolved only her virginal condition on account of giving birth (*partus conditione*) you [Augustine], you assign Mary in person to the possession of the Devil on account of her birth (*conditione nascendi ipsam Mariam Diabolo transcribis*)." The insinuation is viciously inexact and patently false. Augustine did not say and would not say that Mary was born a sinner or "belonged to the Devil" at her birth. Augustine began to write a response to Julian but died without completing it.[185] Julian's incrimination did not go on record as anything but slander, yet inadvertently it opened an issue, for which Augustine ended up on record as being on the wrong side. As soon as the question of Mary's Immaculate Conception was raised, Augustine was interpreted to have said that she was sinless at birth

---

[184] *De natura et gratia* 42, PL 44, 267.
[185] *Opus imperfectum adversus Julianum* 2,22 (PL 45,1417).

but not at conception. He never had a chance to consider the question in this form, let alone to state an argued opinion about it, but the die was cast and it took centuries to clarify in what sense Mary was an exception from our general state of sinfulness at birth. In the 12th century, when the question of Mary's Immaculate Conception appears at the center of an emerging theological debate, Augustine's unfinished dispute with Pelagius and Julian of Eclanum initiates a strange story in which the heritage of Augustine proves itself to be, maybe for the first time, more of a liability than a help. But we might also find later[186] a perspective from which the strange entanglement of his legacy ultimately would seem to have had a beneficial influence on some further developments in Mariology.

---

[186] See Augustine's text to be quoted further down on p. 280 about "Mary and the Church."

CHAPTER FIVE

MARIOLOGY IN LATE ANTIQUITY

This chapter is necessary because of a particular feature of the development of the Mariological dogmas. What appears as an upsurge of doctrinal interest from the 2nd century to the Council of Ephesus was indeed sudden, fast, and substantial. It involved the best leaders and minds of the patristic era and saw the birth of classical texts that remained normative for more than a thousand years. What begins in "late antiquity" (the 5th and 6th centuries) is a sort of change in the intellectual and devotional climate and, consequently, a change of "venue" for Mariological literature and so also of its content, quality, and tone.

While in the first four centuries Mariology develops in close connection with Christology and appears as a special extension of the theology of the Incarnation, there are now only few new topics, and all tentatively formulated. Reflection on Mary's sanctity brings up as if by accident the question of the Immaculate Conception. At the same time the upsurge of the veneration of the heroes of the faith – the Apostles and the martyrs – brings up questions about Mary's death and glorification, as well as her place in heaven. Doctrine again meanders, but without pressure from fear of heresy and with ample support from explicit traditional material linked to Scripture; and this meandering stream peacefully and slowly descends into the devotional life of the late patristic and early medieval centuries. It eventually bears late fruit in medieval times. We will proceed in three steps: First, summarizing the ripe doctrinal statements of the classic patristic era in a Christological overview of Marian theology as *Theotokos*, brought to a synthesis between Nicaea and Ephesus;

then looking at the way the Church in late antiquity anticipated and spoke of Mary's absolute sinlessness (called later the teaching of the *Immaculate Conception*) and began to ask about Mary's share in eschatology, her Assumption to heaven. This latter question, by being more complex and obscure, will bring us to the special topic of the first "emergence" of Christian thought about Mary's death and/or "falling asleep" (dormition) and bodily glorification.

The Theology of the *Theotokos*: A Retrospective Summary

The development of Mariology from the Synoptic Gospels to the 4th century is a unique and easily misunderstood chapter in the history of dogmas. Because we are immediately rooted in the Church as it thinks and acts today, and, in addition, we largely depend on the culture and mentality of the past hundred years, all attempts to frame this history in a correct perspective are rather difficult and problematic. Nevertheless, the material assembled here sufficiently demonstrates that the development of Christology leading from apostolic times to Nicaea (325), then to the first Council of Constantinople (381) and the Council of Ephesus (431), was accompanied by a parallel and sequentially connected movement, which was not merely secondary or fully dependent, but was indeed focused on its own distinct subject. Through the first four Christian centuries the role of Mary, her virginity and divine motherhood, were brought to clear consciousness broadly in all parts of the early Church.

Our story line might appear to go in zigzags, or proceed mostly by the anticipated insertion into earlier times of the interests and priorities of later generations. This might be hard to avoid, especially given the paucity of the documentation on Marian teaching left behind from the 2nd and early 3rd centuries. In some sense, further unexpected discoveries may change our outlook about the sudden surge of Marian doctrine leading from the first two Christian centuries to that great sounding-board of early tradition, the text-collector and synthesizer Origen. In his pioneering work on the Mariology of Origen, Cipriano Vagaggini showed that, in spite of the devastation of the great Alexandrian's literary legacy, even from that meager surviving bit, a true *Corpus Marianum* can be re-constructed. This alone could make it plausible that the pivotal role of Mary and the Incarnation was discovered during the 2nd century with a certain suddenness, and it was then that it earned much attention and prepared for the surprisingly intense growth of interest in Mariology in the post-Nicene era.

With regard to the beginnings of *Dogmengeschichte* (a linear assessment of the increasingly explicit doctrinal tenets in the early Church), and the classical positions it produced by the middle of the 20th century, the era following the Second World War brought important correctives that any impartial study of early Mariology must take into account to revise some hardened and by now obsolete positions that entered the lexicons and the vast textbook production of the early 20th century.

First, the witnesses of Ignatius, Justin, and Irenaeus must not be pushed to the margin and regarded as isolated, sporadic, or even idiosyncratic. Their texts are not negligible. Ignatius of Antioch showed how and why the Incarnation *ex Maria*, in reference to her as a historical person with a name, and an insistence upon her virginal status, had to enter the *regula fidei*. The *regula fidei* is of central importance for the 2nd century Church: it remains in direct continuity with the apostolic preaching by summarizing briefly its most important anti-Gnostic doctrinal elements. What Ignatius provides for us proves that this *regula*, while insisting on the true Incarnation of the Logos ("truly born, truly suffered, and truly risen") had to insist on the inclusion of Mary, with reference both to her name and to her virginal status. For Ignatius, Justin, and other early sources,[187] Mary

---

[187] "He was truly of the seed of David according to the flesh, and the Son of God according to the will and power of God; that he was truly born of a virgin, was baptized by John, in order that all righteousness might be fulfilled by him." (*Letter to the Smyrneans* 1:1). "He became man through the Virgin (διὰ τῆς παρθένου ἄνθρωπος γεγονέναι) in order that the disobedience caused by the Serpent might be destroyed in the same manner in which it had originated" (Justin Martyr, *Dialogue with Trypho* 100). Irenaeus and Tertullian routinely refer to "the Virgin" meaning Mary.

is "the Virgin"; thus the patristic sources manifest that this status is essential for making clear the twofold nature of Jesus: both *ex Maria* and *ex Deo*.[188] If, therefore, in a post-Reformation perspective, one raises the question of Mariology's legitimacy, one must maintain the link with the broader question of the legitimacy of the anti-Gnostic battle, and the theological positions defended by Ignatius, Justin, Irenaeus, and Tertullian while appealing to Mary's role in the Incarnation.

Second, the concern or complaint about the scarcity of Mariological texts in the 2nd and 3rd centuries is misleading. Christian texts from this epoch are few and fragmentary in general. What we have, for example, from Justin about Mary and Eve is important not only for us, but also for him, yet, unfortunately, only one such passage – with a remarkably developed view on the matter – has survived the centuries.

Third, the *Sub Tuum* shows that considering devotional prayer to Mary a "late development" or even non-existent in the 2nd and 3rd centuries was an erroneous supposition. The quasi-dogmatic assertion made by some liturgists that Christians prayed always "to the Father through the Son and in the Spirit" may apply to communal prayer, but certainly not to private prayer. Invocations of the saints appear in numerous graffiti on the excavated 2nd and 3rd century walls of the apostolic tombs in Rome. Moreover, dating the *Sub Tuum* fragment to the 4th century is based on a biased interpretation of the data; paleographically the finding points to the 3rd century; what appears in lexicons dating it "about 300," was the result of "a compromise" to make the dating more palatable. Furthermore, there is yet another proof that addressing Mary in form of prayer comes from the 2nd century: a linkage of two scriptural greetings to Mary, one in Luke 1:28 by the Angel Gabriel and one in Luke 1:42 by Elizabeth. These two phrases formed a single greeting in the way they appear fused in a widely spread variant reading of Luke 1:28 in the

---

[188] καὶ ἐκ Μαρίας καὶ ἐκ θεοῦ πρῶτον παθητὸς καὶ τότε ἀπαθής Ἰησοῦς Χριστὸς ὁ κύριος ἡμῶν (Ignatius, *Letter to the Ephesians* 7:2), "sprung from Mary as well as God, first subject to suffering and then beyond it, Jesus Christ our Lord."

majority of ancient witnesses: "Hail, full of grace, the Lord is with you, blessed are you among women." This cannot be attributed to dittography, because the two scriptural phrases were textually separated by thirteen verses, before the second ("blessed are you among women") was attached to the first ("Hail, full of grace, the Lord is with you"). Since copying mistakes cannot be caused visually from backward, right to left and retroactively (texts cannot be misread before they are read), the two quotations must have been fused first orally, so that then their memorized linkage could interfere with the pen of some inattentive copyist(s). The fusion must come from previous oral (devotional) use. The text of the *Proto-evangelium*, which already quotes the variant reading (dated to 160-190), provides a *terminus ad quem* for dating the origin of the variant reading.[189] This means that Christians began to imitate Gabriel and Elizabeth when addressing Mary in devotional prayer and joined their greetings together, thus paving the way to the composition of the *Hail Mary*.[190]

The fourth corrective can be mentioned here only in a broader way, because of the numerous applications and multiple understandings by contemporary theologians. This regards the earliest, and probably most important, theological tool or *theologoumenon* in Mariology, the Mary/Eve parallel. The custom of reading the Old Testament through Christological "lenses" pervades theology from apostolic times. What Justin Martyr says about Mary and Eve extends what Paul said about Adam and Christ. The Christological reading of God's first self-disclosure to the Jewish people is based on the general principle that all salvation history is focused on a single effective Incarnation distributed in time and space such that it must be taken as an ordered, sequentially prepared, divinely willed, and Spirit-guided history of the manifestations of the Logos, reaching its summit and goal in the Incarnation *"ex Deo"* as Father and *"ex Ma-*

---

[189] This is confirmed by the presence of the variant in all types of the textual tradition and in all languages, including the *Vetus Latina*, also from the 2nd century.

[190] Textbooks derive the Hail Mary from the appearance of its first half in the form of an Offertory Antiphon in the early Middle Ages. But that antiphon is nothing more than the variant reading of Lk 1:28 in the Vulgate. Obviously, this question needs a new assessment.

ria" as mother. Thus Justin Martyr, and after him Irenaeus, initiate Mariology neither by accident nor in response to a psychological need, and even less under the guidance of some pragmatic and pastoral wisdom for the sake of inserting into Christianity a substitute for a goddess or *"Magna Mater,"* no matter how much, indeed, this image of "sacred womanhood" (in the context of feminine fertility) has fascinated all human religions since the beginning of civilization.[191]

Mariology is unavoidable and necessary for whoever intends to explore the mystery of the Incarnation. Treating the event of "God becoming man" point-wise as a nature miracle creates the wrong perspective and can never enlighten the primary data of the Christian faith. It would lead to the conclusion that God gratuitously intended to create the human being whom he, however, would afterward or contemporaneously invade and inhabit, letting the past perish and haphazardly giving a chance for something new to emerge. Such an outlook may seem eminently philosophical and even metaphysical, but in fact it disregards the purpose and context of salvation history. More exactly, it would omit the properly *biblical context* within which *biblical revelation* asserts that the Incarnation truly happened.

In the context of mankind's salvation history the basic issue is the following: God became man in both *continuity* and *discontinuity* with what he had first created. The Mary/Eve parallel expresses the insight that through the Son of God born *ex Maria Virgine* God reached out to all mankind he had created to his image as male and female (Gn 1:27), i.e., as "Adam" and "Eve." Salvation was promised and offered not only to those who, born chronologically after the birth of Jesus, eventually heard his message (the Gospel) preached, and appropriated it by explicit acts of faith and baptism, but to all who responded to grace offered also previously and in many other external sets of circumstances, but, of course, always offered as grace merited by Christ. All who believed and believe with the response of

---

[191] This "beginning" is more often than not said to be connected with the appearance of agriculture, the basis on which a large number of people can become sedentary and live around the same place, establishing the first communal forms of human existence.

their humanity, that is "in body and soul," are incorporated through him into the final output of the divine project of salvation, the Body of Christ. For the whole work of salvation there is but one Incarnation proclaimed by one single *euaggelion* or "good news." Thereafter, there was only one bodily Passion and Resurrection of the Incarnate Son, which took place as historical events. This work of salvation happened only once in human history, not because God is stingy, but because this event is truly comprehensive and definitive. Thus, though single and concrete, it is offered to all mankind, it is extended and thus linked to the rest of history temporally in both directions, past and future, so that it may reach all generations. Christ is the only source of salvation and all people need him, both those who come before and those who come after his physical appearance in the flesh. This is a necessary implication of the well-known principle of the New Testament's soteriology according to which the Incarnate Son died and rose for all so that all salvation be mediated through him, "the only mediator of God and man" (1 Tm 2:5).

What we are saying here is nothing new, except possibly that Mariology was greatly influenced by, and one may even say, activated by this principle. The Mary/Eve parallelism works for both Justin Martyr and Irenaeus in function of the way they understood salvation history as a single and continuous process that, nonetheless, brings about a "new creation." This double statement implies no contradiction, for Jesus is a descendant of Adam through Mary, but, at the same time, in his life, death, and glorification he presents a principle of new birth or "regeneration" for all humanity issuing from Adam and Eve, including his physical ancestors all the way up to Adam, as well as all their descendants. While the first Adam and Eve became the source of all human life in the physical sense, resulting in a single mankind produced through a chain of procreative unions, the second Adam initiated rebirth to the same mankind united with him as the one and same species, linked by common ancestry. For the whole human race he died and rose from death with his body and soul, pertaining to this physically linked community, and provided them a new way of life "in the spirit," a life of sanctify-

ing grace. The same creation as the first – the same concrete nature ·
that had been created on the "sixth day of creation," but had lost its
divine filiation through the first sin – was offered new life in Christ
by being newly created, re-born, and regenerated by the supernatural gift of grace. Grace endows the spirit not physically, but spiritually, i.e., by granting a new assimilation to God for his human image
and thus providing the human being, beyond its creaturely status, a
new participation in the Son's relationship to the Father by receiving
the Holy Spirit.

Generally speaking it is correct to say that the point of departure of Mariology is Christology. However, *in concreto* there is more
to be said about this starting point, in the sense of both systematic
and historical theology. The motor that propelled Mariology for centuries started running when soteriology and anthropology, linked
together, began to open their joint meaning by demonstrating in full
depth the twofold basis of the Incarnation: *"ex Deo"* and *"ex Maria."*
That the Church Fathers understood and responded to this prompting is due to their being deeply grounded in the Scriptures. They
took quite seriously the statements about rebirth and "regeneration"
found in the New Testament[192] and the connections of the first and
second Adam. The latter they appropriated not only from St. Paul
but from reading attentively and in consecutive order the first chapters of Genesis. For these texts point out quite clearly, in a passage
that we may fail to read or speak about, that God could have given up
on man, as he saw man to be irreparably bent to sin:

> When the LORD saw how great was man's wickedness
> on earth, and how no desire that his heart conceived was
> ever anything but evil, he regretted that he had made man
> on the earth, and his heart was grieved. (Gn 6:5-6)

---

[192] See παλιγγενεσία in Mt 19:28, Tit 3:5; "birth from above" in Jn 3:3-5; "being born
again" in 1 P 1:3 and "being born from God" in 1 Jn 5:8. With the controversies
and uncertainties about the acquaintance Ignatius of Antioch had with Johannine
sources, one rarely identifies the last quotation as a possible source for what he
writes in his *Letter to the Ephesians* (7:2). But we see that the idea "re-birth" is a
solid part of the New Testament, an element that obtains its meaning only in the
fullness of the Canon.

We are not dealing here with mythology. It may well be called "mythopoieic" and "anthropomorphic," because in describing God's disappointment with his creation, it expresses something we know only as a human sentiment: the frustration we have with the result of our labor, or artwork or, in closer resemblance, with a child of ours. But the statement is deeply theological: it is about man's chronic failure as he falls back into his devious ways despite the harshest punishments he receives, warranting a sure prompting to discontinue the project. Yet God does not abandon man to his destiny, but begins another plan of redemption. Genesis inserts lists of genealogies leading to new and newer generations populating the earth. But then, in chapter 12, with the call of Abraham, there begins a new brand of salvation history. This is what Matthew's Gospel refers to at its opening, where we find another "Book of Genesis" – this time a beginning with the Genesis of Jesus Christ, Son of Abraham and his descendant, linked down to Joseph, the husband of Mary, of whom was born Jesus who is called the Messiah (Mt 1:1-16).

As the evangelist Luke saw it, the birth of Jesus must be narrated from Adam (Lk 3:24-36) and only thereafter from Abraham; but, in any case, it runs through Mary, because otherwise it is not the Man (Adam) that is being created. Jesus' nature must be identical with the one that was created on the sixth day and redeemed at the fullness of time. Otherwise we speak of another mankind created to fill his place. But Jesus was born from "an Adamite," someone from Adam's race. From Mary the Son of God took our nature; that is why he can be called a second Adam, "the Man" born again. Due to his birth we all are his relatives, his family into which he was integrated in all things except sin. There is but one salvation history and only one authentic Incarnation of the Son. Thus for the sake of a new creation God "who gives life to the dead and calls into being what does not exist" (Rm 4:17) did not annihilate man in order to start, after this failed project, another one. Rather, he started life from the "dead womb" of Sarah and "the dead body" of Abraham (4:19), foreshadowing both the tomb in which he lay and the virginal womb in which he was conceived. By the miraculous origin of Israel he anticipated the virginal conception but only the latter is truly a *fully new* creation (from a brand new soil freshly created: a being untouched by the original disobedience) yet in continuity with Adam and Eve, the latter being called "mother of all living" or simply "Life" (ζωή in Gn 3:20 LXX). The Mary/Eve parallel is a theological sunbeam emitted in the mid-2nd century and illuminating the meaning of Mary's parthenogenesis by inserting it into an apparently brand new frame of reference.

Because of the perspectives described above, this new reading of Luke 1-2 (and Matthew 1-2), which Justin and Irenaeus linked to the narrative about the first man and woman in Genesis 3, has proven itself a powerful incentive to re-read practically every sentence about Mary in the New Testament. Such an approach to all texts about Mary gained popularity and recognition through the use of the Bible among Christians in the first four centuries. It acquired a stable methodology clarified first by Origen[193] and employed as the most widely known pattern of exegesis up to the end of the Middle Ages.[194] In a somewhat similar way, the Christology of the Gospels began to be expanded already by St. Paul in terms of theological concepts and language borrowed from the Law and the Prophets, and so Mary's figure and person were presented already by the early Church Fathers in terms of a universal salvation plan. This plan begins with the history of the first man and woman, their creation in original blessedness, through the loss of Paradise and the divine enterprise of offering a road to salvation for all human beings: it is in this sense *a universal salvation plan offered to all mankind.*

Tertullian coined a strikingly concise and celebrated formula: *caro est salutis cardo,*[195] that is, the human body is the hinge of God's

---

[193] Henri de Lubac, *Histoire et Esprit. L'intelligence de l'Écriture d'après Origène* (Paris: Aubier, 1950). In English: *History and Spirit. The Understanding of Scripture according to Origen*, translated by A.E. Nash (San Francisco: Ignatius Press, 2008).

[194] See Henri de Lubac, *Exégèse médiévale I-IV* (Paris: Aubier, 1960-1964). Partially translated into English: *Medieval Exegesis,* tr. by Mark Sebanc (Grand Rapids: Eerdsman, 2000).

[195] *De resurrectione carnis* VIII,2.

salvation plan. The body's role is neither accidental nor marginal, but essential and central. Nor is it merely passive, as if it were only the recipient of an overflow of grace. Rather, it is an essential instrument without which God's salvific acts could not have happened in the way he willed them. Tertullian formulated this sentence in an anti-Marcionite context, insisting on the reality of Christ's body and thus the reality of his birth, suffering, death, and Resurrection, resulting in the salvation of our body in both sacraments and eschatology. It was on account of this anti-Gnostic outlook that the phrase *"ex Maria"* enters the *regula fidei*. But of course, the Word becoming flesh does not only address Christ's individual human nature. Mary links Christ to Adam: in her child-bearing a link is formed between Christ and the whole human race. Through her he is inserted as a man sharing the same nature with all offspring of Adam and Eve so that he may be crucified and die for us all. Yet he was not born like all the children of the first parents, because these were all born outside of Paradise. Moreover the body of Christ, substantially united to a divine person and thus to the divine nature, is not only a historical *datum* – insofar as it is human – but supra-historical, because *theandrical*: Christ's divinity, to which his humanity is substantially united, assures that his humanity may be accessible for all descendants of Adam and Eve, independently of the point in time at which they were born. Because of his *theandrical* (divine and human) character, Christ is effectively present – we might simply say "available" – for all members of the human race. He is, in fact, Savior of the world (Jn 4:42), since he is both within and above the human race. Christ is the only Savior, for God is available only through the Son: "No one knows the Son except the Father, and no one knows the Father except the Son and anyone to whom the Son wishes to reveal him" (Mt 11:27).

Mary is the one and only immediate ancestor from whose body the Incarnate Logos was formed. Thus she is only the bridge, as it were, for Christ who alone mediates between human and divine natures (2 Tm 2:5) by uniting the two in his concrete existence. Mary's role is not that of a parallel system of mediation competing with Jesus' exclusive role in that capacity. Yet she is the one, single human being from whom God can be born untouched by imperfection, and yet, also so fully human that he can participate in man's tragic destiny: he can suffer – both physically and psychologically – and undergo the most tragic consequence of sin, the death of a creature, at first fashioned to live eternally, in an experience of perishing with a perishing world, no matter how much inferior to him.

The concrete event of the Incarnation cannot be revealed only in the abstract, without the mode in which God chose to let it come about. Thus the Incarnation is revealed together with the way in which it happened: through Mary, the Virgin. Consequently her virginal conception and parturition are to be announced in their mysterious and miraculous character, not as a mere biological curiosity, reserved as some firework in honor of the Son's Incarnation, but as the uniquely fitting mode in which God communicates by both proclaiming to us and conferring upon us his eternal fatherhood, a gift and a revealed truth, announced and distributed to all human beings.

The virginal mode in which God creates and Mary transmits the humanity of Adam and Eve rescued humanity from becoming a failed creature. Rather than letting man run the full course of the path he chose for himself, God revealed his willingness to go as far as he was able to go to pursue his salvation plan up to the end, εἰς τὸ τέλος: "having loved his own who were in the world, he loved them to the uttermost" (Jn 13:1).[196] The mode is linked to the purpose: God joins man in his post-lapsarian condition, namely, by taking upon himself a human nature with all that belongs to its sin-caused condition except sinfulness itself. Paul says much the same about God the Father creating Jesus in such a condition: "For our sake he *made him to be sin who knew no sin*, so that in him we might become the righteousness of God" (2 Cor 5:21). What is added to this with the doctrine of the virginal conception is the realization that a con-

---

[196] ἀγαπήσας τοὺς ἰδίους τοὺς ἐν τῷ κόσμῳ εἰς τέλος ἠγάπησεν αὐτούς. The expression εἰς τέλος certainly means a love that does not cease until it runs its full course both in terms of time and in terms of exhausting all possible ways of manifesting itself.

crete human being after Adam is not only created but pro-created, and thus the second Adam is made to be both a continuation and a beginning. This is the point that Irenaeus' theory of the recapitulation makes explicit: God establishes a new beginning, yet one that resumes the first creation. To achieve that, he truly inserts Christ into the human race, "a man born of a woman," and yet inserts discontinuity into history when, by causing the virginal birth, he makes of this birth a new beginning.

The similarity and paradox between Mary and Eve might be called the foundation stone of Mariology as a distinct discipline. Its antiquity must impress everybody who tries to reduce Mariology to a mere appendix of Christology. Although Justin Martyr is the first Church Father in whose thinking it appears, he does not present it as a novelty, either in the sense of an invention or as a discovery of his own. The roots point not only in the direction of Christology but also toward theological anthropology, a combination of Johannine thought on the Incarnation and Pauline thought on the redemption as parallelism and reversal between the first and the second Adam.

We insert here another thought, also quite obvious from the cumulative biblical and patristic material. It comes from the great figure of Nicaea, St. Athanasius, and possibly his mentor, Alexander of Alexandria. When they speak of the exaltation of Mary above all other creatures, including all the angels, their words convey much more than just a poetic and enthusiastic literary form for Mary, who, as mother of the Son of God, obtained the highest imaginable honor. For this statement introduces into Mariology a new insight that echoes for centuries: Mary's motherhood is that point in history where the deepest humiliation of God and the highest exaltation of man meet. In the case of Mary's motherhood a human being provides fleshly origins to the Divine Son. This is no mere paradox but a mystery. For by this event, he who has no beginning is now born in time ("the fullness of time") and he who is eternally generated by God the Father obtains fleshly origin in time from a woman (Gal 4:4). In this context we may better understand the words St. Jerome uses to open his *Commentary on Matthew*, quoting Matthew 1:1 and

THE MARIAN MYSTERY

pairing it to a variant reading of Isaiah 53:8 as he asks: *generationem eius quis enarrabit?* Jesus' origins are indeed steeped in mystery. The question "who can speak of it?" means for Jerome that the human mind cannot fathom it. In the light of the Nicene dogma, the virginal conception obtains a meaning far beyond a physical "partheno-genesis" or "conception without intercourse." This alone would mean something entirely negative: the absence of the conjugal act before reproduction; this is what we meant above referring to a mere nature miracle. But the virginal conception is an event of a much higher order: in the Virgin's womb the eternal generation of the Logos from God the Father is inserted into the course of history. For a personal being, both motherhood and fatherhood are personal attributes. In Jesus there is but one Person, the second Person of the Trinity, eternally begotten of the Father in a single unceasing action of divine generation. At Mary's *fiat* this divine generation is set into history, hosted in the Virgin's womb, infused into the family of David among the descendants of Abraham. The origins of the Incarnate Son took place in a dialogue of faith and love between God and the virginal Woman, and transcend the realm of human reproduction. In the Incarnation, Mary's motherhood is virginal, not because the sexual union as such is sinful or burdened with the inclination to sin, but because a non-virginal motherhood would obscure rather than express the basic truth to be revealed: that by the Incarnation God's divine fatherhood has been established in Jesus' individual human nature and dwells there in its fullness for all times.

Early Forms of the Doctrine of the Immaculate Conception

While focusing on Mary's divine motherhood and virginity, patristic Mariology also contains some tentative formulation of Mary's Immaculate Conception and opens the door to demanding questions about her eternal glory, questions about her participation in her Son's glory. Of course, such an assessment can be made only in retrospect. After Ephesus, its development began to meander considerably more between the institution of liturgical feasts, the spread

164

of a popular piety with paraliturgical activities, and the expansion of apocryphal literature newly written or newly redacted and translated, exploring Mary's life in the style of the legends much in the same way these were also written and re-written about martyrs and other heroes of the faith.

It is legitimate to begin with the statement that the issue of Mary's sanctity was rooted in the first period of the patristic era and thus the thesis of the Immaculate Conception grew out of a broad background leading to a specific question formulated, as we have seen, by Augustine and Pelagius. Once brought up, this question had to be solved as part of soteriology and the theology of grace; but the conceptual tools were simply missing. Once the basic problems about original sin were clarified, Mary's relation to the sin of Adam and Eve, a question spoken of since the 2nd century, was resumed with more precision. However, the majority of theologians, with St. Augustine in the lead, could not move beyond reaffirming Mary's sinlessness from birth. The question of the Immaculate Conception became trapped in a vacuum: a lack of precision in the reflection on original sin. Thus the issue of when Mary's sinlessness began – at her conception, at her birth, or later – remained dormant for at least five hundred years. For half a millennium after that, on account of unexpected obstacles and thorny problems, the popes felt that it was inopportune for them to define the answer in a dogma.

The Origins of the Doctrine of Mary's Assumption

It may be inappropriate to speak about the emergence of a dogma, as if it were an impersonal and anonymous, even subconscious process, but our present-day knowledge – a sort of *docta ignorantia* – may fully justify the use of such a term. By the late 5th or early 6th century, a multiplicity of traditions surfaced in the Church regarding the ways in which Mary's destiny at the end of her life can be described.

Of course, this era still belongs to the last phase of the patristic period. For the roots of the doctrine and cult about Mary's death with subsequent glorification, or deathless end with glorification thereupon, or just a *transitus*, some sort of a "departure" to heaven, where her body and soul were transported together or with the soul going first and body next – all these various doctrinal claims appear in ancient writings of late antiquity with confusing diversity and a puzzling simultaneity: for our inquiry they seem to "emerge."

Another difficulty particularly applies to the contemporary inquiry into the doctrine's origin. In the second half of the 20th century newly discovered documents – often fragmentary – added further difficulties to dating the origins of the various traditions or the explicit appearance of the doctrine. Some would want to go back all the way to the 2nd century.[197] Others consider the 4th century as the earliest possible *terminus a quo*. However, the data and their diversity have so far resisted all the various attempts to line them up in an evolutionary sequence.

The form in which these traditions are expressed is that of legendary narratives (anonymous or apocryphal) or sermons and homilies for liturgical celebrations in memory of Mary's glorification in soul and/or body, sometimes in succession (first soul, then body) at other times both at once. Most of these texts have their origins in the Christian East starting at least a couple of centuries before the Islamic conquest of the Middle East. Instead of the original Greek or Syriac texts, often only their translations into Coptic or Ethiopian (more rarely Latin, Slavonic, or Georgian) are extant. These carry the traces of repeated editorial changes in a confusing array or a large number of variant readings with significant discrepancies, leaving

---

[197] "Various scholars of the *Studium Biblicum Franciscanum* in Jerusalem, for instance, including Bellarmino Bagatti, Emmanuele Testa and Fréderic Manns among others, collectively share a somewhat similar view that the origin of the Dormition traditions lie in certain Palestinian Jewish Christian communities whose practice and theology were quite distinct from the Gentile church which is much better known from our ancient sources. Bagatti, who is in some sense the founder of this school of interpretation, argued that during or shortly after the apostolic age a group of Jewish Christians in Jerusalem preserved an oral tradition about the end of the Virgin's life." (S. Shoemaker, *Ancient Traditions of the Virgin Mary's Dormition and Assumption* [New York: Oxford University Press, 2002], 18-19). The author rejects the existence of such a tradition concerning the way Mary's life ended.

scholars rather perplexed about their origin, including the question of their original language or the time and sequence of the variations in the texts.[198]

A few basic points, however, stand out as recognized by most historical summaries and systematic treatments of Mariology in the 20th century. In his *Panarion* from 377, St. Epiphanius, who had otherwise claimed to know ancient traditions about Jesus' family and Mary's ancestry, clearly admitted that he could not obtain information about how Mary's life ended.[199] He states, in particular, that nobody knows whether Mary died or was "transferred" to heaven. This statement by a highly respected Church Father was passed down through the centuries and especially in 1950, at the dogmatization of Mary's bodily Assumption into heaven, suggested for the Magisterium great caution. It has made Church authorities refrain from making statements about whether or not Mary ever died. In this way, the threefold variety of options found in traditional sources remained open. These continued to be freely debated among Roman Catholic theologians and also in their exchange with Eastern Orthodox scholars.

The three positions are frequently called Dormitionist, Assumptionist, and Immortalist. The first claims that Mary underwent a deathlike transformation as if "falling asleep" and remained in such a state until some time when she was transferred, body and soul, to share her Son's glory. The second claims that Mary died and was buried, but, just as in the case of Jesus, her tomb was found empty after her body was taken miraculously to be reunited with her soul and brought to heaven. The third is a position that asserts that her glorification in both soul and body happened without any temporary intervention of death or deathlike sleep or trance.

The scholarly debates about these three positions or their denial continue principally on two levels. First, how and why – mostly

---

[198] Detailed information with ample bibliography is found in: S. Shoemaker, op. cit. with a translation of the most important documents in the appendix.

[199] R. Laurentin, *Court traité de théologie mariale* (Paris: Lethielleux, 1959), 45-46.

in what sequence and time periods – did the historical development of the dogma take place? Second, which of the three positions can be best defended with either historical or theological arguments?

Beyond the debate about these three dogmatic positions there looms one basic question: why do we find no trace of a traditional doctrine about Mary's end of life any time prior to the 5th century? Independently of the Franciscan scholars' claims quoted above, who speak of a 2nd century tradition,[200] scholars make the beginning of their investigations the proven presence of a Marian cult in the 4th century, connected with certain shrines in Palestine and especially Jerusalem. This much is usually accepted as beyond reasonable doubt. Equally, there is no reason to doubt the connection of this cult with the traditions about Mary's Assumption/Dormition, proven from both literary and archeological research. What recent scholarship has succeeded in showing is, in my opinion, the simple fact that the tradition we find emerging in the 4th century is not merely the product of imaginative storytelling, but derives from local traditions of the Jerusalem Church, and was already known in the pre-Constantinian period. A lack of earlier documentation about its precise origins and the fact that we cannot reconstruct the theological context in which it was preserved and transmitted may be best explained by the simple fact that neither believing it nor ignoring it was deemed heretical.

Two facts indicate, however, that there was a common kernel for the Assumptionist or the Dormitionist tradition, and that it was kept in silence neither because of a lack of information nor because of a lack of interest on the part of the faithful. First, we notice a total absence of the veneration of Marian relics; there was no claim of relics coming from Mary's body, nor a cult of any tomb containing her remains. As has become fully clear in recent decades, such claims about the tombs of the Apostles Peter and Paul existed with reference to the remains of the Apostles from the early 2nd century.

---

[200] Cf. note 197.

Concerning all imaginable saintly figures of the Christian past, recent or remote, tradition either remembered, or in case of necessity, assumed to know the fate of the remains; yet no relics of the Blessed Virgin have been venerated anywhere in the Christian world. Second, while we are in possession of solid evidence of a cult referring to Mary's Assumption or Dormition in Jerusalem, which reaches back to the 4th century, there was no rival claim pointing elsewhere. It is significant that in antiquity at no place other than Jerusalem was the presence of Mary's (empty) tomb and/or the location of her last dwelling asserted. For in the 19th century certain mystics[201] and, beginning in the 12th century, some Church theologians and scholars, pushed for an alternative place in Ephesus.[202] But for Ephesus there exists absolutely no ancient tradition. The case for a "house of Mary" in Ephesus – the place where Mary would have been under the care of John the Apostle – was made deductively and without reasonable plausibility. After all, from as early as Irenaeus (late 2nd century) the author of the Fourth Gospel was firmly identified with John the Apostle, to whom Jesus entrusted his mother (Jn 19:25) and who, according to fairly unanimous ancient tradition, was said to have written his Gospel in Ephesus.[203] The claims of Mary living for any time in Ephesus under the care of the Beloved Disciple, were based on speculation. John's presence in Ephesus is probable but not

---

[201] The famous visions of Catherine Emmerich, who died in 1824, designated a house in Ephesus where, according to her visions, Mary lived before the end of her life. A group of priests with spades in their hands followed the mystic's directions as described in her visions and in fact discovered the ruins of a 1st century house in the hills above the ruins of the city of Ephesus. The story made great impression mostly because Catherine Emmerich had never left her native Germany, yet her directions led to the discovery of the house in question. But the tomb also described by the same mystic has never been found. See S. Shoemaker, *Ancient Traditions of the Virgin Mary's Dormition and Assumption* (New York: Oxford University Press, 2002), 76. Even if on the basis of Johannine studies some scholars referred to Ephesus as the last place of Mary's life on earth, there is no mention of it in either apocrypha or legends.

[202] According to F.-M. Braun, this hypothesis is first mentioned in the 12th century: *Jean le théologien et son évangile dans l'Église ancienne* (Paris: Gabalda, 1959), 327-332.

[203] *Adversus haereses* III.1.1.

before the last decade of the 1st century, past to which Mary's earthly life cannot be plausibly extended.[204]

Positively, one might say that traditions about Mary's tomb or her last dwelling place attached to her death or Dormition harmonize well with what we know about Mariology in the late 5th and early 6th century and the circumstances following the Council of Ephesus. These include, in general, the need to venerate Mary in the same way in which the cult of the saints (mostly martyrs) began to expand and multiply. In the case of Mary, veneration of her tomb began to be linked to Holy Land pilgrimages and the cult of the places of the Lord's birth, passion, and Resurrection. Recent archeological finds identified several Marian churches, the popular customs of the pilgrims, even souvenir emblems with Mary's name and a primitive bronze image of the Dormition tradition, all testifying to the popularity of the custom of visiting Mary's tomb.[205]

Parallel to this development, while newer and more numerous Marian feasts were being introduced, we see the rededication of a more general Marian feast honoring the *Theotokos* on August 15 specifically to the Dormition or Assumption of Mary, a feast later introduced also in the West and extant to this day. Equally important was the appearance of apocryphal writings about the end of Mary's life. They show a somewhat bewildering diversity of narrative content, but they also carry some important common elements. Their origin is less likely to be reduced to one original composition as in the case of the *Proto-evangelium*. Because of the many theories about their sources and their convoluted relationships, we should not dis-

---

[204] I certainly think that, all things considered, Jerusalem would be a possible place for Mary's life after Jesus' Resurrection. Not only does Acts remember Mary's presence in the Jerusalem Church, but Galatians 2:9 also mentions John together with James ("the brother of the Lord") as "pillars of the Church" in a letter written around 50 A.D. John is, therefore, plausibly assumed to live in Jerusalem at this time when Mary, who gave birth 52-54 years earlier, must be, if still alive, in her seventies.

[205] The so-called *eulogiai* or "blessings" (tokens of obtaining blessings at the shrine) are well documented with pictures of these bronze emblems and their moulds, found at various places in Palestine, in Shoemaker's book cited above.

cuss them in more detail.[206] It may be sufficient to summarize what a majority of experts holds about them and some theologically important aspects that appear in most of them.

There are few historians who would claim that some eyewitness tradition about Mary's death or Dormition was ever transmitted orally or was written down in apostolic times in documents now lost. But there is a rather widespread conviction that Mary's role in the Incarnation slowly and gradually led Christian reflection to some theological conclusions, all similar if not identical in content, concerning the end of her life. Analogous to what happened to her Son's body, the conclusion was formed about what happened to the Virgin Mother: her body did not go through the process of disintegration and decay, but she was, immediately upon (or right after) her death, reunited with her Divine Son's body and soul. That this conclusion was reached only step by step, and was only gradually clarified and expressed, stands in harmony with the fact that the early Church had a large array of firm convictions but only a few well-defined details about eschatology. Details of the destiny of the individual soul after death – the particular judgment, purgatory, the actual time for the just to receive their reward, the way and mode of the general resurrection, the nature of the risen body as part of this world or rather as part of a "new heaven and new earth" – remained shrouded in mystery and recognized as such before they were more clearly formulated and described. Thus, we can say that the apostolic Church lacked the concepts and the technical language with which the question of Mary's arrival to heavenly glory could have been more closely described.

Due probably to the Mary/Eve parallel, but also to Luke 23:43 ("Today you will be with me in Paradise"), the apocrypha about Mary's passing mention the Tree of Life in Paradise, at which Mary's body is deposited in various conditions and by various means. Another common feature is Mary's connection with all the Apostles

---

[206] Extensive coverage is found in the earlier researches of Fr. Jugie, all in French, and in the more recent publications in English by S. Shoemaker.

before she comes to the end of her life: they either assemble miraculously at her deathbed, or accompany her dead body to the tomb as a funeral cortege in which miraculous events occur, or witness her resurrection and Assumption in some way and to some degree.

A minimalistic interpretation would claim that the apocryphal Assumption/Dormition stories are mindful of the little scriptural material they have and so they use Acts 1:14, which follows the list of the eleven Apostles (the Twelve minus Judas Iscariot): "All these devoted themselves with one accord to prayer, together with some women, and Mary the mother of Jesus, and his brothers." But certainly the apocryphal narratives, and probably even Luke, have much more in mind. So, for example, the earliest Greek Dormition narrative[207] describes the arrival of the Apostles, first of John because he is a virgin, then Peter, because he is the head of the Apostles, and next Paul, who still needs to be introduced to most of his fellow Apostles. The Apostles call Mary *their mother* and declare that they want to learn from her, while Mary tells them that this assembly of the Apostles is the fulfillment of a heavenly promise, and so now her departure is imminent.[208]

---

[207] S. Shoemaker, *Ancient Traditions of the Virgin Mary's Dormition and Assumption* (New York: Oxford University Press, 2002), 358-363. The author reproduces in English the text edited by Antoine Wenger. The Greek text is conjectured to originate in the 5th century, but its dependence on earlier Syriac texts remains speculative (Ibid., 25-33).

[208] It is certainly clear that the theological implication of the apocryphal stories point to the role of Mary as a person who between Jesus' Ascension and her Assumption symbolized their unity in Christ, expressing the unity of the Church. The fact that Luke tells us again, at the beginning of Acts, the list of the apostles and ends with a reference to Jesus' family, and within it Mary alone named, shows a similar perception: at Pentecost Mary's presence indicates that what began with the descent of the Spirit upon her at her virginal conception, continues now with a new phase as the Holy Spirit descends upon the disciples and opens the history of the *nascent* Church.

CHAPTER SIX

MARY IN THE MIDDLE AGES

Periodization and Grouping

The time period we often refer to as the "Middle Ages" is notoriously inexact and its definition varies. All the more so what we are speaking about here as "medieval Mariology" must be taken loosely. At earliest "medieval theology" starts *after* the papacy of Gregory the Great and ends before the Reformation or maybe more appropriately with the final collapse of the Byzantine Empire at the Turkish invasion of its last fortress, the city of Constantinople, in 1453. That a rigid understanding of the "Middle Ages" would not work for Mariology is clear from the previous chapter, in which, by using the concept "late antiquity" we considered independently the two centuries following the Council of Ephesus. This was the time when the basic Marian liturgical calendar of the Church was established with the fundamental feasts and texts which, together with the first expansion of the public veneration of the saints, greatly influenced the Christian experience, including Marian devotion, throughout the Middle Ages. As we have seen, the presence of two new elements of tradition became pronounced, leading to a further increase in Mariology: the Immaculate Conception and the Assumption of Mary. However, the development of these two topics began amid imprecise theological formulation and little debate. They never led to disputes in terms of orthodoxy vs. heresy, and advanced in a relatively slow and quiet way, moving few theologians and Church leaders to action, especially in those of the subsequent centuries that saw theologians in diminishing supply.

Furthermore, medieval Mariology in that epoch, which followed the collapse of the Roman Empire in the West, was not "medieval" in some general and uniform sense, but with real diversity and discontinuity. First, the cultural alienation between East and West created a theological gap early on, which kept growing with negative effects on Mariology reaching to the present day. So, for example, dialogue with the Orthodox Churches on the Immaculate Conception failed to develop and is still rather difficult, not so much on Mariological grounds, but simply because the Eastern Churches took little or no part in the disputes concerning the questions of original sin.

Another aspect complicates the application of the concept "medieval" to the different time periods and geographic areas. In one way or another the whole medieval period already represents a series of cultural and political waves aiming to achieve the rebirth of the classical Greco-Roman culture and the long lasting ideal of the "Empire." These efforts occurred in different times, and sometimes in more or less isolated settings. On account of the barbarian invasions this appeared to be an impossible dream: the restoration of the Constantinian Empire. In the West a final collapse of the old order of society happened more suddenly and prepared the emergence of a substantially new Empire, that of Charlemagne. Thus, in a sense, the beginning of Western Europe's Middle Ages begins with the "Carolingian Renaissance" leading to the Holy Roman Empire of the West. In the 9th and 10th centuries a new society with new power structures and new frontiers appears. Church and Empire become intertwined in mutual dependence and never ending conflicts. The coordination of Church and State remains unstable and after lengthy conflicts and both physical and political battles, it falls apart, undermining the assumption that the Christian world is one single religious and cultural whole.

A most important subdivision is often named after Pope Gregory VII as the epoch of the "Gregorian Reform," another attempt to achieve spiritual and cultural rebirth freeing the Church from much of its previous subservience to the Holy Roman Empire with the support by various monastic efforts of revival. As a common thread, these efforts of renewal combine new rediscoveries of the classical Hellenistic culture and the patristic heritage of the 4th and 5th centuries, trying to bring back the philosophical and literary standard of the ancient Greeks and Romans with the piety and purity of the early Church Fathers. It is with such ideals that a special brand of theology, given the name of "monastic theology" in the 1950's and 60's,[209] emerged with a fruitful tension with regard to the nascent or early scholasticism while giving new impetus to theological reflection and literature. In Mariology, the 12th century, characterized by these partly parallel and partly overlapping theologies, kept tight linkage between theology and spirituality and set in motion a broad and wide expansion of literature, theological reflection, art and poetry.

But in the course of the 12th century we also see the emergence of a new intellectual climate centered on a new institution. First the schools of the large monastic foundations and of the cathedrals, then the universities of the cities achieved a new concentration of intellectual talent, interest and work. The universities, like those in Paris, Padua and Bologna and many others which followed, succeeded in gathering an international audience and began to study and teach philosophy and theology on an unprecedented broad stage: the whole of the Latin Christian West. Starting with early scholasticism, this theology sought a deeper philosophical basis and extended itself into many secular, or at least "worldly," undertakings, providing for the emerging national states and omnipresent Church a learned and politically savvy bureaucracy.

Monastic theology flourished in smaller dimensions and in a shorter period of time, first in Benedictine monasteries, especially

---

[209] This concept and era was made famous by Jean Leclercq, a Benedictine monk of Clairvaux in Luxemburg with many important publications. Most important is his *The Love of Learning and the Desire for God* (New York: Fordham University Press, 1982), translated from its original *L'amour des lettres et le désir de Dieu* (Paris: Lethielleux, 1954).

those that fell into the sphere of influence of Cluny (10th through 11th centuries), and reached its zenith in the 12th century, mostly under the influence of the Cistercians, and their greatest saint, writer, and theologian, St. Bernard of Clairvaux. Monastic theology often consciously aimed at giving a rebirth to the classical figures of patristics. It also directly and indirectly influenced the surge of scholastic theology. Scholasticism soon became a major force in the new evangelization of the cities by two new religious orders, the Dominicans and the Franciscans, who produced their greatest theologians in the course of the 13th century.

One must not forget that throughout the Middle Ages returning to authentic texts was a continuous and constant feature of intellectual life leading to a new appropriation of Plato and Aristotle, mostly in translation from Greek (sometimes from Arabic sources) into Latin, and extending this interest from the Greek sources to their commentaries and later derivations of Neoplatonism. The final outcome was, of course, the humanistic transformation of culture in the 15th century, which consciously expropriated the name of a "rebirth," *Rinascimento* or Renaissance.

Rather than going through a long writer-by-writer sequence of texts and the thoughts they represent, we should select just a few representative samples of the main periods and then, at the end, summarize their contribution to Marian thought and devotion. Yet, even with such a breakdown of the material, its immensity remains intimidating and, methodologically, some additional problems surface. To combine the narration of the doctrinal development of Mariology with a deepening theological understanding of its meaning becomes increasingly difficult and any organization of the material may cause serious distortions. The great topics of patristic Mariology keep on being revisited throughout the Middle Ages. There is enough "novelty" in every respect, but only some of the doctrinal issues cause passionate debates and divide the various medieval thinkers. Of course the latter issues are those of the Immaculate Conception and, to a much smaller extent and in a different style, the Assumption of Mary. Yet one must not think that these were the most important questions in medieval Mariology, or, for that matter, at any given time. The new appropriations of the exegetical tradition of Matthew 1-2 and Luke 1-2 is also a rather interesting development, but it includes relatively little novelty. More correctly, these issues shed more light on the history of exegesis than on Mariology as such. Similarly, the slow and steady progress of the apocryphal material inherited in a semi-suppressed state from the patristic Church is typical of medieval spirituality and liturgy. Yet the apocryphal *Lives of Mary* have little direct influence on theology and have not been very well researched, either. The theology of Mary's perpetual virginity, the slow progression with which terms about Mary's participation in her Son's redemptive work (shown by the application of terms like Co-Redemptrix and Mediatrix of graces), the various thoughts and expressions about Mary as the embodiment of virtue and sanctity, Mary as Queen of Angels, Apostles and Prophets and many more ideas and terms of this kind could provide further topics for inquiry, but would make the inquiry mushroom beyond the limits of this book or other even more comprehensive works.

The solution I adopted here may or may not convince the reader, but it should be identified. To illustrate the Mariology of the early Middle Ages, a period otherwise slow in doctrinal developments, I turned to topics for which this epoch stands out. Our most venerable Marian prayers and hymns come from this time period. So I decided to comment in more details on the *Ave Maris Stella*. Next, I turned to the sermons of St. Anselm, a Marian preacher and thinker whom both monastic theology and early scholasticism may regard as their leading figure. For the zenith of monastic theology in the 12th century I decided to highlight the so-called "monastic sermon," a typical literary genre of the 12th century, which represents both a certain kind of spiritual theology (reflection upon the spiritual experience) and theological or exegetical literature for monastic readership. About scholastic theology not much of a choice was needed. High scholasticism became the arena on which the battles about the Immaculate Conception were fought. In this regard, I was less concerned to achieve any resemblance of completeness than showing the way in which the rebirth of ancient philosophical thought influenced the Mariological debates of the day.

Marian Prayers in the Early Middle Ages

As we found by sheer chance in the *Sub Tuum* an early devotional sample for patristic Mariology, so we approach medieval Mariology by analyzing one of the best known early medieval hymns, the *Ave Maris Stella*, as a representative of Marian prayers and poetry in the early Middle Ages (it is usually dated to the 8th or 9th century). With its simplicity, one may even say naiveté, its short and primitive sentences, unsophisticated grammatical constructions, its poetic form based on the rhythm of accented lines rather than on classical meter as well as its primitive but charming rhymes, it represents the Carolingian age at its best. Its success is well documented in the last thousand years by its frequent use in both liturgical and private prayer. Four Jesuits, employed under Pope Urban VIII (1623-1644) at the end of the Renaissance to prepare the hymns for the post-Tridentine Breviary, effectively ruined most pieces of authentic medieval hymnody,[210] but this composition survived all reforms unscathed and is frequently used by the *Liturgia Horarum* issued after Vatican II. Its success may be due to its powerful simplicity and easy grammar, but also to its suggestive imagery. It manifests well that in the center of medieval Mariology we find the principal ideas of the patristic themes: the antithetic notion "Virgo Mater" introduced in the first stanzas in imitation of the Annunciation, but with an immediate connection to the Mary/Eve theme:

---

[210] You find the four Jesuits listed by name (Fr. Strada, T. Galuzzi, H. Petrucci, M. Sarbiewski) by Anselmo Lentini, OSB in his work *Hymni Instaurandi Breviarii Romani* (Rome: Libreria Editrice Vaticana, 1968), p. X. [An Italian edition appeared later under the title *Te Decet Hymnus* (Rome: Libreria Editrice Vaticana, 1984)]. Lentini quotes the summary judgment made by contemporaries about the re-written Latin hymns: *Accessit latinitas, recessit pietas* ("Latinity arrives, piety departs"), but he adds that some of the humanistic poems were, in fact, rather well composed. Lentini based his work, but not his judgment, on the groundbreaking studies by Joseph Szöverffy, *Annalen der lateinischen Hymnendichtung*, Berlin, (I) 1964 (II) 1965. Lentini also composed a few dozen hymns for the post-Vatican II Breviary, some of them rather good.

Ave maris stella,
Dei Mater alma,
atque semper virgo
felix coeli porta.

Sumens illud ave
Gabrielis ore,
Funda nos in pace,
Mutans Evae nomen.[211]

Two elements appear in the first eight lines that are quite new and typically medieval. Let us start with the second stanza, which evokes the scene of the Annunciation. The poet seems to suppose naively that Mary received from "the lips of the Angel Gabriel" a Latin greeting with a word play about her role in salvation history. Moreover, he expects the reader to be familiar with this word play: AVE is the name of EVA spelled backward. Assuredly it was well known for educated Christians. However, we are not dealing with a mere play on words and an Angel's charming wit when speaking in Latin. The AVE/EVA provides a very condensed formulation of the old Marian doctrine so tortuously explained by Irenaeus: what happened at the dawn of history must be unraveled *in reverse order* so that the mighty knot of sin could be untied into salvation and thus obtain the reversal of eternal death into eternal life. The uninitiated modern reader may be confused by the line "mutans *Evae nomen*," but the medieval reader knows that *mutans* means not just "changing" but "revers-

---

[211] We give here a literal translation, which cannot fully express the charm and depth of the Latin text. *Dei Mater* stands for *Theotokos* and *semper virgo* for *aei parthenos* – the two terms which were debated for centuries, but rightly became the foundation stones of Marian doctrine:

Hail, Star of the Sea,
dear *Mother of God*
and *always virgin*,
the happy gate to heaven.
While taking *that* AVE
From the lips of Gabriel,
Ground us in peace,
By turning around EVA's name.

ing." Another sign of medieval thought is the importance attributed to the *nomen*. Also in the present context, the "names" of the two women, Eve and Mary, stand for the *res*, the "thing" they signify, and directly point to the reality which they evoke.

In light of what has been said, the word *felix* in the fourth line seems to have been carefully chosen, for the AVE/EVA or Mary/Eve pair was traditionally used also to highlight Mary's happy or joyful parturition over against the pain or sadness that Eve and other women experience at giving birth. More specifically, in the Latin tradition about Genesis 3:16 we find *tristitia* or "sadness," originating from the old Latin translation (the *Vetus Latina*).[212] In this way the ambiguous χαίρε ("rejoice" or "hail") of the Greek text of Luke 1:26, translated as a mere word of greeting in the Vulgate, retained its link to the message of messianic "joy." Moreover, the image describing Mary as a "lucky gate" (*felix porta*) is suggestive: she is a door both fortuitous and bringing happiness, that happiness which Eve had sadly lost.[213] So Mary as celestial light shining over a turbulent world and the inversion of EVA into AVE stand for a popularized program of Marian spirituality: turning troubles caused by sin into rejoicing as we reach out to Mary, whom the Angel's message has already appointed as our gate to heaven.

Now we may even better understand how the first eight lines of the poem are about "names." Of course the name of Eve anticipates AVE, but the medieval mind also knows that the name of Mary means "star of the Sea." This is medieval etymology of *Maria* or more exactly *Miriam*, which goes back ultimately to St. Jerome, the

---

[212] The Vulgate has *in dolore paries* – you will give birth in pain, but the *Vetus Latina* has *in tristitia*.

[213] The oldest attestation of this image of "the gate" (*coeli ianua* or *porta*) and combined with *coeli fenestra* (heaven's window) is by a hymn of Venantius Fortunatus (d. 601). In this poem the "sadness" of Eve and of her children is emphasized:

Quod Eva tristis *abstulit*
tu reddis almo germine.
Intrent ut astra flebiles,
Coeli fenestra *facta es.*

See further examples quoted by R. Laurentin, *Luc I-II* (Paris: Gabalda, 1957), p. 65 n. 3.

Middle Age's usual guide for explaining Hebrew words. This time, however, there is a twist. While Jerome thought that *Miriam* meant *mare amarum* or "bitter sea," it sounded less than satisfying and was further "interpreted" into *stilla maris* or "drop of the sea." A further change might have been accidental, as it were, but it finally brought about a fully satisfying interpretation: *stella maris* (star of the sea). It was in this form that Isidore of Sevillle (d. 636) incorporated the meaning of "Maria" into his popular *Etymologiae* and passed it on to later ages, inspiring by it countless sermons, poems, and prayers.[214]

The third stanza consists of four somewhat monotonous one-liners, each sounding like some broad generalization and rhyming platitude:

> Solve vincla reis,
> profer lumen caecis,
> mala nostra pelle,
> bona cuncta posce.[215]

After these lines one is tempted to think that the poem is about to lose its original inspiration and may not have much more to offer. But no! The next line makes it again soar to unexpected heights with a thought that was repeated for centuries: *Monstra te esse matrem!* "Show that you are a mother...." No matter how many scholars may be inclined to translate it as "show that you are Jesus' mother," I think such an interpretation is flat and pointless. Rather, it must be read in the light of the Johannine text: "Behold, your mother" (Jn 19:27). And this is so especially because the lines that follow ask Mary to obtain that her Son would accept *our* prayers. After all, the

---

[214] H. Graef, *Mary: A History of Doctrine and Devotion* (New York: Sheed & Ward, 1963), 163-164. The origin of the image *porta coeli* (alternate forms: *ianua coeli, porta paradisi*) may be difficult to determine, but it is present in many prayers of the Carolingian centuries in connection with naming Mary as our intercessor at the hour of death. See H. Barré, *Prières anciennes de l'Occident à la Mère du Sauveur* (Paris: Lethielleux, 1963), 133, 200, 208.

[215] Untie the shackles of the guilty,
bring light to the blind,
chase away our ills,
bring us all that is good.

Lord also has chosen her to be his mother at the moment he wanted to become a man *pro nobis* – for our sake.[216]

> Monstra te esse materem:
> sumat per te preces
> qui pro nobis natus
> tulit esse tuus.

The recall of Mary's motherhood in our regard turns the poem into a passionate plea for heavenly intercession. So we should translate it in this way:

> Show that you are (our) mother:
> through you let him accept our prayers,
> who, when born for us,
> wanted to be yours [i.e., your son].[217]

All this "works" so well because its passionate tone does not diminish the theological equilibrium. Rather it leads back to the basic mystery: the eternal Son when being born for *our sake*, preferred to choose you, or just "did not mind" to be yours. Thus "we" i.e., all humankind to whom also Jesus (God's Son) belongs and you (Mary) are eternally linked in one single human race and one salvation plan achieved by him and through you.

The next line is also both passionate and precise: *Virgo singularis...* – a virgin "unique" or "exceptional." She stands out in every respect and yet she is our mother. Medieval Mariology is full of these

---

[216] No doubt, one could insist that Mary should prove to us that she, as Christ's mother, is indeed powerful. But her status and title as Christ's mother is here not the issue to be proved. Rather "show *us* that you are *our* mother!"

[217] "May he accept our petitions, he who when being born [a man] for our sake, chose to be yours." The specific meaning of "*tulit*" in this context appears obscure. It may mean "brought forward" or "managed" or "chose." Since the subject is the pre-existent Son of God, we may say that he "took upon himself," "did not mind," to become "yours" namely to be born as a child, because he "was willing to undergo" to be your infant child. In this case "*tulit*" would stand for "*sustulit*." The latter meaning may be an echo of the somewhat rough, but basically parallel, statement of the *Te Deum* authored by Nicetas of Rheims in the 5th century: *Tu ad liberandum suscepturus hominem non horruisti Virginis uterum.* ("When you, for the sake of redemption, were to assume man [human nature], you did not loathe the Virgin's womb.")

postures of admiration and pleading, finding security in evoking Mary as that exceptional human being who connects us with God in eternal grace.

> Virgo singularis,
> Inter omnes mitis.
> Nos, culpis solutos,
> Mites fac et castos.[218]

For an epoch filled with violence and sexual excess, the Virgin who is "meek and chaste" in a superhuman way, is a most convincing and badly needed icon. This applies, of course to all ages, but in the Middle Ages the general culture of the *litterati* was able to speak about it in simple and direct terms. Today Mariology, which speaks as it were too much about "Marian privileges," is easily criticized, since we belong to an age craving the democratization of all values. But the Marian privileges are not aristocratic. Rather, she is *singularis* within the Mary/Eve contrast: as Eve's children, we are all losers, but as Mary's children we can all become winners, including even Eve.[219]

Anselm of Canterbury (1033-1109)

St. Anselm was a Benedictine monk who became archbishop of Canterbury. He is often treated as a forerunner of scholasticism. Yet many of his writings fit well into the category of "monastic theology," an extension of the style of writing and preaching of the patris-

---

[218] You, the one and only Virgin,
among all the meekest,
obtain that, once liberated from our sins,
we may be meek and chaste.

[219] The last stanza is like a doxology, somewhat plain and too simple:
Vitam praesta puram,
iter para tutum,
ut videntes Iesum
semper collaetemur.

Provide for us a pure life
Prepare a safe journey,
So that by seeing Jesus
We may rejoice forever.

tic age. His writings about the Virgin Mary are not very extensive but one must admit that they made a great impact on the subsequent century.[220] He wrote about Mary in two treatises, his most famous, *Cur Deus homo*, and his book *De conceptione virginali et originali peccato*. He did not teach Mary's Immaculate Conception, but the arguments he lined up about Mary's absolute purity from sin are quite similar to those which were applied later to deny her sharing in original sin: "For it was fitting that his Virgin should shine with purity so great that no greater purity could be conceived." The statement resembles Anselm's famous "ontological proof" of God's existence, but, of course, it is an argument about "fittingness" (*decet*), a word introduced into mariological parlance already by St. Ambrose as regards the divine motherhood: "Miretur omne saeculum: talis partus decet Deum." This term was time and again re-discovered as the proper word for applying deductive arguments to matters that remain within God's free choice and cannot be a matter of strictly deductive argumentation.

Anselm truly stands between two, possibly three rather different cultural milieux: the Church Fathers, of whom many were bishops and thus official teachers of the faith, the monks with their vowed celibate life patterned after the Virgin Mary, and the scholastic teachers who began to explore systematically the rationality of the faith. To this we can add a fourth dimension: Anselm's deeply personal devotion to Mary, expressed with powerful emotion and poetic force in his seven orations to Mary, which also became widely popular in the Latin West: "Ecce enim virgo homo, ex qua natus est Deus homo ut salvaretur peccator homo!" "Behold the virgin, a human being, from whom God was born as a human being, so that man, the sinner, may be saved."[221]

---

[220] See H. Graef, *Mary: A History of Doctrine and Devotion*, vol. I (New York: Sheed and Ward, 1963), 210-215.

[221] Barré in his famous book *Prières anciennes de l'Occident à la Mère du Sauveur* (Paris: Lethielleux, 1963), 286-337, presents St. Anselm's *Orationes ad Sanctam Mariam* as the peak toward which the literary and theological development of earlier prayers of the Carolingian age and early Middle Ages in general were tending. The quotation is made from sermon VI, 2 on page 301.

This text represents an era marked by a growing emphasis on the human condition: *homo* repeated three times as a threefold anthropological grounding of theology. This moves theological thinking toward the integration of Mariology with patristic thought about free will and original sin, and with the general theological discourse about the mystery of the Incarnation and Redemption. What was said above about the various phases of a continuous humanistic renaissance from the Carolingian age to the 16th century finds its first clear, conscious reflection in Anselm's theology. Redeemed man appears as the center and purpose of the Universe, threatening the equilibrium between an anthropocentric and a Christocentric rethinking of all that the faith teaches.

Marian Cult in Cluny

The so-called Gregorian Reform under the leadership of Gregory VII was closely linked to the monastic renewal centered on the French monastery of Cluny, which, among other things, exercised great influence on the Church in the 10th and 11th centuries with its zealous Marian piety. Two of its saintly abbots must be mentioned in particular: Odo (d. 949) and Odilo (d. 1043). One of the earliest Marian apparitions is attached to the name of St. Odo. As it is described in his *Vita* he converted a thief and led him to monastic life in Cluny. The man, still young in years, became mortally ill and told his abbot of an apparition of a Lady of glorious appearance, identifying herself as *Mater Misericordiae* (Mother of Mercy). The abbot realized that the monk had been visited by the Blessed Virgin and, in fact, three days later the monk died. The biographer says that after this event St. Odo customarily addressed Mary in prayer as *Mater Misericordiae*. Soon thereafter this title was included into the famous 11th century hymn, popular unto our days, the *Salve Regina*.[222]

More substantial is the Marian heritage of St. Odilo, which es-

---

[222] The *Salve Regina* is attributed to a German monk named Hermannus Contractus (meaning "crippled"), a monk of Reichenau, Austria, who died in 1054.

sentially consists of his sermons about Mary. In the footsteps of St. Ambrose (and St. Athanasius, whom Ambrose has often copied) he presents Mary as the "mirror of perfection" (*speculum perfectionis*) by using biblical examples. This is new insofar as it applies a Marian picture of the devout life to that of a medieval monk, with emphasis on what we call today the three vows of religious life: chastity, poverty, and obedience.

Bernard of Clairvaux (1090-1153)

Much has been written about the Mariology of St. Bernard, yet an objective presentation, not to say evaluation, remains to be written. His fame as the peak of medieval Marian piety is possibly rooted in an obsolete image of the saint, as if he was an extremely zealous and pious but uneducated monk, whose charismatic personality was chiefly responsible for the Second Crusade and many extraordinary feats of a political nature. Both the failures of the Crusades or the spectacular successes of the Military Orders, including the Templars, have little to do with his genius or sanctity. At a conference in Dijon, France, at the eight-hundredth anniversary of Bernard's death in 1953, the most stellar French theologians (Congar, Daniélou, Mouroux, Leclercq) of the times proved Bernard to have been an eminent theologian of deep insight and great originality. But at that conference, probably in reaction to the image cultivated mostly in France, Henri Barré treated his Mariology with much expertise but some unexpected consequences. Making a special effort to redesign Bernard's image, by transforming it from that of a "Mariologist" into a theologian of broad and wide interests, Barré wanted to relativize Bernard's Mariology in comparison to the whole spectrum of his theological thought. His main argument was the evidence that only in a small percentage of his work does Bernard speak about Mary.[223] But probably Barré himself tried too hard to

---

[223] "St. Bernard, Docteur marial," *St. Bernard théologien, Analecta S. Ordinis Cisterciensis* IX, 3-4 (1953), 93-113. Barré calculates that only 3.5% of Bernard's authentic texts are about the Virgin Mary.

tip off the balance in the opposite direction. For, already in his life time, Bernard impressed his contemporaries, like his closest friend and confidant and, in some sense, even mentor, William of St. Thierry, as one who speaks and writes about Mary, as if under special inspiration.[224] Barré is probably wrong when he uses a statistical method to show that within the total output of Bernard's writings Mary occupies no special place and therefore his reputation of being "the best ever singing Mary's praises" (*cithara Mariae*) was earned by spurious works and by overlooking much or most of his authentic writings. One of Bernard's first "published" works, four homilies about the Annunciation, with its original title *De laudibus Virginis Matris*, early on obtained extraordinary success and even today is his best known literary work. Although it follows the format of homilies preached on liturgical feasts, it is a word-for-word commentary on the well-known pericope of Luke 1:26-38, and claims not to contain anything that had not been said before by the Church Fathers. Yet these four sermons, amounting to only twenty pages in their critical edition, sound like both a compendium of patristic Mariology and an extraordinary chain of lyrical compositions. They are indeed most refined and perfectly chiseled poems.

What did these four homilies contribute to Mariology? They collected and organized most traditional doctrinal statements into a coherent commentary on the Annunciation. Yet the resulting work does not read as a commentary aiming at intellectual statements, explaining the biblical text, but rather as a personal meditation based on astonishing encounters with the mystery: the reality of the Incarnation.

---

[224] He was Bernard's "best friend," who died before Bernard did, but began to write during Bernard's lifetime the first – obviously unfinished – biography of St. Bernard, the so-called *Vita Prima*. William tells us that he heard from Bernard himself the great Marian experience he had in his childhood. As still a young child, Bernard attended at Christmas the Midnight Mass and, while waiting for the Mass to begin, fell asleep and saw the birth of Jesus in Bethlehem. "Up to this day," William tells us, "Bernard says that he was present at the Virgin Birth." William already thought that this extraordinary experience gave Bernard an exceptional eloquence when speaking about Jesus' Nativity and Mary, and provided him the inspiration for one of his early works (*inter initia operum suorum*), the four homilies about the Annunciation. See PL 185, 229.

The virginal existence and the divine motherhood of Mary may be likened to two pillars of early Mariology. As the title *In Praise of the Virgin Mother* makes clear, those two aspects permeate the whole work. The reader is led by Bernard to see the depth of a mystery that produced the humanity of God's only begotten Son: you see how this took place within the framework of a virginal life, consecrated to and fully focused on God, her Son.[225]

Mary's virginity and motherhood are contemporaneous to each other and to consecrated life lived in the Church. As Bernard states elsewhere, Mary is "full of grace 'and from this fullness we have all received'" (cf. Jn 1:16). For Bernard, Mary is not a virgin whose virginity vanishes *in partu* at her Son's birth, nor is she a mother whose motherhood ceases *post partum*, as if her virginity were replaced by a motherhood that would obscure the unparalleled character of what took place in her flesh. Nor is her motherhood extinguished as the Son dies, as if at that time her role could diminish into merely symbolic significance pointing to the collective motherhood of the Church. Both Mary's motherhood and her virginity continue in a distributive and singularly personal way as Christ's celibate life continues in the Church both collectively (the Church's virginal motherhood) and for the individuals touched by his grace.

We mention four special topics of Mariology connected to Bernard's name: her "martyrdom," her being *mediatrix*, the Immaculate Conception, and the Assumption.

Bernard attributed notable importance to the Virgin's suffering on Calvary. In a sermon preached on the Sunday within the Octave of the Assumption, Bernard describes the Virgin's true "martyrdom" as she participates in Jesus' death: "If he (Jesus) could have died physically, could she not have died with him in her heart (*commori corde non potuit*)?" Bernard's point is, of course, that however Mary's life ended, the "royal crown of twelve stars" surrounding the Mother of the Messiah in the Book of Revelation (12:2), i.e., the glory

---

[225] I chose to quote a famous paragraph of this work when commenting on the Annunciation, the richest text of the New Testament about Mary. See above pp. 31-32.

obtained by her merits and sanctity, include those of all saints, also of the martyrs, because in fact she died on Golgotha, at least spiritually, together with her Son. The verb *commori* ("to die together") might strike us as an important step toward the idea of Mary's role of "co-redemptrix." But the context (Mary under the Cross) only misleads us. Bernard uses the language of the Vulgate: "to die with" Christ is a Pauline expression evoking 2 Corinthians 7:3 (*conmoriendum et convivendum*) and a whole scale of similar Pauline constructions: *consepulti, conresuscitati, conresurgere*, etc. Yet, obviously, Mary was dying contemporaneously with Christ, at the same time as he did, although not physically but only spiritually: a medieval idea which Bernard expresses in biblical language.[226] That the Mother accompanies her Son up to that last event of his life – which happened once in history – and does so in an exclusively spiritual closeness to her Son, would fit all sorts of biblical and patristic texts. Yet it is a true step beyond what patristic texts claim about "the sword which pierced her heart," and in this respect Bernard was often seen as a true forerunner of the problematic term "Co-Redemptrix."

With respect to another term, Bernard prepared later stages of Mariology by calling Mary our *mediatrix*. This term we find in the very same sermon quoted above, in connection with a remarkable comment on the text of the Book of Revelation. We are prostrate at her feet in the same way the Apocalypse describes the moon under her feet (Rv 12:2), as we beseech her to act as our *mediatrix* and intercede with Christ, the Sun of Justice.

Bernard's reputation as a *docteur marial*, which Barré wanted to dismiss or at least diminish, he won early on, and it only gained emphasis with time. The best illustration is found two hundred years later in Dante's having Bernard lead him, the wandering poet, to the Blessed Virgin.[227]

---

[226] The exact same verbal form *commori* appears in the Vulgate in Mk 14:6, when Peter swears that he is ready to "die with" Christ.

[227] In Canto XXXI of *Paradiso* Bernard addresses Mary as the mediatrix of all graces:
"Lady, thou art so near God's reckonings
that who seeks grace and does not first seek thee

But, ironically, a negative result of Bernard's reputation was even more effective. Since in one of his letters he explicitly objected to the feast of the Immaculate Conception[228] his immense authority in Mariology resulted in slowing down for centuries first the celebration, then the dogmatization of the Immaculate Conception. With respect to the bodily Assumption of Mary in heaven, Bernard's influence was also negative, but, due to his cautious reticence on the subject, it had less of an impact, even on other Cistercians during his lifetime. Yet clearly, Bernard preferred to hold to the reservations attributed to St. Jerome by a spurious homily, falsely attributed to Jerome but remaining in liturgical use for the feast of the Assumption for a long time. This text had emphasized that we know little about when and how the saints are to be admitted to the beatific vision, and thus we remain ignorant even about the mode in which Mary's death and glorification occurred. In this sense, as in many other ways, in spite of his celebrated "modern" poetic sensitivity, Bernard not only signals the emergence of "subjectivity" in popular piety, but a cautious conservative attachment to the ancient traditions in theology. He remained suspicious of most innovations that early scholasticism introduced, and showed unwillingness to go beyond the explicit teachings of the Church Fathers.

Other Cistercians of the 12th Century

Bernard's importance for the Mariology of his time is clear from the writings of several of his younger contemporaries: all Cis-

---

would have his wish fly upward without wings.
Not only does thy sweet benignity
flow out to all who beg, but oftentimes
thy charity arrives before the plea.
In thee is pity, in thee munificence,
in thee the tenderest heart, in thee unites
all that creation knows of excellence!"

[228] Bernard disapproves the introduction of this feast in his letter no. 174, addressed to the Canons of Lyons. See H. Barré, op. cit. above, p. 95.

tercians greatly influenced in many other ways by his writings. We mention two of these.

St. Amadeus (1110-1159) was first a monk of Clairvaux and later Bishop of Lausanne. His eight Marian sermons are deeply immersed in traditional piety. While Amadeus follows Bernard's traditionalist negation with respect to the Immaculate Conception, he positively promotes the thesis of Mary's bodily Assumption. Pius XII's encyclical *Munificentissimus Deus* quotes Amadeus as an explicit witness not only of the traditional title of Mary as "Queen of heaven," but also of the doctrine of the Assumption. In this point Amadeus follows neither Bernard nor the homily of Pseudo-Jerome (written probably by the Carolingian theologian Pascasius Radbertus, d. 865) but another "pseudo-patristic" homily, also of Carolingian origin, attributed to St. Augustine, which propagated the thesis that Mary in fact died, but upon her death was soon reunited to her Son in body and soul. This is what Amadeus writes:

> O how precious in the eyes of the Lord was the death[229] of the mother who gave him birth! Whose life can be compared to her death? What amount of joy to her funeral? ... For it meant being freed from the bonds of the flesh,[230] a path to life, entailing no pain, no bitterness, no fear. It gave comfort instead of pain, sweet pleasure instead of bitterness, instead of fear it gave firm assurance to faith. It brought with itself no darkness, because it opened light eternal; nor did it take away life for it opened access to the origin of life. With this kind of glorious death she passed away, if you can even call it death. If I may even call it death, for it must be called life whereby death is dying: where the body is divested of mortality, when the life of

---

[229] The reference to Ps 116:5 is no mere stylistic embellishment, but a solid proof that the death of all the saints pleases God, as their act of final self-oblation.

[230] The Latin text says *absolutio carnis*, and must be taken in the sense of an objective genitive: not absolution from the flesh but the absolution *of* the flesh from the conditions and bonds of earthly existence.

flesh passing on in prayerful peace, is moving into a future enriched by multiple reward.[231]

Another disciple of Bernard, Isaac, abbot for some time of
the Abbey of Stella (Étoile) in France, excels by his originality and
strong philosophical bent. For reasons not fully clear – whether because he had been exiled or was just voluntarily seeking solitude – he
spent years on the abandoned island of Rhé in the Atlantic Ocean.
There he composed sequences of monastic sermons, seemingly not
destined to be preached but to be disseminated as exegetical works.
He died in 1159, six years after St. Bernard. In Mariology he left behind a text for the feast of the Assumption in which he analyzes the
manifold relations between Mary and the Church. He considers the
Church as both the one Body of Christ and the community of individuals in which what is said of the community as a whole, applies
to the members in a distributive sense. This text, referred to in the
document *Lumen Gentium* at Vatican II, obtained belatedly a great
deal of attention and appreciation:

> The Son of God is the first-born of many brothers. Al-
> though by nature he is the only-begotten, by grace he has
> joined many to himself and made them one with him. For
> *to those who receive him he has given the power to become*
> *the sons of God.* He became the Son of man and made
> many men sons of God, uniting them to himself by his
> love and power, so that they became as one. In themselves
> they are many by reason of their human descent, but in
> him they are one by divine rebirth.
>
> The whole Christ and the unique Christ – the body
> and the head – are one: one because born of the same God
> in heaven, and of the same mother on earth. They are

---

[231] Homily VII, my translation (*Sources chrétiennes* 72, lines 213-218). We can see
how for Amadeus the Virgin's death is lacking anything that would be a consequence of original sin. Thus the contrast between the *dormitionist* and *immortalist*
position becomes rather tenuous and is expressed by a search for a definition: "If
I may even call it death."

many sons, yet one son. Head and members are one son, yet many sons; in the same way, Mary and the Church are one mother, yet more than one mother; one virgin, yet more than one virgin.

Both are mothers, both are virgins. Each conceives of the same Spirit, without concupiscence. Each gives birth to a child of God the Father, without sin. Without any sin, Mary gave birth to Christ the head for the sake of his body. By the forgiveness of every sin, the Church gave birth to the body, for the sake of its head. Each is Christ's mother, but neither gives birth to the whole Christ without the cooperation of the other.

In the inspired Scriptures, what is said in a universal sense of the virgin mother, the Church, is understood in an individual sense of the Virgin Mary, and what is said in a particular sense of the virgin mother Mary is rightly understood in a general sense of the virgin mother, the Church. When either is spoken of, the meaning can be understood of both, almost without qualification.

In a way, every Christian is also believed to be a bride of God's Word, a mother of Christ, his daughter and sister, at once virginal and fruitful. These words are used in a universal sense of the Church, in a special sense of Mary, in a particular sense of the individual Christian. They are used by God's Wisdom in person, the Word of the Father. This is why Scripture says: *I will dwell in the inheritance of the Lord.* The Lord's inheritance is, in a general sense, the Church; in a special sense, Mary; in an individual sense, the Christian. Christ dwelt for nine months in the tabernacle of Mary's womb. He dwells until the end of the ages in the tabernacle of the Church's faith. He will dwell forever in the knowledge and love of each faithful soul.[232]

---

[232] *Sermo* 51: PL 194, 1862-1865. See further comments on this text by Blessed Isaac on p. 238, note 284, and on pp. 302-305 below.

The Two Great Dominican Doctors: Albertus Magnus (d. 1280) and Thomas Aquinas (1225-1274)

It is not our task here to describe the great change of Catholic theology in the 13ᵗʰ century. We make only a few introductory comments. The triple basis of nascent scholasticism (the universities, the mendicant orders, and the rediscovery of Aristotle) was itself formed in tentative preparatory phases of the late 12ᵗʰ century, usually referred to as "Pre-Scholasticism" (*Früscholastik*), but once it began to coalesce into a true "movement," they marked the birth of a new renaissance of Greco-Roman culture, quickly transforming the intellectual climate of ecclesial culture and theology. How did it affect Mariology? Certainly there was no "increase" or "decrease" of Marian piety. For centuries both theology and culture remained deeply imbued by deep loyalty to the Virgin Mother. The great intellectual leaders, the Dominicans Albertus Magnus and Thomas Aquinas and the Franciscan Bonaventure, remained equally committed to Mary and took great care to preserve and defend the heritage of earlier Marian teaching. However, one may say that within a more strictly scholarly or scientific pursuit of theology, which was one of the novelties of scholasticism, Mariology, by then certainly committed to many overwhelmingly devotional programs, was pushed somewhat more to the margins. One might even add that, regrettably, the unrelenting enthusiasm for promoting the veneration of Mary in prayer and praise began to produce suspicious fruits, resplendent with all the colors of rhetoric and poetry, but often lacking a more intellectual nature and theological or personal depth.

The "big picture" was also somewhat obscured, at least until the middle of the 20ᵗʰ century, by lack of clear distinctions between authentic and spurious works of various famous theologians. This not only distorted Bernard's image, who became nothing but a Mariologist, but gave undeserved reputation to works popularized under the name of Albertus Magnus, Thomas Aquinas' famous teacher and mentor. Now, however, it is well established that both the treatise *De laudibus Beatae Mariae Virginis* and the even more influential *Mariale super "Missus Est"* were mistakenly ascribed to Albert the Great and were falsely inserted into the timeline of the 13th century.[233] The present-day evaluation of Albert's Mariology, based on his authentic works, proves him an important, but rather sober and traditional, carrier of the Church's doctrinal tradition. By making frequent comparisons between Christ and Mary, while duly distancing their roles in the work of salvation, he is the first to introduce Mariology consciously into the greater framework of Christology. Due to his commitment to both the Augustinian tradition and the scholastic recovery of Aristotelian philosophy, he does not admit Mary's Immaculate Conception. Yet he insists on Mary's sinlessness and claims that her soul was purified of original sin right upon its creation.

With this perspective, the Thomistic school embarked upon the enterprise of arguing for centuries *against* the Immaculate Conception, thus leaving behind a regrettable image of doctrinal rigidity, which, in some cases, ended up paralyzing the development of dogmas.

Thomistic Mariology produced some further problems, which had to be left behind. Under Aristotle's influence, Thomas adopted some "scientific views," coming from a pre-scientific age. In Thomas' *Summa theologiae*, for example, we read the following paragraph about the virginal conception:

> A woman who conceives with the participation of a man is not a virgin. And so it belongs to the supernatural mode of the generation of Christ that the active principle in his generation was the supernatural divine power of God; but it belongs to the natural mode of his generation that the matter, from which his body was conceived, was in conformity with the matter that other women contribute to the conception of offspring.
>
> Now this matter, according to the Philosopher [Aris-

---

[233] R. Laurentin, *Court traité de théologie mariale*, 4th edition (Paris: Lethielleux, 1959), 67-68. L. Gambero, op. cit., 222-223.

totle], is the blood of the woman, but not just any kind of blood, but blood subjected to a fuller concentration by the generative capacity of the mother so that it becomes suitable matter for conception. And so it was from this sort of matter that the body of Christ was conceived.[234]

The issue that Thomas is wrestling with here has little to do with any traditional question of Mariology. It deals with a difficulty introduced by Aristotle's concept of physical maternity, which requires the merely passive role of the female body, receiving its active generative power from the male semen. In Thomas' explanation the role of the male body is substituted by a supernatural influence by which Mary's blood becomes "concentrated" (or "concocted") and thus becomes capable of making a child grow in her womb. When an obscure theory is borrowed from Aristotelian biology and is applied to the mystery of the Incarnation, one feels an embarrassingly close encounter with the ancient concept of a *hieros gamos* – copulation of human and divine beings – which the Church Fathers so vigorously sought to reject or at least avoid with regard to the virginal conception, but which now, after twelve centuries of Christianity, was obviously not perceived as a derivative of pagan thought. It nonetheless feels like a failed attempt to replace the mystery of the Incarnation with a pseudo-scientific explanation, a bad omen for what kept reappearing in modern Mariology.[235] Even more negative was Thomas' comment denying the Immaculate Conception by arguing that in the case of a female offspring "ensoulment" (the creation of the soul) is not concurrent with conception but, according to the same "Philosopher" happens twenty-one days later, so that at conception Mary had no soul as yet and thus could not have been simultaneously cleansed of original sin.[236]

---

[234] *Summa theologiae* III, q. 31, art. 5. English translation in L. Gambero, op. cit., 241-242.

[235] I am thinking about the model of "parthenogenesis" – a non-sexual form of reproduction – which would be a false scientific explanation of the virginal conception as if in terms analogous to modern cloning.

[236] *Summa theologiae* III, q. 27, a. 3. Thomas' other reason for this denial is that "re-

One of the most positive aspects of Thomas' Mariology is the way he integrates Mariology into Christology. Generally speaking this is in itself nothing novel or unique. However, due to the fact that the *Summa theologiae* systematically reflects the view that all Mary's privileges and special graces come from her role of providing the body of the Incarnate Word, it provides a permanent directive for firmly continuing the tradition of seeing in Mary's physical mother-hood of Jesus the heart of all Mariological thinking. Another posi-tive and helpful feature of Thomas' Mariology comes from combin-ing Mary's role in salvation history and the concept of the Mystical Body. He combines the two Pauline images of the Church as "Body of Christ," the one that identifies Christ with the head and the rest of mankind with the body, and the other that calls the sum-total of the members the "whole" Christ. By interpreting the first as the chief metaphor, he explains that all members must have the same mother as the Head, so that Mary's role as "mother of the Church" obtains an intuitively obvious and theologically clear, even easy, explanation.

Duns Scotus (1265-1308)

With Duns Scotus, a Franciscan and younger contemporary of St. Thomas Aquinas, the doctrine of the Immaculate Concep-tion began the last phase of its history and was shortly accepted in the West generally, well before its final and official dogmatization in 1854. Scotus' teacher and mentor, William of Ware, also a Francis-can, was most probably the first scholastic theologian to endorse this teaching. However, it was Scotus' merit to formulate both the doc-trine and its rational support into a convincing chain of theological arguments that eventually overcame all objections and cleared the way to its universal recognition by the Western Church.

One must not forget, however, that on various accounts Scotus

---

demption" is the cleansing of the soul from sin. Therefore if Mary's soul had been created sinless, it would not have been redeemed by Christ. This remained the classical objection to the Immaculate Conception until Scotus reformulated the issue.

needed a solid preparation from earlier medieval theologians who clarified the terms under discussion. Such was Anselm of Canterbury, who consistently spoke about original sin as a privation – i.e., the lack of sanctifying grace – rather than as some sort of collective guilt or individual stain (*macula*) resulting from a sin committed by the first parents of mankind, infecting their children as if by a physical impurity or "evil." Such a clarification greatly reduced the attractiveness of the "purification" metaphor applied by the greatest authorities of the past (Augustine, Bernard, Aquinas) to affirm or explain Mary's state of perfect purity beginning at her birth or right after her conception. In addition, there remained the chief objection to the Immaculate Conception: how can this doctrine be reconciled with Christ's universal salvific action? From ancient times the most influential theologians realized that Jesus' redemptive work had to be understood as retroactive and supra-temporal, for otherwise it would not be truly universal. But they could not see how the immaculate existence, no matter how brief, of any single human being would not contradict the universality of the need for redemption, a need which no one but Jesus satisfied.

Rightly was the title *doctor subtilis* attributed to Duns Scotus. Due to his philosophical sophistication, he was able to dismantle the seemingly hopeless philosophical impasse to which the doctrine of the Immaculate Conception had come by his time. Popular devotion expressing an intuitive sense of the faithful – the *sensus fidelium* – had long overcome these arguments. However, for methodological reasons, the theologians were unable to settle with a statement that appeared to contradict both previous authorities and general statements coming from biblical sources. For St. Paul had written: *Omnes peccaverunt et egent gloriam Dei*, "All have sinned and are in need of God's glory" (Rm 3:23). This powerful sentence was impossible to contradict. However, Scotus' approach showed not only his brilliance and the elegance of a light touch, but a deep understanding of the real issue at stake. He did not lose sight of the context of salvation history: Man has fallen and cannot stand up on his own, he cannot save himself, neither individually nor collectively. Yet the divine salvation plan surpassed man's failure: God sent his Son to achieve infinitely more than was necessary, more than human reasoning could see as necessary for man's redemption. Redemption exceeds our minimal human need to be saved from damnation. When God sent his Son, an unexpected and "unexpectable" event took place: God became man, not just in terms of becoming an *animal rationale* – not just a physical being endowed with intellect and free will – but as a son of the first Adam, a member of the human race. His becoming a man has a double import: he is a human offspring of our race and, at the same time, is the fruit not of man's own act of self-propagation, nor of his self-asserting sexual love, but of a virginal conception. God chose and elevated a woman to be his mother, and thus related himself by blood to the whole human race.

How was this woman chosen and prepared for such a role and dignity? By remaining untouched by sin. A thousand years before Scotus, the heretic Pelagius asked the question: Would you subject the mother of God to the dominion of Satan? Augustine nervously and energetically denied that such had ever been implied by his understanding of the universality of original sin, but he did not come up with a viable answer applicable to Mary's existence prior to her birth. Up to St. Thomas the basic answer remained the same. Scotus excludes the subtle presumption implied in Pelagius' question, and shifts the issue: If God wants to extend all the benefits of his redemptive grace to his Mother, can he not prevent her from being subjected to original sin? Is such prevention from sin not a fuller redemption than any purification, no matter how instantaneously it would follow her conception?

At this point Scotus inserted into his argument a famous phrase, coined before him and at times misunderstood after him, but used quite effectively and convincingly by him: *potuit, debuit, ergo fecit!*[237] "He could have, he should have, and therefore he did!"

---

[237] Jaroslav Pelikan calls this method applied to Mariology by Scotus "maximalism." See J. Pelikan, *Mary Through the Centuries, Her Place in the History of Culture* (New Haven: Yale University Press, 1996), 196. As we have seen above (pp. 1-2), the term "maximalism" received a negative connotation at Vatican II, and,

Formally, this statement runs against a basic logical principle: *de posse ad esse non valet illatio*, you cannot conclude from possibility to actuality. Just because God could have preserved Mary from original sin at her conception, it does not follow that he actually did. But in the argument of Scotus the second verb (*debuit*) is equally important: God "should have done so." Why? Can we deductively prove what God must or should do? Certainly not. Yet, the argument is not just an arbitrary *debuit*. It is a theological "argument of convenience": if God wanted to act in conformity with his eternal saving will, including his willing the Incarnation, and thus wanted to have the most fitting, purest, and saintliest creature as his Mother, but still a mother from Adam's race, then he had to (*debuit*) redeem her as perfectly as possible, i.e., not by letting her be conceived with original sin and then purified right upon her conception, as a second thought. It follows from the joint force of *potuit* and *debuit* that, all the way from the beginning, he preserved her from original sin.

Scotus began teaching the Immaculate Conception as a professor in Paris, and further expanded his thesis when he moved to Oxford. He acted with caution, with no claim to dogmatic certitude, but only expressing a theological opinion. Scotus' students, and especially his fellow Franciscans, took over his teaching and popularized it during the subsequent century. Belief in the Immaculate Conception did not need much popularizing: the faithful at large had readily accepted it as expressing correctly the meaning of the feast of the Immaculate Conception, which was broadly celebrated in the West.

Some hundred years after Scotus' death in 1309 it seemed that the doctrine of the Immaculate Conception had suddenly become general teaching everywhere in the Western Church. In 1439 the Council of Basel (Switzerland) promulgated it as an article of faith to be held as true by all Catholic Christians. However, this sudden and surprising success of the Immaculate Conception was the work

---

therefore, its indiscriminate use in connection with the Immaculate Conception is unfair and may need to be avoided. Yet we will also argue (see below on pp. 286-287) that Mary's unique role in our redemption recommends a re-evaluation of what is usually said and done about "arguments of convenience" in theology.

of an only attempted and unsuccessful "Ecumenical Council." The Council was convoked in the turbulent years following the Council of Constance, which succeeded in terminating the Great Schism of the Western Church in 1417. Constance's great achievement was the termination of an untenable and paralyzing ecclesial situation: by different political and legal maneuvers three Popes had to be put out of office and a new Pope elected, Martin V, who, in fact, brought Church life back to normalcy. However, the Council Fathers electing the new Pope kept on adhering to a program of governance in the Church, today called "Conciliarism," which would have obliged the Pope to convoke a General Council every ten years and provide it with authority to judge the decisions of the Pope and to function as the highest authority in the Church. Before the Council of Constance one such Council had already been convoked in Pisa (1407), but had failed to obtain approval from any Pope and was deemed schismatic. The Council of Basel in Switzerland was the next effort of the Conciliarists. Its lengthy and painfully confusing history made it last a long time (1431-1449), but ultimately all acts of the Council of Basel became invalid because of a lack of papal approval. First transferred to Ferrara in Italy, it was eventually transformed in 1439 by being reconvened in Florence; the Council of Florence was held and concluded under regular papal authority. The unhappy events of the Council of Basel served as a warning for Church authorities, not only at Florence but for centuries to come, not to touch the decrees of Basel. In the 15th century there was no reason to engage in theological debate about the Immaculate Conception – it was well accepted in the Church, yet caused disputes between schools of theology. So this dogma, advanced at Basel, had to retain its status as a theological opinion.

Mariology in the Late Middle Ages

It is rather tempting to paint a negative picture of Marian piety in the late Middle Ages and list it among the just causes of the Reformation implying ecclesial exaggerations, loss of a sound philosophical basis (along with Nominalism and Neo-Platonism), or the loss of a Christocentric vision of the faith. The truth is that, in view of the Marian piety of the 15th century, nobody could have predicted the sudden fury with which certain branches of the Protestant Reformation turned against the veneration of Mary: cultic places like shrines, feasts, popular prayers, and abundant literary material rooted in century-long traditions and generally highly esteemed in every part of the Church became the object of scorn and condemnation. Insipid sermons, exaggerated claims about the "power" of Mary's intercession, a lack of unity and coherence in late medieval theology, the hopelessly disoriented state of philosophy and the general decadence of the culture – all these do not explain why all this decadence would be seen as chiefly expressed in Mariology. After all, patristic writings and splendid works of medieval art reflecting Marian piety remained in evidence throughout the centuries. Even if on the level of popular preaching the 15th century time and again reflects excessive Mariological zeal that applies outlandish qualities to Mary, there was still enough sincere and authentic devotion among the faithful focused on her in full honesty and orthodoxy. The crisis of the Great Schism certainly revealed the lack of forceful, universal leadership in the Church. The papacy, hijacked and banished to Avignon by the king of France, lost much of its prestige and encouraged the rest of the princes similarly to exploit the power of the Church for their own local or national purposes.

Perhaps besides criticizing late medieval Mariology, we should look on a more general level at the deepening crisis of faith that an incipient Renaissance, with its revival of paganism, sponsored first in Italy, the vanguard of cultural progress, and then all over Europe. A famous satirical story in the *Decameron* by Giovanni Boccaccio (1313-1375) might have had more effect in ridiculing Mary's virginal conception than Celsus' pamphlet in the 2nd century did, even if in the 14th century, writer and readers nominally still remained devoted Catholics. This story[238] depicts the amorous exploits of a cleric

---

[238] It is the second story narrated on the "Third Day" about a monk "Fra Alberto" and the Lady Donna Monnetta.

dressed in fancy garb to masquerade as the Archangel Gabriel as he wings his way into the bedroom of an extremely pious yet hopelessly simple-minded Florentine noblewoman. The story remained famous until our own days as a typical forerunner of the Renaissance. Yet one could ask if something were not quite out of balance if, in a society known for its "exaggerated Marian piety," such short stories obtained not only the highest literary acclaim among the *litterati*, but also unprecedented success among all who knew how to read and write. I would submit as a hypothesis that well before the arrival of the anti-Marian program of the Reformation, not only had an important part of the clergy and the religious orders, with all their Marian piety, lost their credibility, but a certain loss in faith began to trickle *down* to lower cultural and social ranks of all the faithful, starting with the intellectual elite and the princely and royal courts they served.

Preachers and theologians might have represented a Mariology in disarray, yet the growing fragmentation of the Church and its highest leadership, which also caused the Great Schism, slowly but surely brought on a more general and further growing crisis of faith. Perhaps consecrated men and women, as well as clergymen, who, while nominally supporting extreme claims of Marian piety, were all too easily and credibly criticized in their personal lifestyles by satirists and humanists and reformers of the age, also motivated further doubts and criticism for their excessive, and often also hypocritical, Marian piety.

The decadence of Mariology, which, according to the Mariologist René Laurentin, is first detectable in the *Mariale* falsely attributed to St. Albert the Great, is probably no particular feature of Mariology, but of theology and ecclesial life as a whole. Yet, as the facts amply testify, Marian teaching and devotion are particularly sensitive to the problems of the day. The politicization of the unsolved doctrinal issue of the Immaculate Conception by the two great mendicant orders, the Dominicans and the Franciscans, resulted in a premature confrontation at an ultimately schismatic "Ecumenical Council" in Basel and almost terminally botched and confused the issue. Other terms and initiatives with a legitimate patristic pre-history, like Mary's "participation in Jesus' suffering" or her special intercessory role based on the special sanctity of her soul and role in salvation history, became further topics of debate with the appearance of newly coined expressions like *co-redemptrix* and *mediatrix*, linked to her image as "mother of all people," or "mother of all graces," or "mother of the Church," but without expressing the depth and weight of what they convey. In spite of an authentic and fervent Marian devotion present in every Christian country, in spite of all claims by all religious orders to a distinctly special Marian devotion, the Mariology of the late Middle Ages shows inflationary symptoms: there is too much of it, with relatively little value, and what value is there keeps on diminishing.

CHAPTER SEVEN

MARIOLOGY AFTER THE REFORMATION

Mary and the Reformers

The "why" and "how" of the Reformation would require a long narrative with the analysis of many cause-and-effect relationships, work that would go far beyond the framework of this book and the competence of its author. But I must at least sketch the way Marian doctrine and piety went through crises and various phases of renewal in the Catholic Church, leading to the threshold of "the Age of Reason," called also Rationalism, or the "Enlightenment," in the 18th century.

Historical surveys of Mariology treat the Reformation in various ways. So for example, the *Short Treatise of Mariology* by Catholic theologian René Laurentin does not even mention the names of Luther or Calvin, while the German Lutheran Walter Delius in his *History of Marian Cult* follows almost year by year the process by which the first reformers (Luther, Melanchthon, Zwingli, and Calvin) gradually distanced themselves from their Catholic heritage.[239] The facts leave little doubt that the initiators of the Reformation confronted first and foremost the veneration of the saints in general, and only afterwards moved to dismantle Marian cult in its devotional

---

[239] W. Delius, *Geschichte der Marienverehrung* (München-Basel: Ernst Reinhardt Verlag, 1963), 191-234.

practice, leaving often both the doctrinal and the biblical questions briefly untouched. Their views on Mary's perpetual virginity and sanctity, even about the Immaculate Conception, initially remained in accord with the teaching of the universal Church. For years the main feast days of Mary (the Annunciation on March 25, the Visitation on July 2, and the Purification on February 2) remained in their calendar. Negative statements began to enter the Reformers' preaching and confessional formulas in connection with praying to Mary or to the saints or with references to claims made of their "merits" playing any, even secondary or participatory, role in "mediating" or "distributing" the graces of redemption. The famous issue of the translation of κεχαριτωμένη (Lk 1:28) as *gratia plena* in the Vulgate was at the beginning no matter of contention. Luther's first German version, found in his Prayerbook,[240] has the equivalent of the Vulgate: *voll Gnade*. Only in his later translation of the full "Luther Bible" does he decide for the expression, *holdselige*, but on a purely stylistic basis: he thought *voll Gnade* was bad German. He had no problem with addressing Mary as carrying in herself, by the fact of the Incarnation, the fullness of all graces.[241]

However, once the separation of the Reformers from the Church of Rome became definitive, more and more elements of Catholic Mariology began to chip off from their theology and liturgy. In the first decades of the Reformation, many of the Catholic feasts are retained in local celebration and preached about. Those which are not based explicitly on a biblical narrative are the first to be abrogated: the feasts of the Immaculate Conception and of the Assumption soon disappear. Only at the end of the 16th century, when under the influence of the Council of Trent the Counter-Reformation begins to show more strength, did Protestant preachers and theologians begin to sharpen their anti-Marian barbs. They accuse Catholics of idolatry because they "worship" or even "adore" Mary;

---

[240] W. Delius, op. cit., p. 217.

[241] Delius quotes the old German comment Luther made: "*Den Gottes Gnade macht sie voll alles guten und ledig alles bösen.*" Ibid. ["God's grace makes her full of all that is good and lacking all evil."]

they forbid the attribution of the term "mediation" to Mary. Just as the saints, so also Mary cannot be praised for what she did or is doing; only God can be praised and thanked for having manifested his greatness in the words or deeds of his holy ones. A whole traditional vocabulary applying the imagery of the wisdom books of the Bible to Mary is excluded; the traditional allegorical reading of these books is frowned upon, and thus Mariology is cut off from the interpretation of the Old Testament in principle.

Mary at Trent and in Post-Tridentine Catholicism

The decrees of Trent say virtually nothing about Mary. On the one hand, the Council decided not to make any statement about the Immaculate Conception; on the other, it considered sufficient the defense of the veneration of the saints in principle and of the Catholic doctrine of justification. This decision by Trent seemed wise and effective. The Council avoided adding fuel to the controversies surrounding the heritage of Aquinas, and remained faithful to the policies of Sixtus IV who, almost a century earlier, had forbidden any further debate about the Immaculate Conception as a matter of orthodoxy vs. heresy.

However, the Counter-Reform championed by Trent initiated a new Mariology fully committed to the traditional doctrine of the Church Fathers and their medieval disciples. Even before a theological renewal of Mariology began, it was clear that the Reform of Trent was in the hands of churchmen fully devoted to Marian piety. Not only was this clear in the exemplary personal story of St. Ignatius of Loyola, but in the spirituality of the Jesuits in general. They were all devoted to the cult of the Immaculate Conception and of the Rosary. At their initiative, "Marian congregations" were formed in all Jesuit institutions, which thus began to spread a renewed Marian spirituality, basic to the Catholic renewal.

Mariology was expanded and further developed by a new generation of theologians like Suarez in Spain and Peter Canisius in Germany, both Jesuits who integrated Mariology into their theological synthesis. At the same time it became clear that theology as a scholarly discipline was tending more and more to split off from "spirituality," such that the history of "Marian cult" and the so-called "Marian theology" began to grow apart with little chance of meeting up again soon.[242] But this increasing split between theology and spirituality also had some advantages. Books written for the sake of spiritual guidance rather than in service of theological studies provided important resources with authentic, orthodox, and prudent Mariological content, as in the new biblical commentaries (like those of Cornelius a Lapide) or in spiritual handbooks like the ever popular works *Philothea* and *Timotheus* of St. Francis de Sales.

The most important aspect of the Counter-Reformation was its hugely successful effort to create a culture by advancing arts and letters, sciences, philosophy, and theology in an authentically Christian spirit in so-called "colleges" (secondary schools) and universities. Together with other religious orders and institutions, the Jesuits of the 16th century signaled a new direction for the last trends of humanism. The development of arts and music in a post-Renaissance style, called today the "Baroque," were soon purified from paganistic tendencies that were certainly present in the first waves of the Italian Renaissance. Thus, without danger of losing its identity, Catholicism would not be left immersed in the cultural backwaters of some medieval immobilism.

Temporarily, for about the last decades of the 17th and first years of the 18th century, an interesting parallel development took place between conservative Protestants and mainline Catholics, which affected also Mariology. A tendency, generally called orthodox or pietistic Protestantism, became more open to Marian teaching and aimed quite openly at reducing the exacerbated clashes between Protestants and Catholics in matters of Marian beliefs and cult. This

---

[242] This development began in earnest ever since Aristotle's concept of "science" as argued and proven knowledge was introduced into the definition of theology. But, of course, as contemporary theologians often emphasize, Aquinas' *Summa* professed to remain faithful to the idea that theology was about an integral understanding of revealed truth, even more specifically, a knowledge based on the *sacra pagina*, the Bible. Cf. *Summa theologiae* I, q. 1, a. 1.

movement of thought did not last for long. The ongoing application of the principle of *sola scriptura*, which Protestants have never left, eventually set up new allegiances between rationalist biblicists and Protestants basing all proofs on the Bible alone, while Catholics renewed their commitment to "the unadulterated word" alone, letting rationalism decide what kind of interpretation it takes to avoid adulterating the biblical word.[243]

In this way we arrive to the threshold of a new epoch of history, beyond which we have just barely progressed: the age of biblical rationalism, in which Mariology too is treated like any other branch or topic of theology. The main characteristic of this trend is the reign of some kind of rationalistic exegesis as the highest norm, and a certain minimalism in virtue of historical criticism, judging all matters by the light of reason, and refusing to accept criticism from any other source than this same light of reason itself.

---

[243] This chapter is obviously much too short and fails by omission to cover a complicated history. As it is pointed out in many books and essays, the young Luther's Marian piety had diminished but never disappeared and in both Lutheranism and the Church of England the cult of Mary survived mostly in the form of liturgical feasts which continued to be celebrated to honor the Blessed Virgin. Also the history of rationalistic interpretation of the Bible is a complicated and troubled story interwoven with anti-rationalistic and even fideistic rejections of most philosophical systems. A good survey of Protestant (and especially Lutheran) Marian theology and piety is found in a book already quoted above: Walter Delius, *Geschichte der Marienverehrung* (München/Basel: Ernst Reinhart Verlag, 1963).

CHAPTER EIGHT

MARIOLOGY OF THE MODERN AGE

A Historical Outline

The whole medieval world came to an end or at least was shattered beyond reconstruction by the French Revolution (1789) and the two decades that followed it. One may boldly state that, although more fragmented than ever before, Christianity not only survived but benefitted from the burning of so much dead wood and the appearance of new shoots with equal, or even greater, faith and zeal than it had seen in ancient times. Even the papacy, first humiliated by Napoleon, and then brought to its knees by all sorts of nationalistic and anticlerical forces that swept across Italy and united it against the Pope, in the end gained such respect and prestige that we can speak of a providential series of losses that led to a great deal of gains for the Christian cause.

For Mariology an even more curious journey began. The main narrative plot is full of puzzling subplots, whose ultimate outcomes are still to be evaluated. Various aftershocks of the French Revolution filled the 19th century, leaving hardly any part of the Church intact. Religious orders dissolved and were reconstructed. Worst was the fate of the monastic institutions in France, where all Church institutions were heavily damaged. Monasteries like Cluny or Citeaux, with all their dependencies, whether decadent or still in vigor, were wiped away; not only were monks and nuns deported, at times guillotined, but their monasteries were often burned to the ground and

211

often the buildings erased stone by stone, carried away and used for new constructions, so that age-old monuments literally disappeared from the cultural landscape. These violent years, undertaken in the name of *liberté, égalité, fraternité* were followed by the Napoleonic wars, which turned the wrath of the French masses into senseless aggression against the rest of Europe. The Congress of Vienna (1814) ended a long era of devastating warfare, but it became clear that history was not reversible: major cultural changes were expected to stay.

Throughout the 19th century religious institutions of the past fell and rose. Country by country new anticlerical governments "secularized" (confiscated) the properties and foundations of ancient religious orders, but, in the aftermath of the French Revolution, powerful modern religious orders emerged with novel structures and renewed spirituality. The religious orders of this new era excelled in Marian piety: all the orders and congregations proudly affirmed their special affiliation to her and set themselves under her protection. The new orders of women and men were usually aimed at specific, urgent needs of the Church in her work of reconstruction. Teaching and missionary congregations were founded by the dozens. Their spirituality soon underwent the heavy influence of the new cultural trend of the time: *Romanticism*, promoting a growing fascination with medieval liturgy and theology. This, of course, favored Marian piety and theology, too. The phenomenal development of science and mathematics kept on recruiting new disciples for humanistic atheism, and, as if it were a balancing force, Marian piety also reached unprecedented levels, though often intellectually impoverished. In periods of political and social upheaval, when many of the Church's efforts and hopes to stabilize Catholic institutions were frustrated, equally "revolutionary" and unexpected episodes appeared that focused the Church's attention on Mary, as if Marian doctrine and devotion were the only resources capable of rapidly meeting the advance of forces transforming the state of culture and civilization on a global level. We mention three such events.

The first may be lesser known today. In 1830, in a small chapel in Paris, Marian apparitions occurred to a nun, Catherine Labouré: Our Lady initiated the use of the "miraculous medal," a medallion to be worn as a sign of special spiritual dedication to Jesus and his mother. Sr. Catherine Labouré, a member of the Order of the Daughters of Charity, originally founded by St. Vincent de Paul, began to spread this new devotion, which quickly obtained popularity across Europe. Some German authors mark the "beginning of a Marian epoch" (*Marianische Zeitalter*)[244] with this apparition, while others think that it was principally the dogmatization of the Immaculate Conception (1854), followed by the apparitions of Mary in Lourdes (1858), that made a large portion of Catholic life focus on Marian devotion.

Certainly the Marian apparitions of Lourdes, a remote village in the French Pyrénées on the Spanish border, had an unexpected and inexplicably huge impact on both the Church and the world. When Mary appeared to an illiterate peasant girl named Bernadette Soubirous, identifying herself as "the Immaculate Conception," a title which the girl did not understand yet memorized and faithfully reported to the bishop, the initial reactions were extremely divided, either suspecting an extreme and most dangerous form of a hoax or an extraordinary "eschatological sign" coming from heaven. Then Mary kept on appearing, and she directed Bernadette to dig into the soil of the site to find an abundant fountain of clean water filling up a pond. Although the chemical analysis of the water showed no special qualities, numerous people coming to wash themselves in it were miraculously cured of their various ailments. Lourdes became the most popular pilgrimage site of all Christian history. Some of the miraculous cures happened under the close watch of medical doctors. One of them was witnessed by the famous though controversial Doctor Alexis Carrell (1873-1944), the winner of the Nobel Prize in Medicine in 1912, who was shocked out of his rationalism by what he witnessed although he retained his agnostic views for a long time afterwards.[245]

---

[244] See Walter Delius, *Geschichte der Marienverehrung* (München/Basel: Ernst Reinhart Verlag, 1963), 258-288.

[245] Alexis Carrell, wrestling with the impact of what he observed finally opened up his soul in turmoil after he developed a personal friendship with Dom Alexis

The apparitions of Lourdes brought about, in the middle of the 19th century, a seemingly new dimension and a new impetus to Mariology. The apparitions claimed to provide direct contact with the very central figure of Mariology, the glorified Virgin herself with miraculous healings connected with messages, warnings, and requests addressing Catholics in large geographic regions. However, this "novelty" was neither sudden nor as genuinely new as it had first seemed. As early as in the 16th century a slower but comparable impetus began to impact Mariology, developing more slowly but effectively in connection with the apparitions of the blessed Virgin to Juan Diego, a native of Mexico, at the present location of the Basilica of the Virgin of Guadalupe in Mexico City. Although less extensively studied by historians and scientists than the story of Lourdes has been, the appearances of Mary to this Aztec Catholic, leaving behind a miraculous Image of the Virgin upon his tilma (mantle or cloak), became eventually widely known. In modern times they drew large numbers of pilgrims to the Basilica built at the site of the appearances where the picture is also kept and is venerated. Since the beatification (1990) and then the canonization (2002) of Juan Diego by John Paul II, the devotion to Our Lady of Guadalupe has greatly increased so that today, on a special feast on December 12 and under the title of "Our Lady of Guadalupe" Mary is venerated as the Patroness of the Americas in both South and North America.[246]

Presse, the Cistercian Abbot of Boquen in Bretagne, France. As a result Carrell embraced again his childhood's Catholic faith. After he published his personal experiences of Lourdes, the medical establishment of Lyons where he practiced medicine ostracized him. He moved to America and as a heart surgeon in New York invented techniques that revolutionized surgery on heart valves. Because of statements he allegedly made about eugenics, Carrell was unfairly accused of supporting the policies of the Nazis. His death in 1944 prevented him from responding to these charges.

He published his story in a book, in English translation, *Voyage to Lourdes* (New York: Harper, 1950). The Templeton Prize-winning Benedictine philosopher and physicist, Stanley L. Jáki re-edited the book and wrote an introduction to it. His remarkable commentary on the evidence of this story is available online under the title "Two Lourdes Miracles and a Nobel Laureate" at www.Catholic-Culture.org.

[246] Cf. Franciscan Friars of the Immaculate (eds.), *Handbook on Guadalupe* (Wait

A third event took place in Fatima, Portugal, in 1917. Beginning on May 13, three young and uneducated children tending their parents' sheep saw "a beautiful lady," who later identified herself as the Virgin Mary. They became her messengers, reporting a universal call to conversion and recruiting other witnesses and pleading for conversion; the apparitions continued until October 13 of the same year. These apparitions have been controversial for some time, yet received increasing endorsement from the Church by all popes, beginning with Pius XII. The unsuccessful assassination attempt against Pope John Paul II in Rome by a Turkish citizen, Mehmet Ali Agca on May 13, 1981, is widely recognized by Catholics as an indirect validation of the apparitions of Fatima.[247]

We mention these three supernatural events, all witnessed by simple and uneducated people, because they eventually influenced the Church at large as incredibly dramatic and unprecedented occurrences that called the attention of Church officials and theologians to the importance of Mary's role in the modern Church. Although believing in so-called "private revelations"[248] has not been nor will be part of Catholic Christian faith, the three events described above motivated a large number of theologians and churchmen to keep the veneration of Mary alive in the Church and prevent it from diminishing.

One might say that these Marian experiences of the modern Church were closely related to the development of Mariology in relation to two extraordinary acts of the Magisterium. In 1854, Pius IX, after consulting the episcopacy of the world, reached back to the "unfinished business" of the Immaculate Conception. This step,

---

Park: Park Press, 1997); Salvador Carrillo Alday, M.Sp.S., *The Theological Message of Guadalupe* (Staten Island, NY: Alba House, 2010).

[247] Agca's bullet, wounding the chest of the Pope, was only millimeters off from being lethal. There is no evidence that Agca knew the significance of the date of his assassination attempt. See the comments of Pope John Paul II on this event on p. 238.

[248] Private revelations mean any revelation received after the New Testament, more precisely, after the passing of the last Apostle of Jesus. The Church claims the authenticity of apostolic revelation but does not declare any further divine communication belonging to the apostolic heritage or the *depositum fidei*.

unusual as it might seem in hindsight, was waiting for some resolution. By the 19th century the so-called "maculist" position – that Mary was conceived with original sin but was cleansed upon her conception – had lost the support of theologians and bishops alike. Disagreements with Protestants, with their increasingly Nestorian Christology (separating the two natures of Christ), was of little relevance: they had no valid theological basis for denying the Immaculate Conception, since they doubted or denied her purity even from personal sin. Their claim that Catholics try to "divinize" or "quasi-divinize" Mary was an old issue which had merely apologetic relevance, but virtually no one was ready to take it into account for defining true Catholic doctrine. Pope Pius' consultation with the episcopate showed that the Immaculate Conception was in fact regarded as correct Church doctrine and, thus, as pertaining to the apostolic deposit of faith. The very fact that this doctrine was recognized four hundred years earlier by the Council of Basel as part of the Church's faith also remained a sign that this teaching was still, for political reasons, without the support it needed of the official teaching Magisterium. To these reasons one must add those more "modern" tendencies appearing in the Church, mostly in Germany, which tried to impose a new model for the history of dogma (*Dogmengeschichte*) demanding that all dogmas taught by today's Church be demonstrably included in the faith of the early Church. By the word "included" they meant either the "explicit" presence of a teaching or a logically implicit presence, which meant that it would suffice only if, by means of mere deductive reasoning, a thesis could be proven as present in some other explicit doctrine of the early Church. Those who denied the Immaculate Conception in such a way might have been relatively few; yet they represented an emerging trend of historicism, which was unacceptable insofar as it methodologically denied true development of doctrine as an organic and living process rather than just a formalistic exercise in logic. The Magisterium's proceeding to declare the Immaculate Conception as a dogma made it possible for a new model to be introduced for the "evolution of doctrines," taking the place of the previous one, which was *ahistorical* and, therefore, unacceptable to the new demands of historians. All historians knew that no explicit statements about such matters as either "original sin" or "God's preventive protection" shielding Mary from it could be found in early Christian writings, neither explicitly or in logically equivalent terms.

Less substantive objections were raised by the schismatic Eastern Churches. These firmly believe in Mary's sinlessness, but their theological anthropology, growing in isolation from the West, did not explore the question of original sin and its transmission in the same way the Western Latin Church did. The influence of St. Augustine, so important for the West, had been of little consequence for them. Their sensitivity was therefore incensed when, in terms poorly known to Eastern theologians, Rome went ahead with a doctrinal decision without their actual participation.[249] Yet, under the circumstances of less frequent and much less intense global communications, the problem remained restricted to small circles. Much was said later on, speculating about a lack of prudence involved in "the dogmatization," but, in reality, the Immaculate Conception created no new obstacle for an eventual future *rapprochement* between the East and West.

In retrospect, another question, more political than theological, can now be answered with a higher degree of certainty. In 1854 the worldly and political power of the papacy was in hopeless decline; the Papal States remained the last political obstacle to a united Italy. A political dilemma between fidelity to the Pope and loyalty to the nascent Italian nation became unavoidable. Under such conditions the declaration of the dogma was a bold step demonstrating that the Pope claimed a spiritual leadership, not over Italians only but over the whole Catholic Church, regardless of the dire storms darkening the international horizon. This is the perspective in which we must appreciate that, fewer than four years after the dogmatization of the Immaculate Conception, the apparitions of Lourdes impacted the faithful as a validation of Pope Pius IX's courage. They came as an

---

[249] The Eastern episcopate, however, was approached and consulted just as it was also invited to the Council of Trent and later to Vatican I and II.

unexpected, supernatural nod of approval uplifting the morale of the Pope and his diminishing "little flock," eventually to be deprived of the badly needed resources of temporal wealth and independence, which the Papal State had provided for so long.

Catholic restoration and a corresponding transformation of the Church – partial, problematic, and full of setbacks – progressed too slowly and was hindered by continuous wars, both cultural and factual, all over the European continent. As an immense blessing coming from internal renewal – by sheer grace and little else – the religious orders and monasteries destroyed by the French Revolution or dissolved thereafter were replaced by a large number of new religious communities founded in the 19th century.[250] This reversal of the state of religious life immensely benefitted the Church, especially if we add the sad story of the Jesuit Order's suppression by Pope Clement XIV in 1773, to be restored only in 1815. In the 19th century almost all religious orders went through a period of "secularization" (suppression by worldly power) resulting in the seizure of their properties or restriction, or often in complete cessation of their activities. However, the 19th century also saw an unprecedented number of foundations of new religious communities for both men and women, often under the explicit patronage of the Blessed Virgin as the model of consecrated life. In fact we can speak of a great recovery and renewal of religious life from the disastrous effects of both the Reformation and the French Revolution. The subsequent upsurge of Marian piety and Mariology owes much to these orders and congregations who, by their very existence, spread the veneration of the Blessed Virgin. Religious life in the second half of the 19th century amply proves the fruitfulness of the dogma of the Immaculate Conception, in harmony with the extraordinary affirmation in the story of Lourdes.

---

[250] Almost all religious orders and congregations of the Post-Tridentine era have something to do with an explicit intention of establishing a special feature of Marian piety. Just to mention some large congregations with a Marian emphasis, we can quote the missionary order of the Oblates of Mary Immaculate (O.M.I.), or the Salesians with their special devotion to Mary *Auxiliatrix*, inherited from Don Bosco, the various orders named by "Notre Dame" (school sisters, canonical orders) or "Saint Mary," all established in special honor of the Virgin Mary.

Mariology in the Past Two Centuries

The period of the European revolutions (1789-1917) overlaps with the history of Civil Wars in Mexico, the United States, and Spain, and the Two World Wars (1914-1918 and 1939-1945), followed by the so-called Cold War (1950-1989). These events affected Catholic theology in unprecedented ways, and Mariology emerged or subsided amid catastrophic blood baths and deep cultural changes. The rebirth of fervor in Marian piety brought about a resurgence also in Mariological thought, although only slowly. The romantic period of the 19th century led to two specific and in themselves remarkable developments: the Mariology of Matthias Scheeben (1835-1888) and of John Henry Newman (1801-1890). Their lives and theological careers are of more opposite than similar character. Yet they contributed to the same cause: a Catholic renewal, mainly through works in education and theology. Both Scheeben and Newman show the positive effects of modern historical consciousness on Catholic theology. In their work a new awareness appeared of the historical dimension of theological development within the framework of culture and Church history in general. This is most remarkable in Scheeben's case, whose work was almost entirely dedicated to "speculative" theology, i.e., a reflection on meaning and systematization, not history.[251] By contrast, Newman consciously focused on the "history of doctrines," which he applied mostly to the study of the Church Fathers. Scheeben was a "cradle Catholic" who entered seminary in Cologne at the age of seventeen. He died at a young age and obtained true

---

[251] In the cultural milieu of Romanticism, Scheeben produced a new approach to theology by which he treated all significant topics in a unique synthesis. Surprisingly he rediscovered the Mary/Eve parallel and presented it with the freshness of his approach but also with an astonishingly succinct and compact manner: "We ought to turn our eyes for a moment to the Blessed Virgin, from whom [the God-Man] received his human nature and in whose womb she wedded the human race and became one body with it.... That is to say, if the new Eve after the model of the old, was to become the mother of the [human] race in its heavenly birth, she had to proceed in her heavenly nature from the side of the bridegroom and had to issue from the sacrificial outpouring of His heart." Matthias J. Scheeben, *The Mysteries of Christianity*, tr. by C. Vollert (London/Saint Louis: Herder, 1946), 464-5.

recognition for his theological synthesis only when discovered much later by other German theologians, in particular by Hans Urs von Balthasar, half a century after his death. To the contrary, Newman was an Anglican, whose career was followed with great interest from early on by his contemporaries.[252] His conversion to Catholicism in 1845 created an upheaval in the Church of England and caused excitement, although mixed with critical reactions, among Catholics. Pope Leo XIII named him a cardinal in 1878, when he was already seventy-seven years old, yet he lived on for more than a decade, dying in 1890. He was rediscovered by the ecumenical post-Vatican II theology, and became an icon and a spiritual leader in the study of the development of dogma in authentic Catholic spirit. His newly-won reputation as the theologian of the development of dogma was earned by his immense erudition in patristics and his deep wisdom, by which he was able to point out the orthodox kernel of Catholic teaching and distinguish it from accidental or transitory forms of expression in various epochs and cultures. His beatification in 2010 by Pope Benedict XVI put him forward not only as a saintly priest but as a theologian in whose work the historical method, a faithful adherence to the Magisterium, and respect for tradition remain consistently linked and balanced.

In the 20th century, before Vatican II, Mariology showed some remarkable signs of health and productivity. What Newman began in the 19th century became a movement after the First World War: the study of patristic Mariology slowly began to leave behind the Procrustean bed of apologetics and the narrow-mindedness of exclusively speculative theology, and so began to concentrate on what the Church Fathers had to say positively about Mary. At the same time, especially after the encouragements of Pope Pius XII's encyclical *Di-*

---

[252] His interest in Marian theology clearly appears in his sermons about Mary, which he preached quite early, still in his Anglican years. He discovered Mariology in the writings of the Church Fathers, starting with Justin Martyr and Irenaeus. From the many publications on Newman's Mariology, that of Nicholas L. Gregoris, "The Daughter of Eve Unfallen." *Mary in the Theology and Spirituality of John Henry Newman*, 2nd revised ed. (Monte Pocono, Pennsylvania: Newman House, 2003) stands out by its extensive documentation and bibliography.

vino Afflante Spiritu (1943), a "biblical movement," parallel to the "patristic movement" started to open its wings. The exploration of the biblical basis of Mariology seemed to offer immense ecumenical potential; this fact was quickly recognized from "right and left."[253] Under this double influence of patristics and biblical scholarship, almost every Catholic theologian of name and fame in the decades preceding Vatican II, regardless of how he was recognized or classified later, felt prompted to publish a book on Mary.[254]

At first sight Vatican II (1962-65) seems to have said relatively little about Mariology. What it said may be regarded as narrowly limited to the confines of age-old tradition and a "middle-of-the-road" approach to theology. Yet the Council exercised an immense influence on the future of Mariology by both what it said, especially with regard to "Mary and the Church," and what it initiated *besides* Mariology through its teaching about the Church. Therefore, I feel we need to treat both the narrative and the analysis of "Mary in Vatican II" in a separate chapter, and do it from a closer standpoint and with more details, in some points even under a magnifying glass.

---

[253] An annotated bibliography of the period 1945-1962 on "Mary in the Bible" is not easily made. See, however, a mostly French selection by R. Laurentin, *Traité de théologie mariale* (Paris: Lethielleux, 1959), 150-151.

[254] To mention the major names of the period, see Y. Congar, *Marie, l'Église et le Sacerdoce* (Paris: Gabalda, 1953), K. Rahner, *Mary Mother of the Lord* (New York: Herder, 1963), E. Schilleebeeckx, *Mary, Mother of the Redemption* (New York: Sheed and Ward, 1963), O. Semmelroth, *Archetype of the Church* (New York: Sheed and Ward, 1964), L. Bouyer, *The Seat of Wisdom* (Chicago: Regnery, 1965), H. Rahner, *Our Lady and the Church* (Logos Books, 1958), J. Guitton, *La Vierge Marie* (Paris: Aubier, 1964). In their first and original editions all these books have anteceded the Council.

CHAPTER NINE

MARIOLOGY AT VATICAN II

Vatican II drew together many leading theologians, gathered as "experts," often as personal advisers to various leading members of the hierarchy; of these, both those belonging to the conservative wing and those who eventually became the "movers and shakers" of the Council had previously made valuable and highly acclaimed contributions to Mariology. Nonetheless, between the announcement of a new Ecumenical Council by Pope John XXIII (January 25, 1960) and its actual opening (October 11, 1962),[255] two antithetical trends quickly surfaced in Mariology. One group saw in the Council a welcome opportunity to declare some new Marian dogma (Mary's role as "Mediatrix of All Graces" or as "Co-Redemptrix"). Others expected the Council to take a stand as it were against Mariology, to assure various Protestant groups of the Council's readiness to oppose devotional exaggerations, pay attention to biblical norms, and ensure strict subordination of Mariology to Christology and ecclesiology. Most observers of the Council pointed out from the beginning the tension that reigned in Mariology between "maximalists" and "minimalists." But in the proceedings of the Council this moved to the forefront only at the second session, in the fall of 1963, when the question was raised whether or not the Virgin Mary should be treated in a separate document or within the document about the Church. Although the vote of October 29, 1963 concerned only a procedural issue, this occasion came very close to being an unsched-

---

[255] The Council opened on October 11, 1962, the feast of the "Maternity of Mary," of which many participants, most importantly the Pope, made a special point.

uled, unexpected, and regrettable showdown between the two par-
ties, splitting the assembly in the middle. With 1,114 for and 1,074
against (five abstained) inserting the question of Mary into a document about the Church, the Council manifested the precarious state
of unity, giving room for a great deal of speculation about the fate of
all future issues.

Due to an intervention by Pope John XXIII, the Council avoided an actual showdown and eventually accepted, with near unanimity, the proposal to treat Mary in the context of ecclesiology, and so
to insert a text on Mary as an appendix in *Lumen Gentium*.

In spite of the frightened forebodings, Marian teaching did not
end up as a major "neuralgic point" for Vatican II. With some opti-
mism one was able to say at the end that the Council had made some
positive contribution to Catholic Marian devotion. At the close of the
third session, on November 21, 1964 – another minor Marian feast[256]
– Paul VI declared Mary "Mother of the Church," an act that met
with only moderate enthusiasm, but certainly did not prompt excessive critical remarks. The new title, shown to be sufficiently rooted
in tradition, has eventually become a good tool for teaching about
Mary's relationship to the Church. After the Council, the framing of
Mariology into an ecclesiological context or speaking about the parallel Mary/Church became a popular topic, either by pointing to the
Virgin Mother as the Church's archetype or highlighting Mary as
both the Church's first building stone and its most eminent part.[257]

The Impact of the Council on Mariology

The post-Conciliar commentaries on this chapter on Mary
give high marks to its theological content, praise its clarity and orthodoxy, as well as its rich biblical and patristic documentation. A

---

[256] The feast of the *Presentation of Mary* in the Temple has for its object the event
narrated in the apocryphal document the *Proto-evangelium Jacobi*. After the
Council, in the new Church calendar, it was retained for its symbolic, non-histor-
ical meaning, but reduced to a feast of the third class.

[257] See the short book by René Laurentin, *La Vierge au Concile* (Paris: Lethielleux,
1965).

quasi-unanimous reception of the document by theologians, lay people, and clergy who dedicated themselves to study the Conciliar documents after the first decade following the Council, commented positively on the last chapter of *Lumen Gentium* as a faithful and insightful rendering of the Mariological teaching of the Church. Only one exception can be made, which, however, does not regard the document itself but the papal act of declaring Mary "Mother of the Church," which was criticized as lacking sufficient traditional (patristic and medieval) background or dogmatic clarity, causing confused reactions about Mary being both "member" and "mother" of Christ's body.[258]

A decline in Mariology must not be attributed to the Council and cannot be regarded as one of its genuine fruits. However, one must not take lightly that in 1983, in the article we just quoted, we find some puzzling sentences by Karl Rahner, who noticed a significant change in Marian devotion, a change he did not directly connect with what critics called "Mariological minimalism," but certainly noticed right after the Council.[259] That this tendency was quite understandable and possibly justifiable is clear from the Council's text about Marian devotion, which points out the dangers of an

---

[258] Typical is, in this regard, Karl Rahner's side remark in his last article on Mariology: "Man mag von dem Titel Marias als der 'Mutter der Kirche,' den das Konzil vermied und den Papst Paul VI dennoch angriff, denken wie man will bezüglich seines genaueren Inhaltes und seiner Verstandlichkeit; die Kirche als ganze hat auf jeden Fall in allen Zeiten, wenn wenn auch in einer wechselvollen Geschichte mit wieder anderen Akzentuierungen, die heilige Jungfrau verehrt." [Regardless of what one may think about the title "Mother of the Church," which the Council had previously avoided but Pope Paul VI has taken up, with regard to its content and intelligibility; the Church as a whole has certainly in all times, although, of course, through a history of many changes and different emphases, kept on venerating the blessed Virgin.] "Mut zur Marienverehrung": *Geist und Leben* 56 (1983), 172.

[259] A closer look at the facts, however, may reveal a somewhat more complicated situation. A telling detail is the article published after the Council's first session under the name of Paul Rusch, the Bishop of Innsbruck, but inspired or (probably written) by Karl Rahner, calling for continued Mariological minimalism: "Marianische Wertungen," *Zeitschrift für katholische Theologie* 85 (1963), 129-131. There is little doubt that the article represented the hopes of many German prelates and theologians preparing for a major ecumenical breakthrough in Catholic/Lutheran relations.

exaggerated Marian focus in doctrine and spirituality, that may end up pushing out of focus the central mysteries of the faith. Furthermore, the agreement about this issue which followed the Council was unanimous and little legitimate debate may question it. In its own immediate context Mariology before and after the Council was a most important and precious part of Catholic heritage, which no significant faction had intended to reduce or destroy. After the Council, the bishops left Rome with a fairly widespread consensus that, in the matter of Mariology, the Council had done its job. They were fully entitled not to expect major problems to develop with regard to Marian theology and devotion.

On the other hand, everybody perceived – many people with justifiable satisfaction – that the Council had opened wide the doors to new trends in Catholic theology. These trends gained decisive influence at the Council and took over the role of leadership from a previous generation with loudly proclaimed hopes of a general "renewal" or *aggiornamento*, mostly in the form of a new dialogue with non-Catholic Christians, but also with other religions and the new culture which began to expand after the Second World War. Unexpectedly, as a kind of feedback, the new theological trend taking over the terrain of biblical, patristic, dogmatic, and moral theology eventually influenced Mariology too and, unfortunately, in a negative way. I refer here, first and foremost, to the sudden dominance of historical criticism over Catholic biblical studies, and a similarly rapid advance of historicism in the study of the Church Fathers. A certain "de-emphasis" of Mariology quickly followed. Strangely, this did not happen so much in the area of the "new dogmas" (Immaculate Conception and the Assumption) but the most ancient doctrinal tenet, Mary's perpetual virginity, which, in a slow erosion, part by part (according to its traditional subdivision: *ante partum, in partu*, and *post partum*), was called into question by various groups and publications.

To trace the logic is easy. By rigid and exclusive application of historical criticism, one arrives to the long-standing position taken by most branches of Protestantism: little or nothing can be known with certainty about Mary's earthly life.[260] From such a perspective, the Evangelists' statements – even if taken literally, but with no place for a theological exegesis of the texts' theological message and motivation – are easily assessed as stating only very few facts. And we mean here only the "dumb facts," meaningful only if supported by hard and unquestionable evidence; nothing can be assumed from the context or from any traditional interpretation, no matter how old it was. "Suggestions" are welcome, but only if paired off with "suspicions." If you say that Luke is suggesting that, at least partly, Mary was his source of information, you should not be naïve, by accepting uncritically what he "seems to suggest." If you suspect that Mark, by calling Jesus "Mary's son"[261] implicitly indicates that Mary was a "single parent" and possibly the victim of rape, then you are *avant-garde*. If you suggest that the sudden transition in Luke 1:5 from elegant Greek to a Semitic style shows that he is turning to a Semitic source, your suggestion is easily dismissed by "statistical evidence" that he does nothing but mimic the style of the Septuagint. But you may rather conclude from the same observation to the suspicion that Luke, as an artist, can and will imitate any style, and this might possibly mislead you (if not intentionally then by accident), and then you are tempted to be equally creative. He fooled his un*suspecting* readers of the last nineteen hundred years, but now he cannot fool us: we know from Acts that he can imitate a Greek narrative about sea voyages and shipwrecks in first person plural just to make us believe he was an eyewitness of the events. Once Luke 1-2 are interpreted in this manner, and most importantly in isolation from other considerations than historicity, the theological "afterthoughts" are riddled with suspicion, so that the narratives of Luke must be subjected to *Tendenzgeschichte*, an inquiry into the "hidden agenda." This has slowly poisoned even the Catholic exegetes of the Lucan

---

[260] Well before the Council a book was published by Paul Gächter, Jesuit professor of New Testament in Innsbruck, presenting a Catholic model for reading the New Testament about Mary in a strictly critical perspective: *Maria im Erdenleben* (Innsbruck: Tyrolia, 1953).

[261] In 1st century Middle Eastern society a man "must" be identified not by his mother's but his father's name, the "patronymic," x son of y.

texts; they began emphasizing clinical issues about the meaning of "virginity," and making us wonder what to suspect: which elements of the concept of virginity, known from Greek and Egyptian polytheism and the history of religions in general, defined the Hellenized Christian agenda?[262]

In response to such an approach by the biblical experts (many of them outdated, but quite new for many post-Conciliar Catholic theologians), many respectable Catholic scholars were ready to "withdraw the *limes*"– the defendable border of their apologetics – and conceded that the virginal conception, as a reality beyond the idea, was not a necessary condition for the Incarnation.[263] Even more easily, after some exegetical hesitations, virginity both *in partu* and *post partum* began to lose importance.[264] Church authorities func-

---

[262] We are speaking of two steps. Historical criticism separates in principle the fact from its meaning. As soon as fact and meaning are separated, the question emerges: Was not the narrative composed for the sake of the meaning regardless of the factuality of its content? Furthermore, the insistence of the exegetes first and foremost upon the *Christological* focus of the virginal conception in both Mt and Lk easily leads to the conclusion that biblical truth (and thus inerrancy) is engaged only for the Christological content, while the separable "Mariological" assertions belong only to the "packaging" (the symbolic expression) of a Christological kernel. René Laurentin tried to counter this logic rather early: *Court traité de théologie mariale* (Paris: Lethielleux, 1959), 97. Raymond Brown, on the other hand, developed the hypothetical separation of fact and meaning into an exegetical system. He assumed that for every biblical topic we must separately ask "what the Bible meant" and "what the Bible means." He applies this system explicitly, as a clear example, to the virginal conception in his *The Critical Meaning of the Bible* (New York/Ramsey: Paulist Press, 1981), 79-80.

[263] "According to the faith of the Church, the [divine] Sonship of Jesus does not rest on the fact that Jesus had no human father; the doctrine of Jesus' divinity would not be affected if Jesus had been the product of a normal human marriage." Joseph Ratzinger, *Introduction to Christianity*, tr. by J.R. Foster (New York: Herder, 1970), 208. Later, Ratzinger, accepting the criticism of H.U. von Balthasar, made it clear that the virginal *mode* of the Incarnation is not separable from the *fact* of the Incarnation. At the same time he had to distance himself from a use of his earlier text by Rudolph Pesch [*Das Markusevangelium*, Freiburg: Herder, 1976, 223-230] who used this text quoted as an argument to the contrary. See Joseph Card. Ratzinger, *Daughter Zion, Meditations on the Church's Marian Belief* (San Francisco: Ignatius Press, 1983), 50-51.

[264] The erosion of this dogma as theologians saw it is illustrated with impressive honesty by Cardinal Kasper's "Letter about Mary's Virginity" in *Communio* 1988 no. 2. In an autobiographical sketch, Kasper narrates a conversation he had with Karl Rahner while traveling on the Autobahn. Rahner agreed that the virginal conception must be held as factual but, he added, "should you encounter some-

tioning on behalf of the Magisterium were anxious not to overreact, but, at the same time, those who oversaw the long enterprise of a vernacular liturgy did all they were able to by emphasizing the orthodoxy of translations. After the Council, while Catholic exegetes felt empowered to explore the various (some of them rather obsolete) attempts to secularize the Infancy Narratives, liturgical texts were forced to retain the recurring title of "ever virgin" (*semper Virgo*) in all texts.

One might say that in the decades before the Council the virginal conception itself (virginity *ante partum*) was rarely called into doubt. On this both Matthew and Luke were so explicit and the Catholic faithful sufficiently informed that interpreting the virginal conception as merely symbolic would imply heresy. Only in some intellectual circles were radical evolutionary models proposed for a kind of development in the Gospel tradition, so that historicity could be fully eliminated. Yet, assuming a late provenance (and thus dubious historicity) for the traditions about Jesus' origins fostered an exegetical climate in which, even for Luke (in spite of Lk 1:1-4), the burden of proof to show that the Evangelists meant real history began to shift over to the exegete. The exegetical language often became slick, calculating the Evangelist's degree of creativity when inventing "stories" for expressing abstract truths.[265] When the "Two-Source" theory about the date and origin of the Synoptic Gospels, previously banned by the Pontifical Biblical Commission,[266] was allowed to be

---

body who does not believe in it, you should leave him alone in peace." Kasper adds that, contrary to Rahner's advice, he found no peace and continued investigating the issue in the early Church Fathers, all attributing very high importance to Mary's perpetual virginity. To be exact, we must observe that Rahner speaks in the story about the virginal conception and not only of *virginitas in partu*.

[265] This is just a step away from Bultmann's position. Originally the *Formgeschichte* spoke of an "unspeakable mystery" as "das Kultmysterium" which needed indirect expression in mythical terms. Hence the expression of "demythologization" (*Entmythologisierung*) came about as a goal for form critics. In the later trend of *Redaktionsgeschichte*, the new paradigm implied that wherever the presence of sources was not clear or not provably certain, one was entitled to *suspect* that the redactor was the author posing as a redactor. This is how, in many eyes, Luke lost his historical credibility.

[266] Denzinger-Schönmetzer, *Enchiridion Symbolorum*, 36th ed. (Freiburg in Br.: Herder, 1976), n. 3573.

adopted by Catholic scholars, it quickly gained acceptance among Catholics, bringing with it the acceptance of the historical and theological primacy of the Gospel of Mark, with no material about Jesus' childhood and mother. This resulted in a further de-emphasis of Mariology.[267]

Therefore, in the minds of the experts in biblical studies, even Mary's virginity *ante partum* was compromised as being of questionable historicity. Yet, for the faithful at large, the dogma was still anchored in history mostly because of the strength of the traditional understanding of the biblical texts and also, at least partly, because of conservative Protestants, mostly evangelicals, who kept on promoting the historicity of the Bible and in particular, the Evangelist Luke's image as a historian.[268]

Excursus: Pre-Conciliar Controversy about Mary's Virginity *in Partu*

That the patristic doctrine of Mary's perpetual virginity began to approach a crisis well before Vatican II can be illustrated by a debate about Mary's virginity that was restricted to relatively small scholarly circles, but was all the more real. It began with a controversial publication by a Viennese physician-priest, Adolph Mitterer,[269] and continued at the Faculty of Theology of the University of Innsbruck in Austria, with a dissertation by W. Zauner lending support to Mitterer's position. The debate quickly obtained additional publicity when a response was written to Mitterer by a rising

---

[267] Joseph A. Fitzmyer lists the bare minimum that a Catholic exegete must hold as historical from the common content of Mt 1-2 and Lk 1-2, with explicit reference to the theory of Markan priority: *Luke the Theologian. Aspects of His Teaching* (New York/Mahwah: Paulist Press, 1989), 27-79.

[268] I. Howard Marshall, *The Gospel of Luke: The International Greek New Testament Commentary* (Grand Rapids: Eerdmans, 1978), 63. E.E. Ellis, *The Gospel of Luke, The New Century Bible Commentary* (Grand Rapids: Eerdmans, 1980), 71. When treating the historicity of Luke's Infancy Narratives, *The New Jerome Biblical Commentary* repeatedly quotes I.H. Marshall.

[269] *Dogma und die Biologie der Heiligen Familie* (Wien: Herder, 1952).

star of Catholic theology, Karl Rahner.[270]

Dr. Mitterer did not mean to challenge any dogma, but he only asked for what he called "a revision" of the concept of Mary's virginity *in partu.* Mitterer claimed that true maternity was in contradiction to the traditional concept that Mary's virginity had been preserved while she was giving birth. A birth-mother cannot be assigned a merely passive role in giving birth as if the infant would simply pass through her body, causing no pain and leaving behind no physical trace. The child's miraculous exit from the womb would be at odds with a sound concept of physical motherhood. In his view, the preservation of Mary's physical integrity is untenable not so much because it is miraculous, but because it contradicts motherhood's important transformative functions in the mother's organism. So, for example, the mother's ability to nurse her child is incompatible with biological virginity.[271] The legendary stories about Mary's miraculous parturition are not only lacking historical evidence, but, besides contradicting medical science, they are also at odds with the dogma of her divine motherhood. Mitterer proposed a simple thesis: Mary bore Jesus by a thoroughly normal process of parturition, which was "miraculous" only insofar as it did not result from previous sexual intercourse.

Rahner, then professor of fundamental theology, was mostly interested in the debate for methodological reasons. Allegedly, the Council of Trent left open the question whether or not Tradition alone – with no scriptural proof – can provide a sufficient basis for dogma. This was, of course, a question closely connected with the "two sources of revelation" (Scripture and Tradition), at the time probably the hottest issue in fundamental theology. Rahner's article was included in a *Festschrift* honoring Joseph Geiselman, the theolo-

---

[270] In English, "Virginitas *in partu,*" *Theological Investigations* III (Baltimore: Helikon, 1966) III, 134-172.

[271] Mitterer as a priest must have been aware of the texts of the liturgy (the old Roman Breviary he was using as a seminarian and a priest) coming from late antiquity about Mary's nursing her Child. These texts were of course assuming that a "virgin" able to nurse her Child was in itself miraculous, part of the miracle of the virginal conception.

gian who claimed to have shown that the Council of Trent left open this issue of the "sources of revelation" so that, contrary to what most handbooks taught, Catholic theologians would remain free to join the Lutherans in requiring scriptural proof for all dogmas.[272] Thus Mitterer's thesis suddenly obtained both additional importance for theology and ecumenism as well as unexpected publicity. In his response Rahner showed all signs of a thoroughly researched study involving, as it seemed, the entire Mariological dossier of the first four Christian centuries.[273] As expected, he showed that Mitterer's thesis did not fully satisfy the standards of traditional orthodoxy. However, in spite of all this ammunition, he abstained from firing the last salvo: he did not clearly and plainly conclude that Mitterer's position was incompatible with the standards of Catholic faith. Instead, he came up with a tortuous non-committal conclusion questioning not only Mitterer but also Church Tradition: the manner in which Mary's "unique, miraculous, and 'virginal'" childbearing is traditionally taught "does not offer us the possibility of deducing assertions about the concrete details of the process in a way that it would be *certain* and *universally* binding."[274] Of course, such a conclusion left the reader unsettled. For in these words Rahner suggested that, at least in this one case, Tradition alone did not manage to produce a fully binding dogma. Moreover, if the Church's Tradition is insufficiently specific, and lacks universally binding force, how can we still speak of "the dogma" of Mary's perpetual virginity? And, we may add, why was this not noticed for the last millennium?

---

[272] Geiselman proved that the Council of Trent intentionally left the question of the two sources open. Thus, contrary to what was taught in many post-Tridentine textbooks, the Council did not teach that Scripture and Tradition were, indeed, two materially separable sources. One may, therefore, without falling into the heretical position of "sola Scriptura," require that all Catholic doctrine be based on *some* scriptural evidence.

[273] In Germany it was well known that Karl Rahner's older brother, Hugo Rahner, also a Jesuit professor of Theology in Innsbruck, was regarded as one of the greatest authorities on patristic Mariology.

[274] Ibid., 172. This text is quoted verbatim from its English translation in order to reproduce the place of Rahner's own quotation marks around "virginity" and *his italics* highlighting *certain* and *universally*.

It seems that from the beginning Karl Rahner felt uncomfortable with some aspects of the dogma. This is manifest in the ease with which, right at the beginning of the article, he admits that the metaphors used by the Church Fathers to illustrate Mary's virginity *in partu* (passing through "closed gates" or "penetrating walls") reveal a "tinge of docetism." This flippant remark, threatening to undermine his own thesis, is left unsubstantiated for the rest of the article. One must also remark that many biblical scholars and Catholic theologians have pointed out that the same metaphors are used in the canonical Gospels about the risen body of Christ (Jn 20:26; Lk 24:31, 36) with no "tinge of docetism."

Throughout the article, in spite of his thorough patristic documentation, Rahner failed to mention the most ancient literary source about Mary's miraculous parturition: the *Proto-evangelium of James*. The reason is easy to guess: in modern Catholic apologetics, the *Proto-evangelium* was held in low esteem, and was handled with considerable embarrassment. As we saw in a previous chapter, before De Strycker's critical edition, most critics followed the conjectures by Adolph von Harnack, claiming that the *Proto-evangelium*, like so many other "infancy Gospels," had no other preoccupation than sprinkling Jesus' origins with miracle stories and providing empirical proofs for Mary's virginity *in partu*.

Rahner apparently never studied the *Proto-evangelium* or the literature about it very seriously. Otherwise he would have known that the text was considered by such authorities as the textual critic Tischendorf to belong to the 2nd century. Also, he would have been surprised that, contrary to the claim that the text was mainly intent on providing a clinical proof of Mary's virginity *in partu*, it narrates that a midwife, attempting to obtain such evidence, had her hand burned off. A careful reading of the document could have convinced Rahner that, already in the 2nd century, Jesus' birth and Mary's virginal parturition were described first and foremost as a *sacred* event beyond the reach of an empirical proof.

Rahner's soft handling of Mitterer might have been based on an erroneous premise. He accepted Mitterer's *status quaestionis* that

Tradition was focusing on physical virginity, and now it had to be treated within the well-defined terms of modern medicine. In retrospect, the Mitterer-Rahner dialogue appears to be based on sheer absurdity: Church Fathers vs. modern medicine discussing questions of gynecology! Such perspectives necessarily make the traditional witnesses, biblical or patristic, appear naïve and painfully outdated. It gave the impression that, when speaking of Mary's "virginal motherhood," the Church Fathers promoted for the Mother of the Messiah a culturally prestigious physical and social status current in Hellenism, while, in reality, either from a Hebrew or a modern point of view (this latter developed by Mitterer), the concept of a person, both "virgin and mother," must be regarded as an abnormal, even unhealthy physical and psychological condition. The debate never focused on the real question: Why did Mary's virginity so quickly obtain such a high importance in the early Church? And conversely, what were the core issues of the classical 4th century heresies about Mary's virginity (Helvidius, Jovinian, and Bonosus) and of the Church Fathers' adamant resistance in response to them? Why was it so important for the latter to assert that her virginity was preserved?

An answer could have been found only by identifying the theological context. We saw that for Rahner the fascination was an issue of theological methodology: Can a dogma be upheld without scriptural proof? Is Mary's virginity *in partu* a valid example of a dogma asserted by the Magisterium with no valid scriptural evidence?[275] The Church Fathers' outlook was different. They developed their Mariology in close association not only with Christology, but also with a nascent theology of Christian perfection, consecrated virginity, and monasticism. Their theological method was also rooted in the concrete graces and gifts of actual Christian lives.

This neglect of the theological context of patristic Mariology was present even at the Second Vatican Council. Its texts about Mary

---

[275] For Rahner the answer he wanted was "probably not." By such evidence he was able to support Geiselman's thesis about the "sources" of revelation: that neither *sola scriptura* nor *sola traditio* corresponds to the teaching of Trent.

quote the Church Fathers with little or no reflection on the context of consecrated life. For example, *Lumen Gentium*, speaking of Mary's virginity *in partu*, quotes a most profound sentence by St. Ambrose: the birth of her Son "did not diminish the integrity of [Mary's] virginity but rather sanctified it" (*non deminuit sed consacravit*).[276] Yet no reference is made to the original context of this famous sentence: the context of consecrated virginity. The Council's decree on religious life, *Perfectae Caritatis*, mentions Mary only once (no. 25), when formulating a pious wish for Mary's intercessions, whose life is "a model for all." This quotation also comes from St. Ambrose, from his treatise *De Virginitate*, stating that Mary's way of life – described in long chapters as that of a consecrated virgin – is *imago virginitatis* (archetype or model of *virginal life*) so that "this *one* (Virgin's) life may become the model of *all* (virgins)."[277] *Perfectae Caritatis* changes what Ambrose meant by presenting Mary as model for all Christians. The result is certainly a true statement, but Ambrose did not say or mean it in this text, while in its original sense it could have had its place in a document on consecrated life.

Post-Conciliar Mariology

The Excursus above might seem disheartening and could even lead to a false impression, misrepresenting the facts. The Council has not only spelled out the basics of Catholic Mariology, it has also given a new incentive to Mariology – exactly by its controversial decision to include its text on Mary in a document on the Church, prompting post-Conciliar theology to explore Mary as exemplar and full realization of what the Church is supposed to be and becomes at the end of times. Pope Paul's deep and filial devotion to the Blessed Virgin was always beyond doubt. Only those who apply "an exegesis of suspicion" to the teachings and leadership of this Pope could speak of a failure of the papacy to defend and promote Marian piety.

---

[276] *De institutione virginum* (PL 60, 320).

[277] *Haec est imago virginitatis: ut eius unius vita omnium sit disciplina* (II, 2. 15).

But Mariology in the post-Conciliar years remains difficult to evaluate, for we lack the historical perspective for discerning the interplay of the forces which had a role in it. We cannot miss the fact that some of the most important names among the representatives of the "new theology" kept publishing on Mary, and some of them, indeed, amidst a slowly growing polarization of Catholic theology into "progressive" and "conservative," were categorized with those shifting to the conservative wing by trying to slow down or even stop the transformation of theology into a pluralistic and open system ready to cut ties with any "school theology" of the past. Publications by these theologians, some of the most shining names of the Conciliar discussions, like Henri de Lubac,[278] Yves Congar,[279] Hans Urs von Baltasar, and Joseph Ratzinger[280] were eventually translated into English as well, so that their pre-Conciliar works had a delayed impact on the new Mariology as it developed.

Yet the personal story of the best known French specialist of Mariology, René Laurentin, quoted in this book's previous chapters, may reveal another side of the story. In his studies, he specialized on the Gospels and Mariology. His book on the Lucan Infancy Narratives suddenly earned him the reputation of a competent biblical scholar. He covered the procedures of Vatican II with well-informed and insightful reports for several newspapers, most regularly for *La Croix*, the largest French Catholic weekly. He was an unabashed supporter of the so-called "progressive" camp, applauding its success in taking over the leadership of the Council. Less than two decades after the Council, Laurentin had to realize that he was "left behind" by new Catholic biblical scholarship, rejecting most of his previous publications and his general approach to the study of the Synoptic Gospels. Teaming up with some other French luminaries (most importantly Claude Tresmontant and Jean Carmignac), he began to

---

[278] *The Motherhood of the Church* (San Francisco: Ignatius Press, 1982), the French original from 1971.

[279] His most important post-Conciliar contribution for Mariology may be also his synthesis of Pneumatology: *I Believe in the Holy Spirit* 1 (New York: Seabury, 1983).

[280] Joseph Card. Ratzinger and Hans Urs von Balthasar, *Mary: The Church at the Source* (San Francisco: Ignatius Press, 2005); originally in German from 1997.

fight the new biblical scholarship in Gospel studies, characterized by redaction criticism and the rapid spread of the so-called Two-Source Theory, embracing Markan priority and relativizing the historical credibility of the accounts about Jesus' origin and childhood (Mt 1-2 and Lk 1-2). By the mid-1980s, Laurentin, as well as Carmignac and Tresmontant, were isolated and declared to be representatives of a reactionary pre-Conciliar scholarship. Laurentin's exceptionally informed theological survey of Mariology was denied international exposure. His *Court Traité de Théologie Mariale*[281] remained untranslated, and even his outstanding post-Conciliar works in Mariology failed to obtain the international attention and recognition they deserved. This may appear to be just a sad, melodramatic story; one should certainly caution against undue generalizations. German publications not only by Balthasar and Ratzinger but several other outstanding scholars like (later cardinal) Leo Scheffczyk[282] or Georg Söll[283] continued to signal that the Council, like a good tree, had borne many good fruits, and ultimately Catholic Marian doctrine was still a vital part of Catholic thought and life.

The Council's teaching about Mary focused, of course, on the topic "Mary and the Church." We will deal with this theme more systematically in the next Chapter. But it must be mentioned right away in this context that in this respect the Council fully carried out the goal set out at its convocation by John XXIII. That Mary is the "Exemplar" or "Archetype" of the Church was an age-old theological insight, which, however, in the course of the centuries had been marginalized and forgotten, mostly because in the post-Reformation times ecclesiology was damaged and distorted by incessant apologetic preoccupations about the human face of the Church, the Church as a human institution. Yet the patristic and medieval texts about Mary and the Church awaited rediscovery and a re-integration into

---

[281] Paris: Lethielleux, 1953.
[282] Leo Scheffczyk, *Die Mariengestalt im Gefüge der Theologie. Mariologische Beiträge* (Regensburg: Pustet, 2000).
[283] Georg Söll, "Mariologie," in *Handbuch der Dogmengeschichte* III/4 (Freiburg/Basel/Wien: Herder, 1978), 193-215.

the new developments in ecclesiology, which culminated in *Gaudium et Spes*, the Council's document on the Church.[284]

What the theologians of the post-Conciliar decades accomplished in Mariology may remain to some extent debatable. In 1983, Karl Rahner called Marian piety of the day, in comparison to earlier times, "abstract and anemic (blutleer)."[285] He was probably right. But he did not live long enough to experience the extraordinary impact that the Pope of his last days, John Paul II, was about to make on the Church during his long years of service at the helm of the Church. The whole world watched in awe, holding its breath, when this Pope returned to his native land and went in procession with a million Poles to Poland's Marian shrine of Czestochowa. Soon thereafter, on May 13, 1981, the anniversary day of the Marian apparition in Fatima in 1917, came the assassination attempt that John Paul II barely survived. He himself said of this event:

> Could I forget that the event in St. Peter's Square took place on the day and at the hour when the first appearance of the Mother of Christ to the poor little peasants has been remembered for over sixty years at Fátima, Portugal? For in everything that happened to me on that very day, I felt an extraordinary motherly protection and care, which turned out to be stronger than the deadly bullet.

This kind of "discourse" may go well beyond the limits of theological discourse within which this book must remain. Yet the extraordinary Marian piety of this Pope, whose election and style of papacy cannot be conceived independently of the Second Vatican Council, might have made the largest impact on the Church's Marian devotion after the Council.

---

[284] Best proof for these statements is the fact that a marvelous text, practically forgotten, by the 12th century monk Blessed Isaac of Stella, was rediscovered and "unearthed" when it was inserted into a footnote of *Gaudium et Spes*, became a permanent part of the new Roman Breviary, and has inspired a number of studies after the Council. See above pp. 192-193 and below on pages 302-305.

[285] "Mut zur Marienverehrung," *Geist und Leben* 56 (1983), 164.

Blessed John Paul II took up an unsettled issue that had been simmering for a long time, flaring up only occasionally in the centuries. When speaking about Ambrose's Mariology we indicated above how a Synod of Rome condemned Jovinian for his denial of the special spiritual value of consecrated virginity and celibacy.[286] The Council of Trent, while ultimately presenting no decree on the Church's teaching on Mary, chose to include into its "Canones" about the sacrament of matrimony a strong defense of religious life, in a language similar to the old Roman Synod of the 4th century: "He who says that the conjugal state is to be preferred to the state of virginity or celibacy and that it is not better and more blessed to remain a virgin or celibate than to enter in matrimony, should be rejected (*anathema sit*)."[287] This "canon" cites in a footnote its biblical sources: Matthew 19:11-12; 1 Corinthians 7:25-26, which in fact provide a context for its meaning. The comparison of these states of life (marriage on the one hand and consecrated life on the other) was, to my knowledge, never taken up at Vatican II and with utmost certainty the statement quoted above from the Council of Trent has fallen into general oblivion. It was a special merit of Pope John Paul II, with his ardent Marian devotion, persuasive ministry on behalf of Christian marriage, defense of a celibate priesthood and vigorous promotion of religious vocations to provide guidance on this issue. Because of its importance, we must quote a whole paragraph from his Apostolic Exhortation *Familiaris Consortio*, published in 1981:

> Virginity or celibacy for the sake of the Kingdom of God not only does not contradict the dignity of marriage but presupposes it and confirms it. Marriage and virginity or celibacy are two ways of expressing and living the one mystery of the covenant of God with His people. When marriage is not esteemed, neither can consecrated vir-

---

[286] See above on pp. 124-125.

[287] "Si quis dixerit, statum conjugalem anteponendum esse statui virginitatis vel coelibatus, et non esse melius ac beatius, manere in virginitate vel coelibatu, quam iungi matrimonio: A.S." (Denzinger-Schönmetzer 980).

ginity or celibacy exist; when human sexuality is not regarded as a great value given by the Creator, the renuncia-
tion of it for the sake of the Kingdom of Heaven loses its
meaning. (II,16)

This paragraph could not have come about without the theological insights on which Vatican II was based. By drawing attention
to the oneness of the Mystery of the Covenant, it has with a sure
hand pointed out that married and consecrated life are not antithetic
and must not be regarded as if in competition. The term "for the
sake of the Kingdom" indicates that the Pope uses the same biblical foundation which appears in the text of the Council of Trent:
Matthew 19:11-12, in which Jesus himself explains celibate commitment and that of some of his disciples, without putting into doubt
the sacred character of a marital participation in the mystery of the
Covenant. One must say that John Paul II completed and advanced
the doctrine of the Council, a legacy of which he remained a faithful
steward throughout his papacy.

While continuing vigorously to defend marriage as a sacred
and covenantal bond, John Paul II's successor, Benedict XVI, further
strengthened the conviction that Catholic Mariology is rooted much
more deeply than any "abstract and anemic" rational discourse that
our present-day culture would force us to pursue. Consider these
words from his homily before the Marian shrine of Altötting in
Bavaria on Sept. 11, 2006, where he spoke of Mary as a "woman of
prayer" at the scene of the wedding feast in Cana:

The "yes" of the Son: "I have come to do your will," and
the "yes" of Mary: "Let it be with me according to your
word" – this double "yes" becomes a single "yes," and
thus the Word becomes flesh in Mary. In this double
"yes" the obedience of the Son is embodied, and by her
own "yes" Mary gives him that body. "Woman, what
have I to do with you?" Ultimately, what each has to do
with the other is found in this double "yes" which resulted

in the Incarnation. The Lord's answer points to this point of profound unity. It is precisely to this that he points his Mother. Here, in their common "yes" to the will of the Father, an answer is found. We too need to learn always anew how to progress towards this point; there we will find the answer to our questions.

With these words, Pope Benedict emphasized the profound and directive truth to be found in the complete reality of Mary's relationship to her Son and God; it is far from anemic. But we certainly need a broader perspective and more time to evaluate closely how Catholic Marian doctrine and piety have developed in these two important pontificates, both so closely linked to and reflecting upon the work of the Second Vatican Council. These participants and promoters of the Council have undoubtedly become the most important and effective stewards of its legacy.

CHAPTER TEN

THE MARIAN MYSTERY: ROAD TO A SYNTHESIS

Obstacles to a Renewed Mariology

In the last years preceding the Second Vatican Council, well before interest in Mariology began to wane, theologians of high reputation opened the investigation into Mariology's "fundamental principle," or, in Karl Rahner's words, *das Grundprinzip der Mariologie*. A first attempt at building Mariology upon such a fundamental principle came from Otto Semmelroth.[288] For some time, Karl Rahner also pursued this question with special interest, and his essays elicited responses and publications from other theologians.[289] During the post-Conciliar years, however, this subject drew little further interest, since a new phase in the history of Catholic theology began in which the method of systematic or dogmatic theology assumed central role and needed to confront much broader questions.[290] Due to the structure and message of the Council's Dogmatic Constitu-

---

[288] Otto Semmelroth, *Urbild der Kirche. Organischer Aufbau des Mariengeheimnisses* (Würzburg, 1950).

[289] In his summary about (speculative) Mariology Fr. Soujeole indicates three basic options: 1. Divine motherhood, 2. Mary as Socia Christi, and 3. Mary the perfectly redeemed creature. Cf. Benoit-Dominique Soujeole, *Initiation à la thèologie mariale* (Toulouse/Fribourg: Parole et Silence, 2007).

[290] *"...die in vollkommenster Weise Erlöste," Die Frage nach einem mariologischen Grundprinzip bei Karl Rahner* (Norderstedt: Grin Verlag, 2005), a dissertation written by Magnus Kerkloh at the University of Münster, summarizes the impact of Rahner's *Grundprinzip*.

tion on the Church, *Lumen Gentium*, Mariology was expected to fall in step with ecclesiology or even enlist in the renewed enterprise of the theology of the Church.

Ecclesiology did indeed unfurl and blossom suddenly, drawing extraordinary interest; but Mariology – which the so-called "progressive wing" wanted to promote as part of ecclesiology – began to wither in the confusing climate of the post-Conciliar transformations of theological method. So the debate on the *Grundprinzip* made little further progress. Regardless of the various positions calling for either a more "positive" or more "speculative" orientation for the Mariology of the future, biblical studies began to dominate it, as historical and critical exegesis imposed its militant agenda upon most theological disciplines. In such a context *biblical* Mariology could only diminish; and, in fact, it became circumspect and anxious, pondering with busy solicitude all exegetical details, but collapsing on the critical and historical evaluation of Luke 1-2 and of a few verses in the Johannine Gospel. Historical critics either found too little about Mary in the Bible, or proposed more or less explicitly the revision of the Marian dogmas. Previous attempts to rescue patristic exegesis by merging it with what modern Catholic exegetes were calling the "plenary sense" of the Scriptures lost credibility. Consequently, a major part of patristic Mariology, heavily engaged in various theological, symbolic, and allegorical interpretations of the Old Testament, lost the little respect they had managed to gain while, in French theology, the *movement biblique* and the *movement patristique* had regarded each other as the major partners in the enterprise of *la nouvelle théologie*.[291] More and more clamorous voices began to denounce the patristic approach to Mariology as arbitrary or even meaningless. Those proposing a Mariology based on the exegesis of the two Testaments became significantly isolated from the mainstream of theological literature.

---

[291] We are speaking of about twenty years (1945-1965) between the Second World War and the end of the Second Vatican Council. These "movements" are still presented as part of a program for the future by Roger Aubert, *La théologie catholique au milieu du XXe siècle* [Catholic Theology in the Middle of the 20th Century] (Paris: Aubier, 1956).

In Catholic Synoptic studies after Vatican II, as also in other camps, the so-called "two-source theory" declared itself the winner of all previous debates,[292] and New Testament theology was forced to rally around the standard of basing all arguments on the Gospel of Mark, Q and the seven authentic Pauline letters (Romans, Galatians, 1 Thessalonians, 1-2 Corinthians, Philippians, and Philemon). While even within these writings not all material was equally "certified" by the critics as historically trustworthy, other writings outside of this group became all the more suspect of being nothing more than the theological constructs of the post-apostolic Church and their respective authors or redactors, mostly anonymous and unusually creative.

Such a theological method was clearly unable to provide the solid foundation that systematic Mariology was seeking; it could never dig deep enough to get past the doubts and difficulties, most of all doubts about the very fact and meaning of Mary's virginal and divine motherhood. Though these surfaced in academic circles as early as the Mitterer/Rahner debate, they were never resolved, but only temporarily silenced. But the practice of silencing debates with authoritarian interventions – still in vogue in the final pre-Conciliar years – was largely abandoned after Vatican II. So the gaping discontinuities in teaching and the wobbling uncertainties voiced by "progressive" theologians destroyed the little confidence still given to patristic Mariology.

In addition to this general methodological impasse, matters of theological anthropology set another huge obstacle in the path of a

---

[292] Markan priority was rejected and not allowed to be taught in Catholic seminaries and universities for quite a few decades by the anti-modernist censures of the Pontifical Biblical Commission. But already under the pontificate of Pius XII, it was treated as an issue open to free debate. In 1956, in an article written by Athanasius Miller, OSB, the secretary of the Pontifical Biblical Commission at the time, it was made clear that "responses" of the Biblical Commission about the Synoptic question, issued some fifty years earlier, were not to be regarded [any longer] as censures but directives and, therefore, those topics could be discussed freely in scholarly debate. The documentation is easily available also in English in Joseph A. Fitzmyer, *The Biblical Commission's Document, "The Interpretation of the Bible in the Church"* (Rome: Editrice Pontificio Istituto Biblico, 1995), 22.

Mariological renewal. On the one hand the thesis of a "helleniza-tion of Christianity" was likely to turn the study of the Mariology of the Church Fathers into a "theology of suspicion" similar to the suspicion that began to surround "biblical Mariology" and exegesis in general. We might say that another set of unresolved issues came from the negative reception – at least negative "press" – that the en-cyclical *Humani generis* had faced in the last years of the pontificate of Pius XII. These unresolved questions included the origin of hu-man life (a debate about so-called *monogenesis*, the origin of man-kind from a single couple), which, as we have seen, is one of the solid assumptions of patristic Mariology and the theology of original sin. But the whole issue of *hominization*, the origin of the human race in history and in the womb, was hijacked by specialists in paleontology and evolutionary biology, because theologians wanted direct con-nection to "concrete facts" and were not satisfied with philosophical renditions of the human soul, the creation of the human species, the individual soul created by God at the moment of conception, and similar presuppositions of the faith. The lack of clarity in these mat-ters continuing to this day was all too nervously dramatized by theo-logians.

An honest analysis, then, must say that a topic as complex as Mariology was doomed to a post-Conciliar crisis: philosophical studies in Catholic seminaries and universities were in serious disre-pair, biblical studies had become aggressively critical, and the patris-tic tradition was likewise subjected to such research, and thus neither the Bible nor the Church Fathers seemed capable of offering a suf-ficiently stable point of departure. At the same time, Mariology, like all other theological fields, needed firm anthropological foundations; otherwise the "biblical material" reduces itself to mere narratives, concepts, and titles with no reference to their ultimate meaning, to their truth and reality. Discussing birth, conception, motherhood, body and soul, creation and eschatology, resurrection and participa-tion in divine life requires philosophically identifiable meaning, or else theology does not surpass philology and textual interpretation. Theology must surpass them, or give the lie to faith; yet few factors before, during, or after the Council were poised to help.

The demise of modern Mariology is also a symptom of another development, fully part of our recent history, though elusive and obscure. There is firm statistical evidence that beginning in the last thirty to forty years of the 20th century, religious life or as we call it today "consecrated life," suffered enormous setbacks. In spite of considerable literature about the topic, hardly anyone seems to know the "real story" of what happened. In a few decades, old and venerable institutions crumbled for no demonstrable, cogent reason, so that one must seriously ask: What on earth happened? We know many details and factors, but a convincing story with clear "cause and effect" relationships has not been told. This directly concerns the state of Mariology. Since the 2nd century, Mary as the archetype of the Church and of Christian perfection has been a constant influence in Catholic Christian spirituality. Consecrated life has usually provided the regular audience of Marian sermons, treatises, commentaries, and theological debates. Religious communities have almost always been the promoters of Marian festivities and celebrations. But all we can conclude with certainty is that revitalizing and reconstructing Mariology is intimately connected to the task of re-awakening religious vocations. But conversely, only a re-awakened religious life can lead the contemporary Church back to a badly needed spring of Marian spirituality and theology.

Mary and the Incarnation

Thomistic Mariology proposed divine motherhood as Mariology's fundamental principle, on which alone a synthetic and systematic vision of the Marian mystery can be based.[293] This is a classical position, easy to accept, provided we take the Incarnation not as a merely theoretical principle but as a fact. Fr. Soujeole, a Dominican who has recently published a mostly speculative Mariology in

---

[293] Fr. Soujeole refers for this thesis to an article by the French Dominican M.-J. Nicolas, "Le concept intégral de la maternité divine" in *Revue Thomiste* 42 (1937).

French, calls divine motherhood the key principle of Mariology (*principe clef*) but quickly corrects any possible misunderstanding by stating that he is not speaking of a theoretical principle, but of a foundational or originating fact (*un fait originel*) on which the rest of Mariology lies. I would advance a further refinement: In its function of "founding" Mariology, the Incarnation cannot be regarded as a static fact, occurring once for all and thus constituting an ontological "state of affairs." Human existence is dynamic. Thus, to consider the Incarnation an instantaneous fact is not false, only incomplete. That the Logos becomes man is *fieri*, i.e., a process. This means that when the Logos became flesh, the Son began to receive his divine nature from the Father in a new mode too. He, the Second Person of the Trinity, subjected himself to a human, historical *becoming*. This began when he entered his Mother's womb. Then, through an extended process of growth and maturation, this individual human nature reached the point of becoming viable. Once born, he begins to run the course of a human destiny, meandering through Judaea and Galilee, a destiny culminating at its τέλος on the Cross (in the cry of τετέλεσται in Jn 19:39); and only then did his humanity enter the glory of heaven and arrive to the bosom of the Father. At that point he transports into God's life a humanity newly made, or more exactly "re-made" (re-born), by the Resurrection. But this return to the Father is also a process: on the morning of the third day it is extended to all mankind, the just of the Old Covenant, those to be evangelized in every time and place, all who previously lived, and all who are to enter life in the future.

As a consequence of this anthropological insight, we cannot treat Mary's place and role in the Incarnation in pin-point fashion, making sole reference to an *assumptus homo*, a human being taken from her womb, such that once her physical maternity terminates in a felicitous birth, Jesus would leave behind her womb and her person, body and soul. God is not merely making the human body and soul of Jesus his own (*Deus assumens*) as an instantaneous act of self-possession, then to begin an independent life apart from a "rented womb." The unfolding of the mystery has its beginning in something far beyond the level of mere human nature and a transitory act of miraculous impregnation. That the eternal Son becomes a human offspring means that *the Son in the bosom of the Father* becomes *a son in the womb of Mary*, emerging into the midst of this world.

It is a post-lapsarian world that the Son enters, a world where suffering and mortality are inseparable from fleshly existence. Yet this is never just a sad coincidence, or an incidental circumstance of the Incarnation; the Fathers repeatedly emphasized its mysterious importance by saying that the Son, incapable of suffering in his divine nature and condition (*impassibilis in suis*), received from Mary the flesh of Adam to become *passibilis* and even *mortalis in nostris* (in our nature and condition). His flesh bears the consequences of sin, but it is not the flesh of a sinner, not even that of a sinner cleansed and redeemed afterwards. Rather, it is flesh taken from a daughter of Adam whom God, in virtue of Jesus' redeeming death, preserved from sin. In order for Jesus to become the Redeemer of all mankind, his humanity originated with no contact with sin and yet carrying all consequences of sin: mortal, vulnerable, knowing every human misery except sin itself.

This human nature, being totally alien to sin, was even more vulnerable and sensitive to all suffering caused by sin. The same is to be said about Mary, whose sinlessness was exposed to the height of suffering at the sight of her Son betrayed, tortured, rejected, physically abused, and unjustly, yet hypocritically, executed. It is neither mere poetic exuberance nor creative imagination for combining unrelated texts that leads the Church to apply Lamentations 1:12 liturgically first to the Lord's suffering then to his Virgin Mother's: *O vos omnes qui transitis per viam, adtendite et videte si est dolor sicut dolor meus*, "O you who pass by on the road, look and see if there is any suffering like my suffering!"

In the Incarnation, then, the Son fully subjected himself to our way of existence and made a tool of salvation out of our way of life. Or rather, our way of death: living his life in a fallen world, Jesus accomplished the work of redemption by going through each and every step of dying, which obliges us all. But he took these steps of suffering freely, with full liberty, and thus lifted our way of existence up into an expression of supreme love: the fullest extent of a love taken to its ultimate end. By suffering with love, he laid a pathway for all the redeemed to enter a "Passover," a *transitus*, a going over from death to life.[294]

Mary is more than merely the first step of this *transitus*: when the Eternal Son becomes her Son, the process of his bearing human life up into divine life remains forever characterized by the humanity of Mary. She is, so to say, the permanent point of departure for the unfolding of the mystery, the link between man's first creation and the re-birth brought about by her Son. In the theology of the two "Adams," "Adam, the first human being" and "Christ, the second Adam" are not merely ancestor and offspring, as if Jesus were just one of the many members of the human race issued from the first Adam. He is indeed a descendant of the first man. In this sense, Jesus is a sharer of the one and same nature endowed by God to the first human man – a nature extended by a procreative chain to all human beings.[295] Each one of us in this chain continues and extends the one single act of God in which he created man, and so we all are taken from the previously created matter of the earth and receive the breath of life that turned Adam into a living being, made to God's image and likeness also in precisely this sense, that we are capable of transferring his life – his specifically defined human life – to newly created members of the race originating with him. The second Adam, being an Adamite, takes his life from this race; but he is sinless, and his created body and soul are in personal union with

---

[294] See Jn 13:1: "Jesus, knowing that his hour had come to pass from this world to the Father, having loved those who were his in the world, loved them to the end" (εἰδὼς ὁ Ἰησοῦς ὅτι ἦλθεν αὐτοῦ ἡ ὥρα ἵνα μεταβῇ ἐκ τοῦ κόσμου τούτου πρὸς τὸν πατέρα, ἀγαπήσας τοὺς ἰδίους τοὺς ἐν τῷ κόσμῳ εἰς τέλος ἠγάπησεν αὐτούς).

[295] This model implies monogenism and excludes hominization as the step-by-step "emergence." One may or may not accept the thesis that one single "first mother" or "Eve" was the first female ancestor of all humans populating the earth today. This is a scientific, not theological theory, made popular by the Oxford geneticist, Robert Sykes, *The Seven Daughters of Eve* (London/New York: Norton, 2002). Based on evidences from DNA research, it allows that we speak about "a first ancestor" of mankind without entering into debates about evolution.

the Son who shares one nature with the Father. He is a son of the first Eve, but was not created from the craving of the flesh ("not born by human parents or by human desire or a husband's decision, but by God"[296]), but as the fruit of a new breathing of life from the mouth of God: an intervention of the Holy Spirit, extending the life of God's Son into the virginal womb of Mary. By Jesus' conception and birth, not only is the life of Adam (and of Eve taken from Adam's flesh) propagated once more, but the eternal filiation of the Son is transmitted into an individual human life. Mary is to be located within this twofold movement of human and divine lineage, which expands, as it were, in both directions: from the outpouring of Trinitarian life into human life, and the assumption of one individual human nature into the mystery of the divine filiation, springs a redemptive stream of life freshening the waters it meets and producing reborn human life – potentially for all mankind.

This movement took on three dimensions, we might say, when the humanity of Jesus was created by God at the Incarnation in the womb of the Virgin, from her body but without the participation of a male sperm. Even for that, Jesus was fully human, developing as a human being in the gradual, surprising, yet destined way that characterizes our maturation into adults. Jesus, however, is hypostatically united to the Godhead, and never becomes a human person apart from his being a Divine Person; the fullness of his personhood is from his Trinitarian relations to the Father and to the Spirit. That is to say, Jesus, though fully human, was not a "developing person," because his personhood does not derive from his being Mary's Son, but from his being that Person who is "the reflection of God's glory and the exact representation of God's being" (Heb 1:3): he is a person in the fullest and absolute sense of personhood on account of being the Son of God. *Homo factus ex Maria* – this is full entitlement to personhood; but it is super-eminently elevated to an absolute entitlement to an infinite degree of personhood – *Deus de Deo*. He is not created, not "made," – there was no time when he was not – and

---

[296] Jn 1:13 in the New English Version.

his personal subsistence did not begin in time.

We are here at the dense heart of the Marian mystery, where gravity seems to work differently and each statement falls back to the same Trinitarian and Christological truths. From this point of view, which is ontological, Mary's divine motherhood happened instantaneously. She was not more the Mother of God on Golgotha or at the Resurrection than she was at the conception of Jesus by the Holy Spirit. Yet this presence of God's Son in her as her Son, as an object of awareness and self-awareness, of conscious knowledge and emotional experience, was a dynamic reality, growing, perceived from different angles, under different aspects, with changing intensity. It was through a constant *fieri* that she learned about her Son and about herself, not in the sense that her Son became God, but because the eternal divine Person subjected himself to the exigencies of an individual nature involved in a normal process of human development. Also in this sense the Word became (ἐγένετο) man, he became the unchanging subject of becoming; he became man as we all do: ontologically in a single instant, but functionally step by step, learning to think, to judge, to decide, and to speak in the normal course of development and growth. In Jesus, a subject of human history, God embraced and appropriated for himself "human becoming." In him, God first becomes unborn, then a fully developed embryo, a newborn, a baby, a toddler, a youngster, a teenager, a man who physically and mentally grows. "Jesus advanced in wisdom and age and favor before God and man" (Lk 2:52).

Mary, elected, called, and carried to messianic and divine motherhood, arrived to the "peak season" of salvation history. There is something far more than private, something truly compendious and comprehensive, in her being the first to greet God among us, and to do so as one who was radically redeemed. Yet in her Child she encountered God as a subject of human growth and of a particular history. Mary's personal history, into which God enters, is the most sacred phase and locus of Israel's history. This is why patristic tradition found such a multitude of retrospective images from the beginnings, all pronounced without reservation: Mary as the Ark, Mary as the Temple, Mary as the chosen Daughter, the beloved Bride, the City of God, the Daughter of Zion, or the People of Israel as a whole. Israel's election is finalized, ratified, and sanctified by Mary's being chosen and made. She was pre-figured in particular by all saintly women of Israel, but also even further back by the very idea of human motherhood. In this sense she is the most beautiful woman in God's creation, and is thus also the woman created like a new Eve "from the side of the second Adam," when the latter fell asleep in his freely accepted sleep of death. The previous phases of sacred history not only prepared for Mary's arrival, but anticipated and pre-figured, indeed even mirrored and proleptically originated from this peak phase of God's dwelling among us in a constantly "developing" intimacy, growing and deepening, between the Lord and his people. As the Son's incarnate life inseparably anchors itself in the flesh, the immediate source and, in human terms, the full source of this flesh is the humanity of Mary. The human soul that animates it, by relating to it as "form to matter," is created in "con-formity" to the "form" (the soul) of the human composite which is Mary: she who receptively and unreservedly offered her being to serve as the source of God's Incarnation. Mary is that place where God becomes man from Adam's humanity. This is why the Church Fathers see in Mary a new Garden of Eden prepared for the new Adam.

Physically, of course, Jesus' body is earthbound and historically conditioned. It moves and changes with regard to space and time. He leaves Bethlehem just as he leaves Nazareth and ends the mortal life he took from Adam through his mother when he dies on the Cross. Yet this is only one aspect of the full reality of Jesus' human life. The God-Man with a human history and destiny sanctifies all phases of human life as he appropriates them as his own, and renews them, so that he may offer them in spotless and sinless novelty to the Father in one thanksgiving sacrifice. In Christ's life, all phases of human growth and all events of the human drama may be incorporated and become divine acts. They become divine as soon as he wills them: they become acts of the eternal Son. Not each in the same way, of course, but in an analogous sense, some only by being permitted, some by being posited in response to other persons, and some by being positively approved and affirmed. But in each case he, the Son of God, is their ultimate personal subject. Through every human act of Jesus, he, the eternal Son expresses himself through *his* human nature, body and soul, which subsists in the Son's divinity.

For Mary, this means that ontologically she is the Mother of God from the very beginning, but her motherhood obtains an ever new, concrete meaning and an increasing depth. As she grows in her understanding of the divine salvation plan, she also appropriates with more understanding and will the divine motherhood that, as a whole, she obtained in virtue of her first *fiat*. This same *fiat* broadens with time, is re-stated, as it were, with greater resonance in the process of her growing self-understanding; she extends the *fiat* to her whole life as part of the unfolding of the mystery. Mary lives in a maternal relationship that keeps developing in the course of Jesus' messianic life, from the Baptism in the Jordan through the various phases of her Son's proclamation of his message. These include encounters with the acceptance and rejection that her Son faces, all the many inner crises that split her family or the community of Nazareth, the Galilean countryside and the whole Jewish nation, bringing about "the falling and rising of many in Israel" and turning her Son's lifetime work into "a sign that is to be rejected" (Lk 2:34). Her motherhood is, therefore, rendered dynamic by its being attached to the events and relationships of Jesus' mysterious personal life, a chain of human experiences lived in consubstantial unity with the Triune God, progressing and rising above the waves of controversy, confrontation, and human failings within that society and historical period into which his life was inserted.

Of course, all this must be considered in accordance with the Johannine words: "He who has seen me has seen the Father" (Jn 14:9). Jesus and his life constitute a process of revelation. Throughout her life, Mary, who treasured the Child's infancy and her own life with him, becomes a receptacle of intimate experiences with her Child, who is the only center of her existence. Thus, her motherhood connects her to her Son's revelatory and redemptive journey. It matters little how much of this is described in the Gospels. Though mere glimpses of her involvement are indicated by one or another Gospel writer, we are privileged to observe her presence on the last trip to Jerusalem. At "the hour of Jesus," prophetically foretold to her in Cana, but now fulfilled as he is publicly executed before his Mother's eyes, we see the ultimate finally happen: she clings to the Beloved Disciple who, in his turn, clings to her, as they experience together what the "new birth" of humanity and the "new human sonship" had to mean. Both take their origin under the Cross: "behold your son – behold your mother" (Jn 19:27).

Messianic motherhood and divine motherhood are intimately connected: both are framed by the Gospel story of Jesus of Nazareth, God Incarnate, who is both Messiah and Son of God. Mary's motherhood of the risen Lord brings these two titles of Mary to a common conclusion, indicated in the briefest way at the beginning of the Church's first gathering after the Resurrection, as described by Luke in Acts. It is the first "plenary assembly" of the nascent Church with "Mary, the mother of Jesus and his brothers" (Ac 1:14) at the end of the list. All wait in expectation of the Holy Spirit, that he may launch the Incarnation of the Son into a worldwide movement of prayer and proclamation.

Beyond Marian Minimalism

To build upon the foregoing synthetic reflection on Mary's role in the Incarnation, we must resolve in some way the tensions of 20th century Mariology. As discussed earlier, shifts in theological thought and method prompted a certain marginalization of Mary in Catholic theology. A new theological "style" emerging after Vatican II led some to think that a new approach was needed in Mariology just as well. The final chapter of *Lumen Gentium* could not serve that purpose, because it was anything but new: it presented well-known, traditional teaching in classical terms. It is largely an echo of the patristic interpretation of the most important biblical texts about Mary, leaving in the shadows most topics about which biblical and patristic scholars did not agree. Consequently, the text was much too traditional for those who, in the name of a first and foremost biblical Mariology, wanted to see a revision of the Magisterium's rigid positions on Mary's perpetual virginity, as well as on the new dogmas of the Immaculate Conception and the Assumption.

Such wishes were discernible at an early point in the Council, among German-speaking bishops and theologians.[297] But a truly new, and revisionist, approach to biblical Mariology appeared only about fifteen years later. Now mostly a historical document, the oft-quoted and wide-spread book, *Mary in the New Testament*,[298] attempted to create a "pluralistic Mariology" as a tool for ecumenism. Its subtitle identifies it as the fruit of collaborative work by an ecumenical "task force." It amounts to a biblically conceived minimalist Mariology,[299] based on a multi-denominational study group's assessment of the

---

[297] See my note no. 259 with reference to an article by Bishop Paul Rusch of Innsbruck, which reads like a proposal or a manifesto for the next session of the Council.

[298] Edited by Raymond E. Brown, Karl P. Donfried, Joseph A. Fitzmyer, John Reumann (Philadelphia, 1978).

[299] The task force's minimalist Mariology is rooted in two statements. I quote them:
1. "The task force agreed that the question of the historicity of the virginal conception could not be settled by historical-critical exegesis and that one's attitude towards Church tradition on the matter would probably be the decisive force in determining one's view whether the virginal conception is a theologoumenon or a literal fact" (291-92).
2. "On the other hand, in the 2nd century, the canonical texts themselves proved open to interpretive developments under the impact of new emphases in Christianity of polemical arguments of one group against another (docetists, Gnostics, Judaizers) and finally of the influence of allegory and typology on biblical texts. The growing ascetic and encratitic tendencies in the churches everywhere prepared for a new, independent emphasis" (257-28).
If consistent with what the introduction claims, in the first sentence "historical-critical exegesis" means the search for "the authorial intent." Now, most exegetes claiming historical-critical exegesis as the supreme norm (including editors, R. Brown and J. Fitzmyer) have established that the authors of Mt 1-2 and Lk 1-2 had thought that the virginal conception was factual. Yet here, the task force is in serious doubt about the historicity of the virginal conception, so it relegates the question to the individual for whom "Church tradition will be the determining factor in the view one takes" (p. 292). "Church tradition" does not mean here the tradition that the Church Fathers represent, but the denominational trend in every church, be it world-wide or local. This is how a "pluralistic New Testament" is conceived in this book, demanding that all traditions, even those that contradict each other, be attributed to divine guidance and differ stubbornly only in emphasis (cf. p. 25).

New Testament's teaching about Mary.[300] The task force proposes a "pluralistic" theology, but draws no perimeters to the theological pluralism it wants to claim. For a patient and attentive reader the book does not achieve the marginalization of Mary. Rather, the task force pays attention to every minute detail about Mary in the New Testament, often with contrary results. The reader remains puzzled: What is at stake in this seemingly endless dispute about whether she did or did not engage in sex, and if she was fully sinless, or could be blamed for some of her actions or attitudes? What ultimate difference would her "exegetically established" perpetual virginity or sinlessness make, if the pluralistic theologian or believer is expected to follow his or her church's stand, regardless of what the evangelists believed to be the apostolic tradition? Furthermore, how can a rigorous application of "the historical method carefully and intelligently applied" (p. 8) *prove by inductive reasoning* that a concretely identified person in antiquity truly was and remained a virgin? And in exactly what sense can we determine that, in Mary's lifetime, no virgin could have meaningfully had the intention to remain in the state of virginity? Is a negative answer to this question not a clear case of the *a priori* reasoning so adamantly rejected by the historical method?[301]

In the second statement the suggestion is made that the biblical texts were equally open to a pluralism of later development, orthodox and heterodox alike. Considering the fact that the "discussion for this chapter was led by E. Pagels and K. Froehlich" (p. 241 under *), the statement is not surprising, but only the suggestion that this statement was the fruit of a discussion. For the program of the chapter in question corresponds point by point to the positions that Ms. Pagels takes in her many publications on Gnostic exegesis. For her John or Paul or the Gnostics all represent one or another legitimate outcome or possible development of the scriptural texts. This is referred back again to a "pluralistic theology" in the introduction (pp. 22-25 cited on p. 242 n. 666) but has nothing to do with theology or pluralism. It is polyvalent interpretation of texts.

[300] Most disturbing is the anonymity of the literary author (or "drafter") of the individual chapters. The reader learns only about the identity of the person who chaired the session of an individual topic but otherwise the committee members abstain from telling their denominational loyalties and we can only guess who is hiding behind the collective mask of scholarly objectivity.

[301] See Raymond E. Brown, *The Critical Meaning of the Bible* (New York/Ramsey: Paulist Press, 1978), 17-22. Brown argues that scriptural inerrancy is not an *a priori* but an *a posteriori*, which would mean that in the name of inerrancy one cannot exclude errors from the Bible. I think this contradicts both unanimous tradition and the very concept of inerrancy, which applies to the Bible not because

And how could we conclude from a historical-critical investigation that none of her actions was ever wrong or sinful? In the end, the book diffuses the biblical data and produces a blurred image of Mary, lacking the focus that could have been obtained only through faith.[302] On account of the task force's single-minded concern for historicity, the book does little more than accumulate doubts, especially regarding Mary's perpetual virginity, so as to bring the reader to a formidable uncertainty, sufficient to eliminate Mariology altogether as a serious theological discipline.

The first impression received in our treatment of Mariology's origins was that Mariology cannot be built up from a minimalistic portrait of the "historical Mary," just as Christology cannot be constructed by historians from their conclusions about the "historical Jesus." Mariology must be rooted in an approach that assumes the bridge of faith connecting Christ, as Son of God, Messiah, and Redeemer, to historical reality; namely, this man, Jesus of Nazareth, had a mother, and this woman had the greatest importance for his origins. This is how, in a basic sense, Paul's words "born of a woman, born under the Law" represent a first, albeit tentative, step toward Mariology. Of course this statement alone could not lead to any kind of Mariology.

Viewed in the light of modern biblical research, Mariology arose in an intuitively far from obvious way. In spite of all the very significant, though short and scattered, comments about Mary in the New Testament (including Lk 1-2), the beginnings of Mariology come into view in a properly theological perspective only when the Mary/Eve parallel explicitly emerges in the time of Justin Mar-

---

we cannot or did not find actual errors, but because, as word of God, the Bible cannot assert errors. However, excluding anything from being historical unless it is in harmony with what we know about a particular culture in a specific time period is also a false *a priori* supposition: there are historical events that are either unique (like the Incarnation or the Resurrection of Jesus) or take place for the first time and thus cannot be validated by previous occurrences.

[302] The study group's participants are named on p. 4 but without naming their "church affiliations." Exceptions are the Catholics, whose religious orders (two Jesuits and one Sulpician) or title (Msgr.) identify them as such.

tyr.[303] Thereafter, this theme exercised never-ending fascination on all Church Fathers, and the force of its influence continued up to our times. The "hellenization" of Christian thought would not adequately explain this theological development. It was intimately linked to a specifically Christian theological anthropology, implicitly present in apostolic times, and to an approach to the interpretation of the Hebrew Bible in view of the words and deeds of Christ presented by the Gospels. One must add that it was brought to the forefront of theological reasoning by the Church's anti-Gnostic struggle.[304] The concept of a "redemptive Incarnation" began to enrich the old Pauline paradigm of "Christ as the new Adam": God was seen to have been *born* in order to *die* and, at the same time, to bring man to *rebirth*. This opened the way for a growing synthesis by linking Synoptic and Pauline concepts with the Johannine writings, which focus on the concept of being born anew and from above. So, properly speaking, Mariology came about in the 2nd century's synthesis of Pauline and Johannine thought reshaped by anti-Gnostic Church leaders and bishops, a development we best know from the *Adversus Haereses* of Irenaeus.

In the two-Adam, two-Eve paradigm of this soteriology, redemption means "being reborn" by faith and baptism in the Pauline and Johannine sense: rebirth through union with Jesus' truly human death and Resurrection, and attaining ontological access to his true and fully revealed divinity through the double instrumentality of faith and sacrament ("water and Spirit" according to Jn 3:5; "water and blood" according to 1 Jn 5:6). It is remarkable that in the extant texts of Justin Martyr the only identifiable reference to the Fourth

---

[303] Mary spoken of as the "woman" in both Cana (Jn 2:1-10) and on Calvary (Jn 19:26) connects the Mary/Eve theme in Justin Martyr with a Johannine expression of the same theme in symbolic language and with the use of irony; thus Mariology is rooted in biblical revelation.

[304] In an indirect way, the book *Mary in the New Testament* proves this point. Going against its own logic, it consecrates a whole chapter to "Mary in the Second Century" with this reasoning: "We hope that the attempt to hear the voice of the earliest Christians on Mary's place in God's salvation plan will be useful for others who seek to understand and evaluate the later Church traditions" (p. 8).

Gospel evokes one of these verses: "I say to you, no one can enter the kingdom of God without being born of water and Spirit" (Jn 3:5).

Justin also saw the reversion of human history as in a panorama. He cites the story of the Annunciation from the "memoirs of the Apostles," in this case from Luke's Gospel, as the reversal of Eve's – "an undefiled virgin's" – tragic loss of life through disobedience, for which an act of obedience by another Virgin, Mary, compensates, when she gives assent to the Incarnation. In her body she receives the Son who then "frees from death those who repent of their sins and believe [in him]."[305] This outline sketched by Justin connects not only Christ to Adam, but also Mary to Eve, "the mother of all the living" (Gn 3:20). Thus Mary is drawn into the center stage of redemptive history. For in God's plan, the first couple's creation served not only to provide for the physical, procreative beginnings of a multiplicity of human beings to populate the earth, but also to initiate the transmission of the life that God had granted from his own mouth to the first man, made from clay. He wanted man and his companion to enjoy and nourish a life of intimacy with him and with each other in the Garden of Eden, where they would be sustained in this state of immortality by the Tree of Knowledge and by the Tree of Life, both offered not as payments due to man, but as gifts granted by God. The loss of Paradise by Eve (and Adam), was followed by the pro-creational multiplication of mankind; to this same chain of procreation Christ's birth from Mary was added, resulting in the gift of redemption and the restitution of Paradise. These are, in fact, two parallel and antithetical beginnings that the Mary/Eve parallelism was first capable of bringing to light.

A merely historical-critical reading of Genesis 1-3 and Luke 1-2 would not be capable of establishing this. In such a reading the meaning of the trees from which God forbade the first couple to eat would be blurred, as also God's perseverance with his original

---

[305] See this text quoted above; the reader may want to see this text again in its context on p. 67.

project in spite of the first couple's being ejected from Paradise. Of course, a whole host of further ambiguities would surface in such a fuzzy picture, even if by some superhuman power our historical-critical lenses could be combined with miraculous clairvoyance, and we could extend our historical-critical vision to see how God intended to respond to the Fall with a hidden salvation plan. But according to our present assessment of revelation there is still abundant opportunity to complete the vision of the Old Testament with the New. So, for example, the multiple layers of the biblical text about creation are progressively revealed: we have two (or more) creation stories in Genesis, the "breath of life" given Adam by a mysterious primitive action of mouth-to-mouth resuscitation makes him a "living being," obviously in a sense superior to the life in animals. We also have the introduction of a sexual relationship with the aim of procreation after man is barred from the Tree of Life.[306] We find also an insistence in the whole Bible (the Torah and the Prophets) on the primacy of God's word, which saves and nourishes us because it has come from the mouth of God (Dt 8:3; quoted in Mt 4:4; 2 Ch 35:22; Is 1:20, 34:16, 40:5, 58:14, 62:2; Mi 4:4; Jr 9:11, 23:16). The ultimate meaning of this would remain obscure were we to neglect that in Mary the Word becomes flesh, given her adherence to it with acceptance and obedience. Small details – like one of the parting statements of the dying Savior on the Cross, pointing to an immediate reunion with the repenting criminal who dies along with him: "Amen, I say to you, today you will be with me in *Paradise*" (Lk 23:43) – indicate a connection with the first couple's original state of happiness, to which the death of the Lord brings us back.

Some may wonder if a mosaic or collage of references to human origins proves anything. Indeed, Scripture only rarely offers deductive proofs; but canonical re-readings of the two Testaments must be continued, so that, under the guidance of the Spirit and the Church,

---

[306] "See! The man has become like one of us, knowing what is good and what is bad! Therefore, he must not be allowed to put out his hand to take fruit from the tree of life also, and thus eat of it and live forever" (Gn 3:22).

they may disclose *what they meant and what they mean.*[307]

If a reading of the Annunciation linking Eve and Mary inaugurated Mariology in the middle of the 2nd century, what is its contribution to a systematic overview of Marian teaching? Its most important contribution was not the window it opened to a Christian exegesis of Genesis 1-3, but the strengthening of ties between soteriology and the theological understanding of Mary's virginal motherhood. The anti-Gnostic Church Fathers focused on the "flesh" taken from Mary, nailed to the Cross, and raised from the tomb, and thus demonstrated the importance of Mary – and her virginal humanity – in a role that was assigned to her alone: to be the proper locus of the Incarnation. What both Luke and Matthew assert in an unmistakably historical and factual sense challenged the earliest Christian thinkers. By their understanding of what the Gospels teach, they walk the narrow path around the Hellenistic philosophers' aversion from the realm of the flesh and a corresponding Gnostic propensity to formulate salvation as liberation from the burden of the body. Thus Christian theologians were called to face up to the truth of Christian revelation in the Gospels by equally asserting Jesus' birth as a son of Adam and yet as a human being begotten in a manner unlike that of any other descendant of Adam and Eve. Between these two constraints we find the first and foremost thesis of Marian teaching: virginal motherhood.

Mary: Virgin and Mother

Mary's virginal conception was the first mariological statement to obtain dogmatic status; it was professed in the so-called *regula fidei*, a patristic formula distinguishing Catholic Christian doctrine from Gnosticism, developed from the primitive baptismal formulas from which the "Apostles' Creed" also took its origin. The first im-

---

[307] I intend here to reconnect what Raymond Brown in his *The Critical Meaning of the Bible* (New York/Ramsey: Paulist, 1978), 21-29, separates: "what the Bible meant" treated in separation from "what the Bible means."

portant theologians of the Church, Irenaeus, Tertullian, and Origen, do not attempt to deduce Mary's virginity at Jesus' conception. Even when they state that Jesus was conceived by a virgin, they report it as factual content of the apostolic faith and tradition to which the Gospels testify. The abstract distinction between a proof *per necessitatem* and a proof *per convenientiam* does not manifest itself in their arguments; they continuously point out why the facts of salvation that we know have fittingly happened in the divine dispensation. The "fittingness" of an assertion is not only its meaningfulness in some particular sense or its beauty, but its profound harmony with other truths we know and with basic presuppositions of scriptural statements. That is, such a proof *per convenientiam* refers to the coherence and compatibility between assertions of the faith. So for the early Church Fathers, the principal import of the virginal conception is its "revelatory" significance: Mary's virginity, and the absence of a human father who would initiate Jesus' conception, point to God's exclusive and sovereign fatherhood. They likewise manifest that Jesus' origin does not involve the force of sexual passion, which is otherwise a necessary ingredient to sexual reproduction. This we find expressed in the threefold negation of John 1:13 describing divine Fatherhood: "οὐκ ἐξ αἱμάτων οὐδὲ ἐκ θελήματος σαρκὸς οὐδὲ ἐκ θελήματος ἀνδρὸς ἀλλ' ἐκ θεοῦ."[308] Modern translations emphasize one or another aspect, but the "want of the flesh" cannot be interpreted away, for it refers to a fleshly desire.

In their theology of Mary's virginity, the texts of the 2nd century adhere not only to the texts of Matthew (1:8-23) and Luke (1:34-35), but also to Isaiah (7:14). As we repeatedly stated here, in the Septuagint, Isaiah's text goes beyond the Hebrew text, which means only "the young girl" (*ha'almah*) and not necessarily "the virgin" (ἡ παρθένος). The Septuagint, made by Hellenistic Jews of Alexandria, seems to imply that the conception is not just some sort of a

---

[308] At this point it matters little if we accept the singular or the plural reading as original. Ultimately even in plural the believers' participation in divine sonship comes from the Incarnation, i.e., the virginal conception of Jesus that brought about our participation in being sons of God.

sign, but a miraculous one. The Christians of the 2nd century, however, went even further, seeing here yet another reference to the Book of Genesis. Tertullian compared Mary's virginal womb to "the virginal earth" as it is described in the so-called "second creation story" of Genesis (2:4b-7):

> At the time when the LORD God made the earth and the heavens – while as yet there was no field shrub on earth and no grass of the field had sprouted, for the LORD God had sent no rain upon the earth and there was no man to till the soil but a stream was welling up out of the earth and was watering all the surface of the ground – the LORD God formed man out of the clay of the ground and blew into his nostrils the breath of life, and so man became a living being.

Tertullian comments on this in the following way:

> For if the first Adam was created from a barren soil of clay, "not yet subjected to cultivation and with no seed sown into it," and thus not capable of producing life, then Christ, whom the Apostle calls "the last Adam" (*novissimus Adam*), when he became a living spirit [reference to the resurrection in 1 Cor 15:45], must have been created in the same way: from a soil (that is from flesh) not yet assigned to procreation.[309]

This describes Mary's body as "flesh not assigned to procreation (*generationi*)." We must admit that Tertullian comes dangerously close to asserting that Mary's virginity is a merely (or chief-

---

[309] We gave above a paraphrase of Tertullian's text, too compact for a word-for-word English translation. Here is the passage in Latin: "virgo erat adhuc terra, nondum opere compressa, nondum sementi subacta: ex ea hominem factum accipimus a deo in animam vivam igitur si primus Adam ita traditur, merito sequens vel novissimus Adam, ut apostolus dixit, proinde de terra (id est carne) nondum generationi resignata in spiritum vivificantem a deo est prolatus." *De Carne Christi* XVII (CCL 58, 19-24). See above p. 84.

ly) bodily condition, for he speaks of a "virginal flesh." But in the present context he wants nothing more than to emphasize that the creation of the second Adam from a Virgin introduces no discontinuity into salvation history: mankind whose beginnings come from the first Adam obtains another genuine second "beginning" – a life extended to God's own inner life, a life once given, but lost, and now breathed into man a second time through Christ.

Similar thoughts appear in Irenaeus in a rich language, equally complex, and often poorly understood. We must revisit here the metaphor of the two knots on one single string which must be untied in reverse order.[310] He tries to show that first the sequence is that of fleshly descendance: Adam → Eve → Mary → Jesus. But then the arrows are reversed, because Jesus becomes the "last" Adam in the sense of the "newest," i.e., the "latest" or "most recent" one, from whom new life begins to flow. Chronologically, of course, Mary's virginity antedates Jesus' conception, making her the counterpart of Eve, a second Eve and "the mother of all human life" (meaning the life of grace). So, the whole life of grace flows from Mary's virginal motherhood. But Mary's pure and unblemished being came about in view of Jesus' redemptive death (*praevisa morte*)[311] so that the flow of supernatural life is poured into mankind from Jesus as the second Adam, who also caused his mother's sanctity and transferred redemption retroactively to all children of Adam in the past and even to Adam himself. This is how the order of spiritual parenthood is reversed: Jesus → Mary → Eve → Adam.

It seems that when the Church Fathers first began to pay attention to the virginal conception as the source of "regeneration," little was said about its subjective or "experiential" aspect. But as a rule, in such ancient texts the subjective aspects of the mysteries of the faith are usually not explored; that aspect is normally detectable later, in medieval or modern writings. Even in the *Proto-evangelium*, no matter how much attention one pays to Mary's living the life of

---

[310] See pp. 72-73.

[311] See below about the dogmatization of the Immaculate Conception on pp. 282-290.

a consecrated virgin, it is a certain spiritual ideal that is described in objective and external terms, and not subjectively. Although acts of asceticism, pious activities of prayer, self-denial, and perfect sexual continence are strongly emphasized, little show is made of the intellectual or emotional motivation that animates them. From the *Proto-evangelium* we learn to appreciate all the more the biblical accounts of the Annunciation and the Visitation. These Lucan passages show the importance of Mary's faith, presented not so much under an emotional, personalized aspect but in terms of consent and readiness to act. The canonical Gospels' "virginal spirituality" characterizes much less the story of a single mother, than that of a woman for whom – in a singular, unparalleled, unrepeated event – the experience of the virginal single-mindedness of loving God and nobody else, and the maternal dedication to her Child simply coincided. This is the meaning of the statement by St. Ambrose, echoed in *Lumen Gentium* yet faring poorly in post-Conciliar spirituality: her giving birth did not take away or reduce her virginity, but rather consecrated it, *non deminuit sed consecravit.*[312]

The *Magnificat* too illuminates substantial elements of Mary's life of faith. Her spirituality mirrors that of "the poor of the Lord," with an emphasis on humility, essential for defining her as the Lord's maidservant. In the center of her prayer we find the praise of God, who rejects those who seek to reign by power. Finally, there is the connection she sees between herself and Abraham, since the promises first made to him now come to fulfillment. Each of these themes is closely linked with her motherhood, and so is a sign of God's having exalted her, lifting up a powerless virgin after she gave a firm and unhesitating response to her call in faith.

It is worth asking when and how the Annunciation was transposed into more personalized terms. A forerunner to such an understanding is the antithetic use of terms like *tristitia/laetitia*, comparing the devastating effect of Eve's sin with the fulfilling joy radiating from the Child through Mary into the redeemed world. But only

---

[312] See above pp. 130-131.

relatively recent authors begin to consider the relationship of Mary and her Child not only, or not primarily, in terms of an ontological miracle, but also by bringing to the foreground her existential encounter with God the Father as the Mother of his Son. The ontological side has been commented on, explicitly and frequently, from Nicaea all the way to the late Middle Ages: Mary gave body and birth to her own Creator. A medieval antiphon, written in the form of an elegant *distichon* ("elegiac couplet") captures the "Mariological paradox" with eloquent beauty: *"Virgo Dei Genitrix, quem totus non capit orbis, / In tua se clausit viscera factus homo."*[313] But modern writers – theologians, devotional authors, and papal encyclicals – began exploring the extraordinary implications of virginal motherhood in a new light, the light of modern personalism and Catholic existentialism.

The theology of marriage, the theology of the body, the unique intimacy of spousal and maternal relationships aimed at individual fulfillment, led the Church little by little to realize more fully the astonishing relational riches linking the Virgin Mother to her God. She was carrying a Child in her womb who, while consubstantial with God the Father, received every element of genetic heritage from Mary alone to be of identical nature with us. This meant, among other things, that the human soul of Jesus, which for other human beings would be created concomitantly with and in response to a human couple's fertile, procreative union, was created in response to her act of faith and obedience, her *fiat*, in a sublime spiritual encounter with the Father in the Spirit. Thus it was that Jesus' human soul, the holiest part of all creation, came about in her womb. This grants us some insight into the meaning of a famous statement by Augustine, quoted frequently after him, that Mary conceived Jesus by her faith and obedience before conceiving him in her body: *"prius mente quam*

---

[313] "Virgin, Godbearing: the one whom the whole world cannot hold / Shut himself into your womb as he became a human being." This antiphon is listed by Henri Barré as originating in the early Roman liturgy. Originally the Roman liturgy used it for the third Sunday of Advent, but it became a favorite and was inserted into several new feasts. Cf. H. Barré, *Prières anciennes de l'Occident à la Mère du Sauveur* (Paris: Léthielleux, 1963), 36, 284 n. 27.

ventre."[314] Mary's part in the conception of Jesus is not only passive; that it was "virginal" means something positive, although the negative connotation is clear, that there was no human intercourse. Hers was to give herself fully and unreservedly in response to her call, to which corresponds on God's part a divine act of complete self-giving to mankind as a whole. One might speak of Mary's act as purely and fully receptive, but only in the sense that by this act she establishes her full availability for motherhood in specific regard to her divine Son and her positive acceptance of the divine will of participating as mother to son in the destiny and work of the Messiah. This act consisted of a single statement involving all her natural and supernatural aspirations. In the one act of her *fiat*, as if in a single move of her will that summoned her whole being – her being called to be woman, spouse, *and* mother – she accepted her role as that human being who was to accept in the name of us all the gifts of the Incarnation.

To each insight pertaining to Mariology there emerges from us, human beings, an intuitive component of self-understanding. We understand ourselves as being potentially infinite and thus endowed with limitless capacity to advance in knowledge, to act freely, and thus we discover a desire rooted in our nature to transcend ourselves, specifically by giving away the sum total of our finite participation in the gift of life for the sake of others and, ultimately, for the sake of life eternal. In the experience of our humanity's embarking in search of both completeness and procreation, there is an instinctive discovery of how truly it is not good for man to be alone (cf. Gn 2:18), and thus we sense that we can be completed only in communion with "others" (understood as intelligent and free beings). This openness to and desire for other persons is never verified in a distributive sense – in relationship to this one or that one other human being – but remains unfulfilled, or only inadequately fulfilled, while tending to a share in

---

[314] This is one of Augustine's more frequently quoted lines. The full sentence is *illa fide plena et Christum prius mente quam ventre concipiens.* Sermon 215, 4: PL 38, 1074. See Paul Coathalem, *Le parallélisme entre la sainte Vierge et l'Église dans la tradition latine jusqu'à la fin du XIIe siècle* (Rome: Univ. Gregoriana, 1954) 27.

the fullness of God's life. Encompassing both body and soul, every human being who grows into adulthood discovers that full maturity does not happen without relating to others, and the mystery of the "otherness" of other human beings moves us on in search of the fullness of Being. Unless we are handicapped in some way, this desire for the other is constantly at work, directing us to roads that lead to all sorts of community forms: a family by procreation, bonds of lasting and nurturing friendships, and, ultimately, seeking to find God while searching for perfect fulfillment. This is precisely the dynamic by which God may lead us to hear a call to consecrated life. Cultural history shows how, in man, personal self-awareness is inseparably linked to the experience of discovering physical and emotional attraction to others through marriage, of the community of nuclear and larger families, and also of religious life. Such a desire, when unobstructed, tends to explicit and outwardly expressed communion with other persons in acts whose intentionality is to establish stable, full, and lasting relationships, toward and beyond procreation and parenting, but also toward spiritual community, in which we can participate in other human beings' inner life by reciprocal trust and love.

That is why in human existence motherhood is essentially linked to a spousal experience. Since the human being is naturally a body-soul composite, ordinarily a sexual relation between a man and a woman seals and crowns, expresses, completes, and finalizes a spousal relation by which two separate existences seek to merge into one and give origin to new human beings. With virtually infinite variations, two sovereign personal realms of knowledge and liberty (intellect and will) seek ways to merge through some joint and reciprocally intimate journeys of trust, of giving and receiving. In the case of spousal encounters between two "postlapsarian" (fallen) human beings, our finitude, our sinfulness, our limited resources, and our mortal destiny set bounds on each and every side of the dynamics we have mentioned above. The initial logic of this path would seem to lead naturally to the creatures' search for God – seeking to discover God's image and likeness in "the other" human being. But the creatures often have to settle for less, facing boundaries imposed upon them. Even in vowed virginity or consecrated celibacy, a form in which the search for God by-passes the road to procreation by choosing more direct pathways, man ends up a beggar asking to be exalted to a way of life in which the understanding of the self and love and service of the neighbor would harmoniously progress to a growingly Christ-like love of other human beings and of the Father.

In the Incarnation, God elects a woman for a similar but in its radical nature totally different, unique journey: Mary follows the path of a "consecrated virgin." For a personalistic analysis it matters little how clearly at her time such a thing could have been or was culturally defined as such. In any case, Mary was called to make herself available to a spousal union with God the Father, who intended to make his eternal Son the personal subject of a true human birth. He wanted his Son to be born from a woman (see Gal 4:4), not by renting a womb and borrowing an ovum that he would then use for this sovereign project. Rather than engaging in some "divine act" of cloning, he called a woman to total self-giving, physical and spiritual, while he miraculously caused her to become a mother in the intimacy of a direct encounter with the Absolute Being in a mystical, unspeakable way. Such an encounter we can describe only analogously. Her spousal encounter with God is more dissimilar than similar to what we experience in interpersonal relations, because Mary's call and consent resulted in motherhood to a human child, an utterly unique experience; it does not pertain to anyone else's experiences of God or of parenthood. Yet this encounter turns out to be the fountainhead of all gracious encounters between God and man: it is this event of grace from which all other graces take their origin. In such a participatory sense, Mary's call is the *primum analogatum* or chief example of any other encounter with God by grace, though itself unique. Nobody encountered God in the way Mary did, and yet Mary's encounter with God in the Incarnation is the *archetype* of all our encounters with God in grace.

Only at this place can we resume an issue we left behind as a seemingly grammatical problem. In the translation of Luke 1:28, some criticize and some support the expression "full of grace" (κεχαριτομένη), which has indeed been the matter of interminable disputes. However, the question goes far beyond grammar and vocabulary. The grace that brings about Mary's motherhood is the source of all graces for mankind. We all participate in it, but she stands alone before God to accept the gift as she represents all human beings. No footnote or comment on the angelic messenger's role and words can diminish the importance of the act of acceptance by which Mary alone is brought, by the Holy Spirit, to a fullness of creaturely receptiveness. In her act of acceptance and faith, the Father entrusts to her whole feminine being his Son, the Logos through whom the world was made. The Virgin cannot generate the Son on her own; through her response of obedience, she performs an act in which, in his turn, the Logos "takes the form of a slave," and becomes an incipient human being, "obedient until death, death on a cross" (Ph 7:2). As God's Son begins his journey of becoming like a human being in every way, Mary's fullness of grace is revealed in both the fullness of her humility and of her exaltation. All that is perceptible "outwardly" to human senses is this: in her body a non-fertilized *ovum* is turned into the initial stage of an individual human nature. But that human being subsists in God, is a man starting his developmental growth toward becoming a fully grown male child, who from that point on is "God become man." In the words of the late antique Christian hymn *Te Deum* addressing the divine Son in his act of humiliation: *non horruisti Virginis uterum* (you did not disdain the womb of the Virgin).

In this event unparalleled in salvation history God's condescension reaches all levels of human existence. It embraces the human being as a whole in Mary, in whom the fullness of creaturely truth becomes capable of receiving the fullness of divine mercy intended for the human person. In the scriptural perspective, uncovered by Paul in Romans 4:19, this is analogous to what happened in Sara's dead womb due to Abraham's faith. Dead as it was for bringing about new life, it was turned into the source of procreation. Similarly, as Paul also insinuates (Rm 4:24), this is what happened to the dead body of Jesus lying in the tomb when it was lifted miraculously to risen life in the Spirit. All these events manifest the one and same Divine Agent who "alone does great wonders" (cf. Ps 136:4) when exercising his mercy. Indeed, in the account of the Annunciation, the Angel Gabriel describes such a divine act, by which Mary's virginal being will be exalted to the dignity of divine motherhood, in Trinitarian language: "The Holy *Spirit* will come upon you, and the power of *the Most High* will overshadow you. Therefore the child to be born will be called holy, the *Son* of God" (Lk 1:35).

Of course we are not speaking of a mere "language," but about the matter at hand: in an ultimate sense the Marian mystery is Trinitarian. According to John 1:14, it was the Logos who became flesh: he who was from the beginning, he who was one with God from the beginning, and through whom all salvation history came to be. Similarly Hebrews 1:1-2 links the Father's self-expression, first made through sundry utterances in prophetic events and words, with the point in history at which the Son, acquiring his human mouth in the Incarnation, becomes that direct channel through which he can address the human being in a new and ultimate immediacy. Thus the Father begins speaking through the Son's humanity, in fully human terms and in full condescension to us, yet still from the height of the Supreme Being. For to no other did God ever say: "You are my Son, this day I have begotten you" (cf. Heb 1:5, quoting Ps 110:3).

We began from the particular interest of experts in Mariology who, in the first half of the 20th century, sought to find the "fundamental principle" of Mariology without coming to a consensus. Yet we may say that both historically and logically Mariology arose in an organic and unified process from the realization of Mary's role in the Incarnation. We are not speaking *in abstracto* of a conceptual truth, but of a concrete personal life: that of the Virgin, elected and prepared, preserved immaculate and virginal, to become God's Mother. The virginal divine motherhood is not simply *Grundprinzip* but may be called the seed, the seminal truth, from which Mariology grew. Of course, the seed needs fertile soil in which to grow and develop. That fertile soil was constituted by the Christological, anthropological, and soteriological context in which the Mariology of the first three centuries blossomed into a resplendent appreciation of Mary's role and importance in God's salvation plan.

The eventual objections always opted for marginalizing or fragmenting, reducing or restricting Mary's virginity into a momentary or transient event, while both the authoritative teaching of the Church and a corporate consensus of the faithful asserted it as a perpetual paradigm. Mary's virginity emerged from these confrontations by being asserted as the persistent mode and permanent locus of the Incarnation. Behind the attempts to restrict or eliminate her virginity there often lurked the wish to reduce the motherhood of the divine Son to the motherhood of his human nature, or attempts to separate the Son of God from the Son of Mary. At times a seemingly faith-based outlook also sought to identify Jesus' virginal conception with a "nature miracle" and thus considers it an external issue testifying to the Incarnation as some "divine work in course," but not revelatory of what was internal and essential to it. From this point of view, Athanasius and Ambrose in the 4th century and the passionate protagonist of Ephesus, Cyril of Alexandria, had immense merit. They showed that for the fact and meaning of the Incarnation the virginal conception and birth were essential. Without Mary being recognized *as the Virgin*, and thus her having a virginal status that lasts in perpetuity, the conception of Jesus at the moment of the Incarnation could have been easily misunderstood as another merely human step forward or up on some evolutionary scale, but a step with no impact on all mankind; thus it would veil rather than reveal the divine filiation of the Son of God. If he had been born from a man's instinct, from the joint procreative wish and will of two human beings, and by the moving force of eros and human concupiscence, Jesus by his "becoming" would not have expressed the eternal birth of the Son and God's transcendental, fully free love toward his Son and toward us, his children. Had Jesus' birth been followed by Mary's further pregnancies and parturitions, Jesus' divinity would have been left fully obscured and hidden (also improbable). Had Mary and Joseph returned after Jesus' birth to their "plan A" of a married life, how much rationality could we have discovered in this interlude of virginal matrimony, if it was only a prophetic interruption allowed for nine short months, as if it took place to cede to some transcendental *ius primae noctis* represented by the angelic visitation, a short postponing of the marriage's consummation? What would we say about the Holy Family if one of the, say, five children was the Second Divine Person, but all the rest were "normal human beings"? How could we reproach James and Jude and their two sisters for not believing in their big brother's divinity, if he was apparently born from the same marriage, with identical background and the same credentials? The naïveté with which dogmatic theologians admitted on a purely ontological basis the possibility of the Incarnation without virginal conception is rather surprising. Of course, not excluding it as ontologically impossible means little or nothing, since the issue under discussion is such that without divine revelation it could not have been known in any way.

In this perspective, Christ, Mary's Son conceived by the Holy Spirit, was unmistakably the first fruit of a new creation; yet as a son of Adam, he was also rescuing-redeeming the first Adam and Eve. Mary renewed and revindicated for herself the previously lost role of "the Mother of all the living," the mother of a regenerated mankind. The new Eve through whom the Lord makes a sign with full sovereignty (cf. Is 7:14), introduced as "the Virgin" in Matthew 1:23 and Luke 1:35, Elizabeth names "the Mother of the Lord" (Lk 1:43).[315] To that Mary responds by singing that mankind should embrace this event with praise in all generations (cf. Lk 1:48).

---

[315] If we choose a minimalistic interpretation of "my Lord" on Elizabeth's lips we would recognize Mary's Son only as a messianic king. But Elizabeth's words must be read in continuity with what the Angel Gabriel said in Lk 1:35, immediately before he referred to Elizabeth's pregnancy: "Son of the Most High." We may see here another importance of the patristic linkage of the two greetings, Gabriel's and Elizabeth's, in the frequently copied variant reading of Lk 1:29.

The Center of the Marian Mystery

Virginal divine motherhood is the *raison d'être* of all the Marian privileges and attributes, and in this sense we can call it the "foundational principle" of Mariology. The "foundation of this foundation" is the anti-Arian Christology of the Council of Nicaea, which finalized the Catholic understanding of Jesus' divinity in such a way that Mary's dignity as Mother of God logically had to follow. Mary was not only the mother of Jesus' humanity, because, from the very moment of the Incarnation, Jesus' human nature subsisted in the *person* of the Son and was in this way united to the divine nature: motherhood refers *to the person, not to the nature* of the child, and the Person Mary bore was divine, the Second Person of the Trinity. Such an understanding is reflected in the early use of the term θεότοκος, a term appearing in the *Sub Tuum* well before Ephesus. But this term and the truth it expresses bring us only to the gate of the mystery. A deeper look is required.

The Incarnation took place so that the Son might be the subject of actions and events taking place in time. The defense line drawn in Nicaea intended to protect and support the ancient faith of the Church: the eternally begotten Son was truly born, suffered, died, and rose from the dead. This statement is like a bridge reaching from Nicaea to the anti-Gnostic Fathers of the 2nd century and all the way back to the New Testament. The implications were clear to the Fathers. If the Son of God is also the Son born from Mary, then he knows two births, one as God and one as a man, one from the Father before all times, and one from Mary in the course of history. Both are covered in a proper although analogical sense by the concept of "birth," for both are births in a more than metaphorical sense. Insofar as the Son of God became[316] a human being in time, the same

---

[316] In ancient Greek manuscripts ἐγενήθη (from γίνομαι meaning to become) and ἐγεννήθη (from γεννάω meaning to "generate") are easily confused due to the non-standardized spelling of Greek in antiquity. This problem is even worse in Latin with *factum est* which may be a form of *facio, facere* (to make) or *fio, fieri* (to become). The latter confusion appears as an inexcusable mistake of translation in the modern English liturgical mistranslations of Jn 1:14 from the Latin (*Verbum*

subject was born in time from a human mother and was born eternally by the Father.[317]

These Christological clarifications brought the Church to reflect more on Mary. The consent that led to her conception of Christ was the first act by which a human being welcomed and introduced the Son of the eternal Father into the realm of time and history as the subject of human acts. The eternal birth from God the Father and the temporal birth from Mary are analogous, yes, but with an infinite difference. One is the unfathomable relation of the Father to the Son not just before all times but beyond all temporal or material dimension, not comparable to anything in the world. Yet the subject in each case – the person born – is fully and strictly the same. Hence that mood of astonishment permeating our ancient texts, most of them patristic, some medieval, many preserved only in the liturgy. Due to the classic Mariological paradox of the mother giving birth to her Creator, and the Creator who rules heaven and earth and yet hides in his creature's womb, such texts succumb to a certain ontological dizziness, switching from the language of theological precision to a hyperbolic poetic idiom, and finally to a sense of being at a loss in contemplating the mystery: *quibus te laudibus efferam, nescio,* – what sort of praises I should utter, I do not know![318]

St. Athanasius expressed this sense of the mystery when he wrote: "O noble Virgin, truly you are greater than any other greatness. For who is your equal in greatness, O dwelling place of God the Word? To whom among all creatures shall I compare you, O Vir-

---

caro factum est) as "the Word was *made* flesh" although the Greek text makes it sufficiently clear that it should be "the Word *became* flesh."

[317] We use here almost literally the terminology of Ignatius of Antioch, *Eph.* 7:2: Εἷς ἰατρός ἐστιν, σαρκικός τε καὶ πνευματικός, γεννητὸς καὶ ἀγέννητος, ἐν σαρκὶ γενόμενος θεός, ἐν θανάτῳ ζωὴ ἀληθινή, καὶ ἐκ Μαρίας καὶ ἐκ θεοῦ, πρῶτον παθητὸς καὶ τότε ἀπαθής, Ἰησοῦς Χριστὸς ὁ κύριος ἡμῶν. "There is but one Physician who is both of flesh and spirit; both made and not made; God existing in flesh; true life in death; both of Mary and of God; first passible and then impassible – Jesus Christ our Lord."

[318] Although in first person singular, this text comes from the Roman liturgy, possibly from that old Marian feast celebrated in Rome on the fourth Sunday of Advent in honor of Mary's maternity. See H. Barré, *Prières anciennes de I Occident à la Mère du Sauveur* (Paris: Lethielleux, 1963), 36.

gin?" And Ambrose continued in his "Ambrosian" iambic lines, we quoted above: *"Miretur omne saeculum / talis partus decet Deum."*[319] As we mentioned in connection with Athanasius (cf. p. 114), seeing Mary in such closeness to the Trinity leads our mind to place her above the nine choirs of angels, for she is the Mother of the Logos, through whom all things were created. The medieval image of "the Queen of Angels" follows logically. In an "ontological hierarchy of beings" – a very important principle for ancient and medieval thinking – the appearance of ever new titles in the superlative praising and honoring Mary becomes a crucial issue, promoted because it elevates the human being above the angels not only in Christ but also in Mary. But later on most brands of Protestantism, with little trust in reason and no appreciation for philosophy, became contemptuous of this kind of rhetoric in Marian preaching and devotion, while, quite to the contrary, post-Tridentine schools of spirituality, which promoted the baroque revival of scholastic philosophy and started a new school of aesthetics, delighted in ontological meditations on Mary's divine motherhood.

Miretur omne saeculum, indeed; but as we look back we are turned off by the excesses. The Marian literature of the late post-Tridentine age is full of pastiche: it often engages a hollow, repetitious rhetoric with a measure of mannerism resulting in stylistic exercises, expanding the literary form at the expense of rational content. The eventual failure of post-Tridentine Mariology is partly due to its strong alliance with a less and less enlightening scholastic philosophy and an increasing neglect of biblical realism. In addition, the broader context of traditional sources was lost as the reading of ancient texts was replaced by the use of abbreviated quotations or *florilegia* of patristic passages.

However, in spite of partial neglect or oversight, the truth remains: Mariology carries in itself the principle of its own renewal because of its stable and deep access to the mysterious well-spring of the Incarnation. Mary, in her whole being, is the point of connection

---

[319] "The whole world should be in admiration: such is the birth that befits God!"

between the eternal filiation from the Divine Father and the human filiation in the flesh from a human Mother. Most importantly, the *Grundprinzip der Mariologie* must not be turned into an "idea," like an axiom for abstract mathematics or formal logic. It is not really a principle but a fact or an event: the union, freely chosen by the divine Son in obedience to the Father, of the divine nature with an individual human nature taken from the flesh of Mary, who, when called to partake in this union, freely gave her consent. *Miretur omne saeculum*: yes, the mystery must be a source of wonder, we must marvel at how this event which affects us so profoundly is founded not on a mere idea we can master, but on a mystery of love whose boundaries exceed our imagination: *talis partus decet Deum!*

The Marian Mystery means that the entire work of salvation is linked to the event of the Annunciation, and thus we are all connected to Mary as to our common mother in the order of grace. Just as all grace flows from the Incarnate Son, so is our salvation linked eternally to the grace given to Mary. That is why, with a correct outlook, but admittedly awkward word choice Mary is sometimes called the "Mediatrix of all graces" or "Co-Redemptrix," that is, she is associated to all acts by which her divine Son promotes our redemption. Beyond this mention of them, neither of these two titles will be discussed. Both are clearly fit for use within orthodox Catholic teaching[320] while they easily lead to excessive forms of pious comments against which Vatican II warned[321] should they signify any doctrinal truth beyond the traditional statements about Mary. Yet we should treat separately the theme "Mary and the Church," a topic which the Second Vatican Council underlined and advanced when Pope Paul VI declared Mary "Mother of the Church."

---

[320] I abstain from treating these titles mostly because they could distract us from the central issues of this book and because they would make a number of additional studies and discussions necessary.

[321] The danger consists of picturing Mary, a creature, on the same level as the Creator in partnership of divine power. Because of the prefix in "Co-Redemptrix," this term is especially awkward. The pair of nouns "Mediator/Mediatrix" have a similar effect. With a correct explanation the orthodoxy of both is assured, but without an explanation, the transparency or intelligibility remains questionable.

Mary and the Church

The Church Fathers as early as the 2nd century referred with increasing clarity to some similarities connecting the individual person of Christ's Mother and the Church as mirror images. These similarities first occur in very early, at times fragmentary texts for which one cannot even clearly discern if the symbolism attributed to "the Virgin Mother" refers to Mary or to the Church as a whole. As we saw above, St. Paul already saw the Church as both Virgin and Mother. Then, in the early Fathers, the figure of Mary and that of the Church merge together or, we might say, are superimposed so that their attributes match. For example, Clement of Alexandria seems to speak only about Mary as he writes:

> The Lord Jesus, fruit of the Virgin, did not proclaim women's breasts to be blessed, nor did he choose them to give nourishment. But when the Father, full of goodness and love for men, rained down his Word upon the earth this same Word became the spiritual nourishment for virtuous men. O mysterious marvel!

In this text, however, the discourse suddenly changes and it turns out that the source of all nourishment for man is both Mary and the Church:

> There is one Father of all, there is one Word of all, and the Holy Spirit is one and the same everywhere. There is also one Virgin Mother, whom I love to call the Church. Alone this mother had no milk, because she alone did not become a woman. She is virgin and mother simultaneously; a virgin undefiled and a mother full of love. She draws her children to herself and nurses them with holy milk, that is, the Word for infants. She has no milk because the milk was this child, beautiful and familiar: the body of Christ.[322]

---

[322] *Paidagogos* I, 8 (PG 12, 115).

The comparison is bold, because Clement seems to imply that he has developed the parallel ("I love to call…") to the point of identification. But we find similar passages in the texts of St. Hippolytus, a Roman contemporary of Clement, and soon thereafter, in the 3rd and 4th centuries, Mary and the Church are said to be carrying the same mystery: divine motherhood. Of course in terms of salvation history, Mary's role is primary: there is but one Incarnation, the one which took place in Mary's womb. But what took place in Mary's womb continues at the baptismal font; the Easter liturgical texts for blessing the baptismal water repeat this comparison. Since the faithful collectively form Christ's body, they are born from the womb of the Church and ultimately from Mary. But the Church is both virgin and mother as she gives birth to new members in baptism and nourishes them with the Eucharist. At times a patristic source may line up a whole row of parallelisms between Mary and the Church, as Augustine does in this text, commenting on the creation of Eve:

> These words [of Genesis] are a great mystery: here is the symbol pointing forward to the Church that is to come: she is fashioned out of the side of her spouse in the sleep of death. Did not the Apostle say about Adam that "he was a figure of the one to come" (Rm 5:14)? And is it not also true of the Church? Listen then, understand and realize: it is she that will tread down the Serpent's head. O Church, watch for the Serpent's head![323]

The topic retains its relevance throughout the centuries. In the Middle Ages, it still retains its vigor, but after the Reformation developed a more and more apologetic quality and adapted to an ecclesiology that often considers the Church as a hierarchically and juridically structured "collegium."[324] Then Romantic theology rediscovered

---

[323] *Enarrationes in Psalmos* 103,6 (PL 37, 1381).

[324] In the sense of Roman Law a separate juridical person may be built above the individual members if three persons agree about the purpose and lay down its statutes: "tres faciunt collegium."

the deep meaning of this ecclesiological model and began to collect and organize the relevant images under various headings.[325] The discovery of the early Church's teaching in this regard reached a high point at Vatican II, even if the Council's contributions remained incomplete. We may cite paragraphs 60-67 of *Lumen Gentium*, which extend Mary's maternity of Christ as head of the Church to a maternity of the members, and thus attempts to balance two views of Mary and her maternity: one over and one within the Church. It is clear that the metaphors used in tradition cannot be pushed beyond the limits of their particular symbolism. The distinction between Christ and the believers as head and members is based on a scriptural metaphor that does not allow the head to be treated without the members, nor the members without the head. The image of Mary as both member and mother of the Church must not be extended beyond its natural limits into some grotesque portrait of Mary as her own mother. These limitations do not arise from incorrect theology, but from the mystery – the Marian mystery – that lies behind and beyond the images. It is by the Immaculate Conception that Mary becomes a worthy Mother of the Savior; a redeemed mother who antedates her Redeemer, the Son whose redemptive acts caused both the sinlessness that qualifies her as Mother and the remission of our sins by which we became brothers and sisters of Christ, sons and daughter of his Father.

Where there is mystery, there is a paradox, an apparent contradiction to be solved by both resolving and dissolving the metaphors. This is all the more important regarding Mary's motherhood because the paradox is scriptural, based on irony in John's Gospel, the only scriptural source that consciously indicates two meanings for the word "mother" as applied to Mary. We should re-read this text: "When Jesus saw *his mother* and the disciple there whom he loved, he said to his mother, 'Woman, behold, your son.' Then he said to the disciple, 'Behold, *your mother*'" (Jn 19:26-27). This Gospel text

---

[325] H. Rahner, *Our Lady and the Church*, tr. by S. Bullough (Chicago: Regnery, 1965). The first German edition was published in 1951.

applies two different possessive pronouns ("his" and "your") with apparently contradictory meanings. Grammatically speaking they might indicate two successive motherhoods: Jesus dies and so she is not his mother any longer, so a second motherhood begins in relation to the Beloved Disciple. But that is not the meaning that the context suggests or the tradition the Church supports.[326] If we take seriously what Augustine (in unison with a whole tradition) suggests, namely that, as Eve from Adam's side, so the Church is born from Jesus on the Cross, we can see how in a twofold sense of the word, Mary is Mother of the Church. First, suddenly, by her painless virginal parturition in Bethlehem, and then as the first and foremost fruit of redemption, and thus first member of the Church, "the mother of all the living." She as the second Eve was brought forth from the body of Jesus, as the spouse of the second Adam, and yet was made also the mother all members of Christ, the rest of the Church, when the Church's sacramental life was founded by the water (baptism) and blood (Eucharist) poured from Jesus' side, as it was witnessed by the Evangelist, who was called her "son" at the same time (Jn 19:26).

The Immaculate Conception as the Beginning of Redemptive Incarnation

Our considerations about Mary's divine and virginal motherhood have led us to the issue of the Immaculate Conception: the full redemption of Mary before redemptive acts could even have been posited. In fact, some theologians sought to locate the *Grundprinzip* of Mariology in the thesis that Mary was the "perfectly redeemed human being." The idea had its merit in that it pointed out that, from her Conception, Mary represented, on the one hand, redeemed humanity in its original purity and, on the other, anticipated the eschatological Church, the spotless Bride adorned for her wedding feast.

Systematic reasoning about this matter would proceed as fol-

---

[326] This is an excellent example where we need the positive leadership of the Church to obtain the correct sense of the scriptural text.

lows. Divine motherhood does not allow that the human being chosen to become the locus of the Incarnation be subjected to human sinfulness for any period of time. More specifically, Mary's becoming the "mother of all" i.e., a second Eve in the supernatural order, implies a "new creation"[327] which, on the basis of Pauline terminology, was explicitly announced by all the New Testament in its canonical unity. The mother of newly created humanity cannot have any trace of Adam's sin, because that would be incompatible with a new beginning.

We spoke above about the ironic way in which an apparently old tradition, about which consensus reigned, unexpectedly surfaced under the pen of Pelagius when he shrewdly saw that a "universal statement" concerning the inheritance of Adam's sin is untenable if it means that some sin tainted Mary for even a moment.[328] From the confrontation between Pelagius and Augustine it is clear that both realized at once that admitting any sinfulness in the Mother of the Savior would contradict Church tradition. So Augustine replied that Mary's case is an exception; when speaking about the universality of original sin he did not want to make any statement about her. But how was this "exception" achieved? Augustine died before formulating his answer. Both in the East and the West, Mary's sinlessness was generally assumed. This can be seen especially by the Church Fathers' remarks about some Gospel passages that observe a certain lack of faith in Jesus' family. These were explained as not implying unbelief on behalf of Mary.[329] By the 4th century such controversies

---

[327] "So whoever is in Christ is a *new creation*: the old things have passed away; behold new things have come" (2 Cor 5:17). "For neither does circumcision mean anything, nor does uncircumcision, but only a *new creation*" (Gal 6:15). "In his great mercy he gave us a *new birth* to a living hope through the resurrection of Jesus Christ from the dead" (1 P 1:3). "We *await new heavens and a new earth* in which righteousness dwells" (2 P 3:13). "Then I *saw a new heaven and a new earth*. The former heaven and the former earth had passed away, and the sea was no more" (Rv 21:1). "The one who sat on the throne said, 'Behold, I make *all things new*'" (Rv 21:5).

[328] See above pp. 147-150.

[329] These texts became matters of contention in post-Tridentine confessional controversies and were even routinely called "anti-Mariological" texts without amounting to sufficient evidence that any of the Gospels had wanted to accuse Mary of

had mostly disappeared, as it became clear that the texts in question never raise specific charges of unbelief against Mary. By the time of Augustine the only question that remained open was if Mary (whose nativity was celebrated by a feast), had been purified of original sin in the way John the Baptist or Jeremiah (cf. Jr 1:5) were believed to have been cleansed, namely, still in the womb.[330] For many people these "parallels" gave satisfactory explanation for Mary's sinlessness at her birth. However some wanted to see how and why Mary's lack of original sin at birth could be assumed, and whether it were perhaps more convincing to assert that from the first moment of her conception she was sinless. The issue was complicated by the fact that Aristotelian philosophy assumed that a certain number of days occurred between physical conception and "animation," and therefore purification could not have taken place at conception. One might note that the position of the "maculists" included philosophical issues, and that pre-scientific notions about the biological process of procreation also remained an obstacle for further advancement.

From an interest and even an urge to celebrate liturgically the appearance of redeemed life eventually there arose the desire for a feast of Mary's Conception on December 8, nine months before the feast of Mary's Nativity (September 8). So the issue was brought up in liturgical terms: should we or should we not celebrate this day? In the 12th century, this movement reached Lyons in France, where the canons of the Cathedral adopted the feast. Bernard of Clairvaux reacted against it, calling it an unwelcome innovation. A century later, Thomas Aquinas also joined the opponents of such a feast, and

---

unbelief. Nonetheless, they became repetitiously present in Catholic/Protestant controversies, mainly for suggesting that Mary's high perfection, postulated by Catholics, was "non-biblical." After Vatican II a certain fatigue can be seen: both sides began to realize that centuries of mariological controversies based on biblical literalism and insinuations were unproductive. Similarly, calibrating the degree of "fault" some patristic authorities find with Mary became stale. What appear as "imperfections" manifest a belief in ongoing growth in holiness or Mary's eventual experience of temptation, a topic with no doctrinal relevance for fighting Mary's sinlessness, since nobody ever denied the presence of temptation (in the Judean Desert) or crisis (in Gethsemane) in the life of her Son.

[330] Ancient exegesis interpreted Is 6:5-7 as purification from original sin too.

its future seemed doomed. And yet six centuries of relentless effort brought it about that this feast was not only accepted as optional, but was then imposed as a compulsory solemnity, and its object as part of the faith of all believing Catholics.

The history of the dogma, summarized earlier, including the fiasco of the first efforts of its dogmatization at the Council of Basel, is unparalleled in the Church's history and is usually narrated without further explanation. Why did it happen that, at the zenith of Christian faith and culture in the 12th and 13th centuries, at the advice and under the leadership of two charismatic saints, Bernard and Thomas, this dogma could not reach acceptance by the authorities of the Church? How is it to be explained that generations later, Scotus, a theologian of lesser significance, and up to this day not canonized,[331] was able to convince a Church suffering serious symptoms of decay amid never-ending crises, that the position of Augustine and his famous followers was in error and it behooved the Church to reconsider the case so as to turn around the official position?

The peculiar history of the dogma of the Immaculate Conception calls our attention to the particular delicacy of this issue. The ontological analysis of the term "redemption" made it clear that only something already existent and in need of redemption can be redeemed. Therefore, the sober Thomistic consensus generously conceded Mary's sinlessness only after she was cleansed by Christ's redeeming death on the Cross, so that she had to be declared immaculate immediately upon her conception, but, of course, *after* she was created. Any other approach would have seemed to introduce a being *de facto* perfect without being redeemed, or, in other terms, a being who participates *de facto* in redemption before participating in being. No theologian wanted to postulate a person's being re-created before being created the first time. Such a conclusion seemed to contradict blatantly the universal salvific character of Christ's redemption and, therefore, had to be rejected. On this basis St. Thomas' rejection of the Immaculate Conception appeared to stand on a firm ontological

---

[331] Duns Scotus was beatified by John Paul II on March 20, 1992, but has not been canonized.

foundation laid down by Augustine and defended by Bernard as the Church's well-reasoned, traditional position.

The fault that Scotus, along with other Anglo-Saxon thinkers, saw in this reasoning, might make us tremble: is it possible that in some other area, in fact in several other cases, ontological arguments may lead us to false conclusions, sealed by consensus? The insertion of finite, spiritual beings into a chain of temporal causality easily misleads us, making our reasoning drift toward the assumption that the *temporal sequence* of the *effects* of divine acts upon finite beings would necessarily impose limits on the acts of the Absolute Being as if in a compulsory constraint on an absolute time line. But if, in the case of divine acts moving finite beings, time and causality do not necessarily follow the same order, God might anticipate the effects of certain of *his* acts and let them obtain their effects in anticipation. So, for example, by unanimous consent of Catholic tradition, the Patriarchs and Prophets enjoyed the fruits of redemption in anticipation: they were justified by their faith and a baptism of desire before the Incarnation and the redemptive death of Jesus. In the same way it is thoroughly possible, even plausible, that Mary could be exempt from any trace of original sin in view of Jesus' meritorious redemptive work, which on a historical time line occurred at a later point.

Dealing with this unique case concerning original sin, Scotus applied a general principle. He argued that Jesus' redemptive work had a universal value, and that this value applied in the case of Mary in a proleptic manner granting preventive protection against any trace of sin to the Savior's only immediate parent. Truly to be the Mother of God, Mary had to be completely saintly and pure. Before her conception the purpose of her existence was determined by her election to be the Mother of God. Her *raison d'être* determined the mode of her conception, which came about *praevisis meritis*[332] of her

---

[332] The expression "praevisis meritis" appears in *Ineffabilis Deus*, the Bull of Dogmatization by Pius IX. The language of the Bull avoids mentioning if Mary's sinlessness at her Conception was the result of being shielded from sin in spite of a universal *debitum peccati* (a sin she should have occurred as a "debt" on account of being a descendant of Adam), owed by every human being, or on account of

Son. The Christological paradox discovered by the Nicene Church led the medieval theologians to see the Mariological paradox: Mary's Immaculate Conception is both the result and the antecedent of redemption. Mary's Immaculate Conception takes place before she is born, before she matures enough to receive God's Son in her womb. To reach this goal, in a preview that this goal in fact will be reached, she was conceived sinless and became the Mother of God-Become-Man, who died for the sake of obtaining her sinlessness at conception. The Immaculate Conception takes place in anticipation of her own response to the Angel's greeting, the birth in Bethlehem, and the death on Calvary. This temporal sequence of events contains causes that physically happen *after* their effects, but in God's eternal and unchanging sovereignty over all beings, the whole chain is "fore-seen" at once. Consequently it is well possible for God, whose causality remains transcendental to time all along, to make her conception happen as the fruit of her Son's redeeming work. This is the basis on which Scotus stated his famous *potuit*, insisting that the Immaculate Conception contained no contradiction to Jesus' universal redemption. The rest of the argument (*debuit*,[333] *ergo fecit*) was relatively limpid: from Augustine to Thomas it was agreed that Mary is the closest to God in the order of grace, therefore she must be formed at the furthest possible distance from sin and evil. Scotus made all see that the furthest possible distance entailed for her an absence of sinfulness from the first moment of her existence.

We see here how Mary's Immaculate Conception implies a correct relating of categorical causality to transcendental causality in every action characterized by the simultaneous, not sequential working of divine and human causalities, operating not concomitantly as if by temporal coordination but on different levels of causality, so that divine causality always remains unambiguously sovereign and supremely free, while human action is likewise always free in its own

---

being the beginning of a "new creation." Cf. René Laurentin, *A Short Treatise on the Virgin Mary* (Washington, NJ: AMI Press, 1991), 188.

[333] See above on pp. 199-200 the explanations concerning its misleading logical language: moving from *posse* to *esse*.

order, so that the act of the human being that is involved may be, indeed, a human act, *actus humanus*.

The doctrine of the Immaculate Conception also makes explicit that Mary is the first beneficiary of redemption, not in the temporal order, but as the one who is first and foremost entitled to the fruits of what God achieved through her and entrusted to her, namely his Incarnation. As Mary declares in the *Magnificat*, "God has done great things for me." That God has provided her with every fruit of salvation is not a maximalist statement of irrational enthusiasts; it is not a Romantic idyll of people whose hearts are captured by the little girl suddenly elected to be the Mother of God, as if, to use the language of the American dream "you can be anything you want to be, even the Mother of God." Instead we are talking here about a certain order of redemption, willed by God when he decided to realize the Incarnation: filiation from a real human mother and motherhood in the flesh, but with the full exclusion of concupiscence and all other residual effects of original sin, so that a fully pure and sinless fountain for the life of grace might be established on earth to bring about rebirth: παλιγγενεσία (Mt 19:28). This event that places Mary at the top of the table at the Wedding Banquet in heaven is not at all different from what the Lord foretold: "For behold, some are last who will be first, and some are first who will be last" (Lk 13:30). This is what Mary expresses about herself in the *Magnificat*: "He has thrown down the rulers from their thrones but lifted up the lowly. The hungry he has filled with good things; the rich he has sent away empty" (Lk 1:52-53).

The failure of the definition of the Immaculate Conception in 1435, and its slow but ultimately triumphant comeback in 1854 makes a fascinating story with important implications. When Pius IX declared Mary's Immaculate Conception, he faced a Church in political and theological disarray, yet this Church was mostly enthusiastic for the new dogma. The image of Mary that emerged was enriched on several levels. Her representation without the Child in her arms (at least visibly not with the Child, for often there is a hint that she is pregnant with her Son) recalls not only the Mary/Eve parallel but also her being the image of the Church, pregnant with the whole Body of Christ. In paintings and statues with the Serpent under her feet, the figure represents her unambiguously as the Second Eve triumphant over the Devil, who was seen after the French Revolution to have staged incessant waves of persecution against the Church all over the world.[334] When the First Vatican Council was interrupted by the last phase of the Italian *Risorgimento* (the revolution toward unification) and the Papacy was shut into the Vatican, one hostile regime after another tried to continue the program of the French Revolution by putting the Church "out of business." But the miracles of Lourdes did their job, reflecting a new radiance of Catholic faith upon a world almost fully convinced that supernatural events are impossible. Contrary to all expectations, a Marian epoch opened in the Church, not in any "well prepared" or organized way (nothing would suggest that it was either staged or foreseen) but in the form of an uneducated "grass-roots initiative." Lourdes itself began with a totally uneducated girl's prophetic visions in the most backward regions of the French Pyrénées. Soon thereafter, during the bloodbath of First World War, new visionaries emerged, this time Portuguese children guarding their parents' sheep. The visionaries were even less educated, but their visions were more spectacular. In the 20th century, more densely filled with concentrated human brutalities than any previous century, Marian devotion spread and recruited the less educated classes, the poor and the simple. The papacy, Catholic theologians and the episcopacy made heroic efforts "to reset (by moving ahead) the clock of the Church" when the Second Vatican Council launched a movement of *aggiornamento* (updating the Church), seeking to make the Church more sensitive to contemporary needs. The large Catholic masses partly succumbed to a harsh, new secularization of society, or tried to cling to the simplest forms of piety (the Rosary, for example) while the leadership dedicated its

---

[334] We make here a reference to many events of history. The waves of secularization extending delayed effects of the French Revolution over all Europe must be seen together with the sufferings of newly converted churches in the Far East (Japan, Korea, Vietnam, China).

research to bringing the Church closer to everyone, to establish "the Church in the Modern World" (the subtitle of a main document of Vatican II, *Gaudium et Spes*), helping it to stand on its feet and listen more responsively to contemporary human needs while remaining faithful to its religious mission.

In the second half of the 20th century a "Marian message" was distilled by Pope John Paul II with the extraordinary impact of his leadership on both the Church and the world: Mary can save the family, Mary can provide perseverance for the persecuted, Mary can keep priests and lay people faithful to dogmatic and moral traditions – and Mary can even save the life of the Pope, as happened on May 13, 1981, the anniversary of Mary's apparitions in Fatima. On that day the life of the energetic, young Pope John Paul II was saved from an assassin's bullet, which missed his heart by mere millimeters, and his vibrant pontificate continued until 2005. Following two visits by the Polish Pope to his home country, European Communism collapsed in a dramatic sequence of events as if, to quote Origen, the walls of Jericho had crumbled at the trumpet sound of the Gospel. The message of Vatican II about Mary as Mother of the Church appeared with special force at the threshold of the third millennium, due to the leadership of John Paul II and Benedict XVI, both extraordinary champions of Marian theology and devotion.

We found that our consideration of Mary's virginal Motherhood in terms of the Incarnation led us to discuss the beginning of her own human life, her Immaculate Conception, and that, in turn, with the Immaculate Conception we find ourselves not merely ruminating some particular theological technicality, but exploring a mystery that draws together the earliest foundations of Mariology, their unusual and peculiar development, and the latest movements and even upheavals in the life of the Church.

Mary's Bodily Assumption

Much like Mary's Immaculate Conception, her Assumption to heaven was widely believed by the faithful and regularly celebrated in the liturgy before there was any thought of "dogmatizing" it. As for the Immaculate Conception, so also for this dogma, theological precision was long lacking and so the doctrine underwent various formulations. On the one hand, ancient apocryphal sources seemed to provide many legendary details, not often supported by the majority of the Church Fathers; on the other hand, theologians had to sort out their disagreements on various issues of eschatology like the ontological explanation of human death, the separation of body and soul, the general and particular judgment, and other matters pertaining to the "last things" like the destiny of the soul immediately after death, purgatory, the resurrection of the body as a cosmic or individual event, the role of the body in the beatific vision, as well as the anthropology of the risen human being in general. In the meantime, naturally, a few basic questions concerning Mary's glorification after death remained open. Did she die? When, where, how? Did she go through the "normal" process of corporal death or some other experience reserved to her alone? Was her body dead and then resurrected, or did her death resemble a peaceful "falling to sleep," the kind of painless death that most human beings wish for themselves? In Chapter V we dealt with the various traditions and their emergence in the history of the Church without attempting to summarize and systematize the answer, which theologians eventually proposed and also propose in recent times.

The rough road leading to the dogmatization of the Immaculate Conception was not promising for the doctrine of the Assumption. After the dogma of the Immaculate Conception was promulgated in 1854, the Church was again thrown into political crises and the intellectual chaos of modernity, so that nobody seemed to be ready to take any steps toward defining Mary's Assumption with a similar papal intervention. But Church life took new turns. The miracles of Lourdes and later of Fatima provided unparalleled support for rebuilding Marian devotion and resisting the pressures of rationalism and modernism that otherwise tried to eliminate, or at least reduce to a minimum, the manifestations of the supernatural in Catholic teaching. In the mostly painful, yet ultimately healthy chain of events leading to the First Vatican Council, with its dogmatization of papal infallibility, enough security accrued for a renewed battle against militant atheism, bringing new confidence to the organs of the Magisterium. In this respect the so-called "modern Popes," beginning with Leo XIII, undertook enormous initiatives to upgrade scholarly competence in the ranks of the Catholic clergy and the hierarchy, as well as in the realm of Catholic institutions of higher learning. Times were changing altogether. The exaggerated claims of rationalism came to an end, even if the "consuming" masses and Western culture in general failed to register what was happening. Classical physics, formalistic mathematics, and the crude forms of Darwinism promulgating ever new charts for man's unaided "emergence" from the Animal Kingdom were replaced by new and more sophisticated models of scientific thinking. In physics, Einstein's theory of relativity and Heisenberg's principle of uncertainty, and in mathematics Gödel's proof of incompleteness, dramatically changed the outlook of scientists about religious faith. Even in evolutionary biology the discovery of new types of hominoids revealed the complexity of the process of "hominization," and the schemes for the emergence of man became increasingly hypothetical and less hostile to religious faith. The original and therefore ultimate unity of mankind once again became a possible and even attractive hypothesis as genetic research itself started realizing that all humans living presently on the planet belong to one single biologically connected family.

How well the Church at large has learned to carry out her task of defending and explaining the faith is, of course, not a topic we can treat here. But it is important to see the cultural and intellectual climate in which, after the bloodiest wars of history, when half of Europe was still in ruins and half the planet burdened by the additional misery imposed by Soviet Communism, the aging Pope Pius XII undertook the dogmatization of Mary's bodily Assumption as a pastoral initiative to make one more significant step in clarifying Mary's role in the history of our redemption. Pius XII used the model that worked well for Pius IX almost a century earlier. He officially asked the episcopate and registered a deeply rooted and quasi-unanimous teaching of all bishops that Mary was taken into the glory of God in both body and soul, so that her body was not exposed to the curse pronounced over Adam: "You were made out of dirt and to dirt you shall return" (Gn 3:19). The dogmatization happened on November 1, 1950, the feast of All Saints, another tool for demonstrating the Pope's intention to show that what was at stake was Our Lady's communion with the other saints, and not only her distinction from or superiority above them.

The Bull *Munificentissimus Deus*, which promulgates the dogma, gave a useful, new clarity to the question; about Mary's death or the nature of the change that carried her from this life into the next, no pronouncement was made. Those who objected to the definition of the dogma voiced little disagreement with its content. Some part of the episcopate regretted it, as if it signaled a new obstacle for the unity of the Catholic Church with Orthodox Christians and the Protestant denominations. The issue of the Orthodox was more nominal than real: in all quarters of world-wide Orthodoxy (Greek, Russian, Armenian, Syriac, Coptic, Ethiopian, etc.), an explicit belief in Mary's Assumption had reigned for at least a thousand years. The complaint was more about the mode in which the dogma was proclaimed *ex cathedra* by a reigning Pope in Rome and by a papal Bull. The Pope, however, made ample references to the Byzantine Greek tradition as witnesses of a commonly held tradition. For a long time, in fact, Catholics had used the universal acceptance of this dogma as a proof that this article of faith was part of their common apostolic heritage. Protestants saw in the dogma another proof of the ongoing "love affair" of the Roman Catholic Church with Mary, and took it in the same way as they had earlier handled the Immaculate Conception. Nor was there any apparent change in the strategy of building defensive fortifications on behalf of the new dogma upon the typical process of the so-called *Schultheologie* of those times,[335]

---

[335] This expression was used with predilection by Karl Rahner. He reacted to the new dogmatic definition in an article which shows that, for him the issue was again first and foremost a task in theological methodology: How to use Tradition when arguing about a dogmatic teaching not found explicitly in any biblical passage?

a "theology of the textbooks" that still spoke of the two sources of revelation (Scripture and Tradition) as adequately distinguishable entities.

Catholic theologians, both those who formed the entourage of Pius XII and those who dissented, reacted in articles and books, but they were well prepared. They had known for quite some time that the step of dogmatization was imminent and unavoidable. For mostly practical reasons, of course, some wished that the dogmatization would have been postponed, leaving a wider area of dogmatic "no man's land" between Catholics and various ecumenically minded Protestant denominations. Others took the challenge of a serious, new reflection on eschatology as a timely and urgent question, and attempted to design a broader and wider context for Mary's glorification in newly reworked treatises on the "resurrection of the body and [its] life everlasting."

Most helpful of all were the incentives that the new dogma gave to the topic of "Mary and the Church," which patristic theology had just recently begun to investigate again. In the decade following the Second World War, ecclesiology had received a new impetus from both the human sciences and the astonishing effects of the most catastrophic war of all history, in which man's addiction to violence was idolized, and mass murder systematized, as proven beyond any doubt by the ideologies of Nazism and Communism, and cataclysmic destruction was made possible by the atomic bomb. The best minds of the post-war decades avidly turned to sociology and, within the realm of theology, to ecclesiology, seeking ultimate redemption not only in Christian social thought but in the central truths of Christian doctrine about the communitarian aspects of man's sin, redemption, and final salvation. From such a point of view the dogma of the Assumption easily implied a reference to mankind's full salvation in the redemption of the body and the fulfillment of the eschatological hope of the Church: mankind's full unity and the arrival to glory in the fully realized Kingdom of God.

1. The New Eve Suffers No Decay

Rather than exploring the social implication of Mary's Assumption, we need first to see how Mary's *body* shares the destiny of the body of the Child she bore. This is the correct way to reconstruct the theological thought implicit in the tradition that maintained from time immemorial that Mary's body suffered no decay. Psalm 16:10[336] is applied to Jesus' body in two programmatic sermons of Acts, first by Peter in Jerusalem on the day of Pentecost (2:22-37), second by Paul during his first apostolic journey in Antioch of Pisidia (13:16-41). The argument taken from the Psalm is presented in a deductive form with the conclusion: "it was impossible" that the nether world would hold Jesus' body (Ac 2:24) and that he was "never to return to corruption" (Ac 13:34).

Obviously, a "corruptible" vs. an "incorruptible" body appears to refer to pre-scientific concepts; but in the language of the New Testament we are here faced with a quasi-technical expression that has a specific meaning. It first appears in the Book of Wisdom, but Paul extends its use as he applies it to the risen body of Christ as well as to the glorified eschatological body of the faithful (1 Cor 15:42; Eph 6:24). It obtains central importance in Christian eschatological language when the 2nd century Church Fathers begin to quote 1 Corinthians 15:50 as a basic principle: "Flesh and blood cannot inherit God's kingdom, nor can *corruption* inherit *incorruptibility*."[337] While the Gnostics insist on this principle in the sense of denying that man's bodily nature can ever obtain divine life, the anti-Gnostic Church Fathers make it clear that the authentic Pauline sense of the term implies exactly the opposite: truly born, truly died, and truly risen, the Savior, who took upon himself man's true flesh in corrupt-

---

[336] In Acts, Peter (2:27) and then Paul (13:35) quote in parallel manners Ps 16:10 about Jesus' Resurrection. The Psalm states that "your Holy One" will not see the nether world nor experience corruption or decay. The word "corruption" corresponds to what we find in the LXX (διαφθορά), while the Hebrew text has "the Pit," a standard image of "Sheol" or "nether world" (it would be Hades in Greek).

[337] "σὰρξ καὶ αἷμα βασιλείαν θεοῦ κληρονομῆσαι οὐ δύναται, οὐδὲ ἡ φθορὰ τὴν ἀφθαρσίαν κληρονομεῖ" (1 Cor 15:50).

ibility, carries it with himself in a transformed and thus incorruptible state into the realm of the divine, by transforming and glorifying it.

We spoke above[338] about the connection of Mary's incorruptible virginity with her sanctity and participation in divine life through sanctifying grace. This virginity does not exclude motherhood, but quite to the contrary results in motherhood, because precisely in virtue of this virginity and not just in spite of it, she becomes the Mother of God. Her virginal motherhood is a tie binding her to the divine nature more closely than any other link could. Fundamentally, then, those who exalted the dignity of the *Theotokos* were also the first to begin the cult of Mary's Assumption. They extended the logic of the sermons we quoted from Acts and applied Psalm 16:10 not only to the body of Mary's Child but also to her own flesh. The one from whom the Word took flesh could not have seen her physical integrity fall under the power of death and return to the dust from which the body of the first Adam was taken.

Here we arrive to the realization of how powerful a tool the Mary/Eve parallel eventually became. As the second Adam could not stay "in the belly of the earth" (Mt 12:40), i.e., in the Hades that swallows all the living on account of the first sin, neither could the second Eve, mother of all to be re-born, all those living God's life, have seen decay and corruption, either. A new heaven and a new earth with newly risen humans can be called the "new creation"; Christ, the firstborn of the dead, and Mary of whom Christ was born, are inseparably the first physical bodies of this new creation. The first was Christ at his Resurrection, but temporally Christ's redemptive power preceded the Cross and the Resurrection at Mary's Immaculate Conception. Thus Mary, as the link between the first and second Adam and the only immediate ancestor of Jesus, cannot undergo destruction. She is fully redeemed at her conception and only her body needs to follow Christ, the body he took from her and brought into incorruptible life ahead of her. That body does not need to enter Hades and become dirt before it is created anew. Her chil-

---

[338] See pp. 116-119.

dren are destined to an indestructible life, and their Mother too has a life that cannot be extinguished.

But could she have undergone death? As the second Adam's flesh and blood died as an instrument of redemption, but physical destruction did not take hold before his body was created anew, so the body of the second Eve could have come to a full stop in the infralapsarian world before becoming "incorruptible" – a body belonging to the world to come, a body transferred into the world to come: eschatology come to its full.

This open-ended line of thought left tradition and theology in the state of "wonder" about the form and manner in which the blessed Virgin's life ended. We saw above how, in an extraordinary sermon, St. Bernard of Clairvaux saw the paradox about Mary's death with more lucidity than most others. He thought that the moment of her Son's death was an experience of death for her too.[339] There is no need to postulate any martyr's death for her, or any physical journey into decay. In other words, the end of her life remains a mystery, beyond the experience or understanding of the rest of human beings, born with original sin and bound to natural death as part of the collective destiny of "returning unto dust." At the end of her life, which she lived in our fallen condition and in a world of corruptibility, the mode of her transfer to the realm of her Son's risen condition is not known, and may not be knowable. This is so, not chiefly on account of a lack of historical data, but because we lack experiential basis for knowing what she experienced.

2. The Woman Clothed with the Sun: an Eschatological Vision of Mary and the Church

As long as we focus on Mary in her individual role as the virginal mother of Christ, the image of her Assumption easily blurs, for in the eyes of those who accept only "the critical meaning of the Bible," the "historical Mary" disappears on the first pages of the Acts

---

[339] See above, pp. 188-189.

of the Apostles. As an unintended and ultimately myopic outcome of the dogmatization of the Assumption, for many theologians and most laypersons, raised in the apologetic traditions of the immediate past, the chief question became the existence of a reliable historical tradition about something like an empty tomb of Mary. It is true that the apocryphal writings of patristic times provided too much imaginary material about the gathering of the Apostles at the hour of her earthly death or "dormition," but the dogmatization did not intend to increase credence in such material or investigation into this kind of evidence.

The acceptance of Mary's departure from this earthly life into her Son's glory is a theological statement. Its "physical implications" in terms of observable material facts open to sense perception cannot be proven beyond reasonable doubt. In fact, the doubt is reasonable unless one accepts divine revelation and deeds, and the Magisterium as the authority that describes and explains – although with no claim of completeness – the basic statements of revelation and the contours beyond which we have no information. In the case of the Assumption, the content of the dogma is best defended as possible and even probable by a single empirical fact: according to the memory of the Church, Mary's relics or bodily remains have never been venerated.[340]

But the clarity of our vision improves as we focus on the Marian mystery coming to completion in the Church. We have touched upon this in previous chapters, especially in passages with an eccle-

---

[340] It is probably helpful to state that the "Immaculate Conception" or Mary's virginal conception or the description of the birth of Jesus that do not destroy but sanctify her virginity and Mary's preserved virginity *post partum* (i.e., *all* dogmas of Mariology) are statements whose nature excludes empirical verification. Questions of their empirical proof are therefore out of the question, but their denial can be urged by *suggesting* that (a) she could have been raped and made pregnant (Celsus), (b) Joseph could have been the father of Jesus (Ebionites), (c) she might have been the mother of Jesus' "brothers and sisters" (Tertullian, Bonosius, most Protestants); (d) she could have been cleansed from sin after conception (St. Augustine *et alii*), (e) she could have died, been buried, and *not be risen* (most outside of the Catholic or Orthodox Churches). From this point of view, Mariology cannot be promoted very successfully with a theological method that pursues empirical facts for supernatural events perceived in the most private realms of human existence.

siological focus. In the present perspective, the ecclesiological aspect of Mariology would focus on the work of redemption as an extension of Christ's presence not only through the only Son of the Father being born, put to death, and risen, but also through the birth of many children of God issued from Christ's redemptive work and continuing in ongoing waves of further children, all participants in creation through the same Logos and in redemptive new birth through faith and sacrament. In this direction, of course, we could probe deeply into the heart of ecclesiology, going in a direction which would go beyond the perspective of this book. But a number of important issues must be signaled.

It seems that the Marian exegesis of Revelation 12:1-10 has been a great help for this topic throughout the centuries. Although the Book of Revelation says little or nothing directly about Mary, it would be a mistake to ignore its Marian dimension and meaning.[341] The question is not what Revelation 12:1-17 says about the Blessed Virgin's individual person and earthly life – about that it says very little – but why such a cosmic portrait of the Mother of the Messiah is drawn in a book that uses hardly any identifiable earthly person to illustrate its message about the Church's destiny and struggle before the Second Coming. As becomes quite clear in the last words of the passage (v. 17), the "Woman" is the result of the superimposition of two persons called by this name in the Bible: Mary and Eve. The Woman clothed with the sun in Revelation 12:1 is in the travail of the "messianic birth," an Isaian image of salvation. Her birth pangs result in the birth of a male Child to whom a verse of a messianic psalm (2:9) is applied. The male Child is "caught up to God," while the Woman is brought to the desert. The Child is expected to "rule the nations with an iron rod" (i.e., to come as judge), while the Woman is evacuated to the desert to witness a war between the Dragon who had tried to destroy her first Child and the rest of her offspring. In this picture the Woman is both the mother of the Messiah, portrayed as an individual, and the mother of many children. After the

---

[341] See above pp. 46-48.

Dragon loses out in his attempt to snatch the messianic first Child, he fights the rest of the children. In this panoramic view of salvation history the Dragon is identified as Satan and the Devil and the "ancient Serpent,"[342] and thus his significance reaches beyond the first of his prey; so also the Woman who gives birth to the one who is the exalted Son, a Son unique to her at the beginning, has many other children too. That is to say, the Woman confronting the ancient Serpent evokes again what we had suspected in reading the Fourth Gospel, the parallelism between Mary and Eve.

Here we return to a theme constantly present throughout our study: Mary obtains significance, importance, and a unique role in the Bible because the biblical sources about God's great deeds for man sweep a huge arc from alpha to omega, from a first Adam and Eve to a new Adam and a second Eve, encompassing thereby a canonical presentation of Creation and Redemption, in which the parts and the whole retain their interrelatedness. The textual units of the single books lose their meaning as soon as we isolate them: from a mosaic you can knock out hundreds of colored pieces of stone and consider them in themselves; they are still shiny and their color is still retained, but the picture's meaning is irretrievably lost. The "Woman" in Cana, under the Cross, giving birth in travail, becoming the mother of the Beloved Disciple, cosmically elevated above the moon, clothed with the sun, surrounded by twelve stars: they all belong together.

Of course we could fragment them. We can talk about the "Johannine Jesus" addressing as "woman" most every female, we may point out all the zodiac symbolism in the twelve stars or that the "messianic birth" – the painful travail of the mother – has little or nothing to do with the historical Mary (if we hold to her perpetual virginity); we may create several Johns as mistakenly believed authors of the Fourth Gospel and Revelation. We may join Eusebius

---

[342] The threefold naming of the Dragon provides it with three identifications. He is the Serpent of the Garden of Eden (Gn 3:1-6), Satan ejected from heaven (Lk 10:18), and the symbol of all enemies against whom God's children must fight (cf. Eph 6:11-12).

of Caesarea in calling Papias a man of feeble mind, we can assume that Justin Martyr knew little about Revelation or the Apostle John when he said that the Apostle John authored it; we are free to call this a meaningless fact or plain hearsay; we might think that the views of Irenaeus are certainly anti-Gnostic and pro-millenarist, also pro-hierarchy and pro-Marian but anti-feminist, and, finally, we may suspect that his Johannine ties are problematic and his knowledge of Polycarp needs another critical review. I go on repeating this caricature of an "exegesis by suspicion" in order to compare two views. One would say that, a good hundred years after the death of the historical Mary, a confluence of interests, manifest through the birth of an apocryphal literature and through the emerging Mary/Eve theme, gave rise to Mariology and guided its ascendency until it penetrated and corrupted early Christology. But I proposed another path. The presence of Mary in the apostolic Church and firm tradition about Jesus' virginal origins began a process of reflection that can be followed along two avenues. In the Gospels of Matthew and Luke, the literary documentation of the traditions relating to the origins of Jesus was channeled through some members of his family and became part of the standardized written record of the Jesus tradition. While this tradition was built around Isaiah 7:14 and many other texts related to the Davidic origin of the Messiah, another set of traditions, finding its way eventually into the Johannine writings, focused on Jesus' virginal conception in the framework of a new birth and its meditative comparison to the first chapters of Genesis, especially Genesis 3. This second set of themes, expressed with allusions, irony, and symbolism in the Gospel of John and Revelation, obtained strong support and impulse in the 2nd century as the Mary/Eve parallel and the first Adam/second Adam parallel began to engage the first theologians of the Church.

I choose for us to follow the second avenue, seeing the beginnings of Mariology in the Woman clothed with the Sun as portrayed in the Book of Revelation, another proof that this parallelism showed itself from apostolic times to be the most congenial biblical source of Mariology through the ages.

In an extraordinary text quoted by the Second Vatican Council, Blessed Isaac of Stella, of whom we briefly talked above, wrote a sermon for the feast of the Assumption.[343] The sermon is long, but essentially it is a Marian commentary on a verse from the book of Sirach: "I will dwell in the inheritance of the Lord" (24:11). Isaac shows that this text can be equally applied to Mary, to the Church, and to each individual soul. He justifies such a threefold commentary by presenting the similarities between Mary, the Church, and each believer, all participating in the same mystery of the Incarnation, though in different ways. At first, Isaac explains the term "Son of God" in the singular and plural. It is astonishing that Isaac, who could hardly have known about the ancient pre-Vulgate variant reading of John 1:13 in singular, uses this same Johannine verse to explain how the "many sons" are born in the course of redemption – the human rebirth – so that, as a result the many sons and the only begotten Son, mentioned in the Johannine Prologue, are both many and one:

> The Son of God is the *first-born of many brothers* (cf. Rm 8:29). Although by nature he is the only-begotten, by grace he has joined many to himself and made them one with him. For *to those who receive him he has given the power to become the sons of God* (Jn 1:13).... When he became the Son of man, he made many people sons of God: he united them to himself by his unique love and power, so that they became as one. In themselves they are many by reason of their fleshly origin, but in him they are one through their divine rebirth.

After that, the relationship of the one Son and the many sons is defined in terms of two filiations. Yet the only begotten Son and the many sons, redeemed by a rebirth, have one Father in heaven and

---

[343] The Council's document *Lumen Gentium* refers to Isaac in a footnote attached to no. 64 of Chapter VIII: Isaac of Stella, *Sermo* 51 (PL 194, 1863A).

one mother on earth. "The whole Christ and the unique Christ – the body and the head – are one: one because born of the same God in heaven, and of the same mother on earth. They are many sons, yet one son." This leads to a special Mariological point, linking Mary and the Church: "Head and members are one son, yet, many sons; in the same way, Mary and the Church are one mother, yet several [mothers]; one virgin, yet several [virgins]."

Isaac sees a complex picture: these two, Mary and the Church, both represent virginal mothers: Mary as an individual, the Church as a collectivity, yes, but for the members of the Church these dovetail together, by their individual participation in several (*plures*) virgins and mothers. What is the foundation of this oneness and yet plurality of virginal motherhoods?

> Each of the two is a mother, both are virgins. Each conceives of the same Spirit, without the sexual drive (*sine libidine*). Each brings forth to God the Father a child without sin. Mary gave birth to Christ, the body's head, without any sin whatsoever, and the Church gave birth to the Head's body with all its sins forgiven. Each is Christ's mother, but neither gives birth to the whole Christ without the other giving birth.

Both Mary and the Church are made mothers and virgins in order to remedy fallen man's condition. Each conceives of the same Spirit, without concupiscence. Each gives birth to sinless offspring of God the Father. For Mary, motherhood produces an utterly sinless Child, while the Church gives birth by a sacrament that effects the remission of all sins. Each is Christ's mother, but neither gives birth to the whole Christ without the cooperation of the other; the image of head and body points to some mysterious but real connection.

These introductory thoughts are familiar from the Church Fathers. At this point, however, Isaac introduces a hermeneutical point, more sophisticated and generalized than anything formulated earlier.

> In the inspired Scriptures, what is said in a universal
> sense of the virgin mother, the Church, is understood in
> an individual sense of the Virgin Mary, and what is said
> in a particular sense of the virgin mother Mary is rightly
> understood in a general sense of the virgin mother, the
> Church. When either is spoken of, the meaning can be
> understood of both, almost without qualification.

This text belongs to the best pieces of medieval Mariology: it joins
a patristic inspiration with the sophistication of early scholasticism.
It provides a system by which texts taken from the "inspired Scriptures" can be applied all at once to Mary, to the Church, and to the
individual believer, three participants in the triangular relationships
resulting from the Incarnation.

> In a way, every Christian is also believed to be a bride of
> God's Word, a mother of Christ, his daughter and sister,
> at once virginal and fruitful. These words are used in a
> universal sense of the Church, in a special sense of Mary,
> in a particular sense of the individual Christian.

Finally Isaac arrives to the point where he begins applying
Sirach 24:11 specifically to Mary, the Church, and the individual
believer. The "I" of the scriptural sentence is "Wisdom," the Son
of God. His dwelling in "the Lord's inheritance" is threefold. His
dwelling in Mary lasted nine months, in the Church it will endure
until the end of the ages, and in the faithful alone his dwelling place
lasts forever.

> They are used by God's Wisdom in person, the Word
> of the Father. This is why Scripture says: *I will dwell in
> the inheritance of the Lord.* The Lord's inheritance is, in
> a general sense, the Church; in a special sense, Mary; in
> an individual sense, the Christian. Christ dwelt for nine
> months in the tabernacle of Mary's womb. He dwells un-

til the end of the ages in the tabernacle of the Church's faith. He will dwell forever in the knowledge and love of each faithful soul.[344]

As we see the relationship of Mary and the Church is rooted in the unique oneness of the divine filiation extended through the Word's Incarnation to other sons who, therefore, are all sons of the same Father and of the same Mother. But while the divine Father is one, single Divine Person, the human mother is a finite historical being whose personhood is anticipated in the Old Testament (Daughter of Zion, the Daughter of Israel – the community of the "saints of old") and expanded into the collective community of the Church, held together as members of Christ by their head and thus related to the Church as Mother and, once more and in a different way, to Mary, Christ's Mother, who brought *them* into the redeemed life obtained in the historical Jesus and participated in through the glorified Christ.

In such a system of analogies, both "motherhood" and "virginity" are predicated in similar ways of Mary and the Church. Most importantly, however, in this vision Mary and the Church are closely linked with regard to their eschatological status of glory. From her Immaculate Conception, through the lifelong growth of her participation in her divine Son's earthly history and final glorification, Mary walked in front of the Church as the first one who believed in the Incarnation, as the one who accompanied the various stages of her Son's life and witnessed his life's final consummation on the Cross. This is how we understand and can appropriate a somewhat rare title, Mary as "Mother of the Church" and yet pre-eminent member of the Church. The two concepts must not be understood as mixed metaphors. They remind us of the double use of the Pauline concept of the Church as "body of Christ." Christ is both the Church as the fullness of human participation in divine life and one pre-eminent part of it, the Head of the Body, which the members

---

[344] *Sermo* 51 (PL 194, 1862-1865).

form in unity with each other. Mary is mother of Jesus, thus also of the Church, the full Christ, and of course Mary is one of the redeemed. In particular, her role as "mother of all the living" is the preeminent fruit of redemption, just as Jesus' humanity and his many brothers redeemed and presented to God his Father, all generated by his sacrifice, are fruits of his act of obedience to the Father in accepting the form of a slave and humiliating himself not only to the level of human existence but to mortality and death, death on a Cross.

BIBLIOGRAPHY

Aubert, Roger. *La théologie catholique au milieu du XXe siècle* [*Catholic Theology in the Middle of the 20th Century*] (Paris: Aubier, 1956).

Barré, Henry. "Saint Bernard, Docteur marial," *Saint Bernard théologien, Analecta S. Ordinis Cisterciensis* IX, 3-4 (1953) 93-113.

Bastero, Juan Luis. *Mary the Mother of the Redeemer* (Dublin: Four Courts Press, 2011).

Bauckham, Richard. *Jude and the Relatives of Jesus in the Early Church* (Edinburgh: T & T Clark, 1990).

Boring, M. Eugene. *Mark, A Commentary: The New Testament Library* (Louisville/London: Westminster John Knox, 2006).

Bouyer, Louis. *The Seat of Wisdom* (Chicago: Regnery, 1965).

Bovon, Francois. *Luke 1, Hermeneia* (Minneapolis: Fortress, 2002).

Brakke, David. *Athanasius and the Politics of Asceticism* (Oxford: Clarendon Press, 1995).

Braun, F.-M. *Jean le théologien et son évangile dans l'Église ancienne* (Paris: Gabalda, 1959).

Brown, Raymond E., Karl P. Donfried, Joseph Fitzmyer, and John Reumann (eds.) *Mary in the New Testament* (Philadelphia: Fortress; New York: Paulist, 1978).

_____. *An Introduction to the New Testament, The Anchor Bible Reference Library* (New York/London/Toronto/Sidney/Auckland: Doubleday, 1996).

_____. *The Birth of the Messiah. New Updated Edition* (New York: Doubleday, 1993).

_____. *The Critical Meaning of the Bible* (New York/Ramsey: Paulist Press, 1981).

Capelle, B. "La liturgie mariale en Occident," in D. du Manoir, *Maria*, I, 221.

Carrell, Alexis. *Voyage to Lourdes* (New York: Harper, 1950).

Coathalem, Paul. *Le parallélisme entre la sainte Vierge et l'Église dans la tradition latine jusqu'à la fin du XIIe siècle* (Rome: Univ. Gregoriana, 1954).

Congar, Yves. *Marie, l'Église et le Sacerdoce* (Paris: Gabalda, 1953).

_____. *I Believe in the Holy Spirit* 1 (New York: Seabury, 1983).

Culpepper, R. Alan. *Anatomy of the Fourth Gospel: A Study in Literary Design* (Philadelphia: Fortress, 1983).

Davies, W.D. and Dale C. Allison. *The Gospel According to St. Matthew* (Edinburgh: T & T Clark, 1991).

de la Potterie, Ignace. *Mary in the Mystery of the Covenant* (New York: Alba House, 1992).

de Lubac, Henri. *Exégèse médiévale* I-IV (Paris: Aubier, 1960-1964), vol. I and II translated into English: *Medieval Exegesis* tr. by Mark Sebanc (Grand Rapids: Eerdsman, 2000).

_____. *The Motherhood of the Church* (San Francisco: Ignatius Press, 1982).

_____. *Histoire et Esprit. L'intelligence de l'Écriture d'après Origène* (Paris: Aubier, 1950). Eng. *History and Spirit. The Understanding of Scripture According to Origen*, translated by A.E. Nash (San Francisco: Ignatius Press, 2008).

de Strycker, Emile. *La forme la plus ancienne du Protoévangile de Jacques* (Bruxelles: Société des Bollandistes, 1961).

Delius, Walter. *Geschichte der Marienverehrung* (München-Basel: Ernst Reinhardt Verlag, 1963).

Ehrman, Bart and Zlatko Pleše. *The Apocryphal Gospels* (Oxford: University Press, 2011).

Eliade, Mircea. *Patterns in Comparative Religion*, tr. by R. Sheed (London: Sheed and Ward, 1958).

Bibliography

Ellis, E.E. *The Gospel of Luke: The New Century Bible Commentary* (Grand Rapids: Eerdmans, 1980).

Farkasfalvy, Denis. "Prophets and Apostles, the Conjunction of the Two Terms Before Irenaeus" in *Texts and Testaments*, edited by E.W. March (San Antonio: Trinity University Press, 1980) 109-134.

_____. "Reconstructing Mariology," *Communio* 37 (2010) 47-68.

_____. "The Presbyters' Witness on the Order of the Gospel as Reported by Clement of Alexandria," *Catholic Biblical Quarterly*, LIV, 2 (April, 1992) 260-270.

Fitzmyer, Joseph A. *Luke the Theologian. Aspects of His Teaching* (New York/Mahwah: Paulist Press, 1989).

_____. *The Gospel According to Luke I-IX, Anchor Bible* 28 (Garden City, NY: Doubleday, 1981).

_____. *The Biblical Commission's Document "The Interpretation of the Bible in the Church"* (Rome: Editrice Pontificio Istituto Biblico, 1995).

Gambero, Luigi. *Mary and the Fathers of the Church*, tr. by Thomas Buffer (San Francisco: Ignatius Press, 1999).

Graef, Hilda. *Mary: A History of Doctrine and Devotion* (New York: Sheed and Ward, 1963).

Gregoris, Nicholas L. *"The Daughter of Eve Unfallen," Mary in the Theology and Spirituality of John Henry Newman*, 2nd revised ed. (Monte Pocono, Pennsylvania: Newman House, 2003).

Guitton, Jean. *La Vierge Marie* (Paris: Aubier, 1964).

Johnson, Luke Timothy. *The Gospel of Luke, Sacra Pagina*, vol. 3 (Collegeville: Glazier/Liturgical Press, 1991).

Jouassard, G. "Marie à travers la patristique": Du Manoir D'Hubert (ed.), *Maria: Etudes sur la Sainte Vierge*, I (Paris: Beauchesne, 1949) 69-157.

Kasper, Walter Card. "Letter about Mary's Virginity" in *Communio* 15/2 (1988) 262-266.

Kerkloh, Magnus. *"...die in vollkommenster Weise Erlöste."* Die *Frage nach einem mariologischen Grundprinzip bei Karl Rahner* (Norderstedt: Grin Verlag, 2005).

Koch, Helmut. *Adhuc Virgo, Mariens Jungfrauschaft und Ehe in der altkirchlichen Überlieferung bis zum Ende des 4. Jahrhunderts* (Tübingen: P. Siebeck 1929).

_____. *Virgo Maria – Virgo Eva. Neue Untersuchungen über die Lehre der Jungfrauschaft und der Ehe Mariens in der ältesten Kirche* (Berlin-Leipzig: Walter de Gruyte, 1937).

Laurentin, René. *A Short Treatise on the Virgin Mary,* tr. by Charles Neumann (Washington, NJ: AMI Press, 1991).

_____. *Jésus au Temple. Mystère de Pâques et foi de Marie en Luc 2,48-50* (Paris: Gabalda, 1966).

_____. *La Vierge au Concile* (Paris: Lethielleux, 1965).

_____. *Luc I-II, Études bibliques* (Paris: Gabalda, 1958).

Leclercq, Jean. *The Love of Learning and the Desire for God* (New York: Fordham University Press, 1982).

Lentini, Anselmo. *Hymni Instaurandi Breviarii Romani* (Rome: Libreria Editrice Vaticana, 1968); in Italian: *Te Decet Hymnus* (Rome: Libreria Editrice Vaticana, 1984).

Lyonnet, Stranislas. "Χαῖρε, κεχαριτωμένη" in *Biblica* 20 (1939), 131-141.

Marshall, I. Howard. *The Gospel of Luke, The New International Greek Testament Commentary* (Grand Rapids: Eerdmans, 1978).

Maunder, Chris (ed.). *The Origins of the Cult of the Virgin Mary* (London/New York: Burns and Oates, 2008).

McHugh, John. *The Mother of Jesus in the New Testament* (Garden City, NY: Doubleday, 1975).

Metzger, Bruce M. *A Textual Commentary on the New Testament* (London/New York: United Bible Societies, 1970).

Mitterer, Albert. *Dogma und Biologie der Heiligen Familie nach dem Weltbild des hl. Thomas von Aquin und dem der Gegenwart* (Wien: Herder, 1952).

Neumann, Charles W. *The Virgin Mary in the Works of St. Ambrose* (Fribourg: University Press, 1962).

Nicolas, M.-J. "Le concept intégral de la maternité divine" in *Revue Thomiste* 42 (1937).

Pelikan, Jaroslav. *Mary Through the Centuries: Her Place in the History of Culture* (New Haven: Yale University Press, 1996).

Rahner, Hugo. *Our Lady and the Church,* tr. by S. Bullough (Chicago: Regnery, 1965).

Rahner, Karl. "Virginitas *in partu,*" *Theological Investigations* III (Baltimore: Helikon, 1966) III, 134-172.

_____. *Mary Mother of the Lord* (New York: Herder, 1963).

Ratzinger, Joseph. *Daughter Zion. Meditations on the Church's Marian Belief* (San Francisco: Ignatius Press, 1983).

_____. *Introduction to Christianity,* tr. by J.R. Foster (New York: Herder, 1970).

Robert Sykes. *The Seven Daughters of Eve* (London/New York: Norton, 2002).

Rusch, Paul. "Marianische Wertungen," *Zeitschrift für katholische Theologie* 85 (1963) 129-131.

Scheeben, Mathias J. *The Mysteries of Christianity,* tr. by C. Vollert (London/Saint Louis: Herder, 1946).

Scheffczyk, Leo. *Maria, Mutter und Gefährtin Christi,* Augsburg: St. Ulrich Verlag, 2003.

_____. *Die Mariengestalt im Gefüge der Theologie. Mariologische Beiträge* (Regensburg: Pustet, 2000).

Schillebeeckx, Edward. *Mary, Mother of the Redemption* (New York: Sheed and Ward, 1963).

Semmelroth, Otto. *Urbild der Kirche. Organischer Aufbau des Mariengeheimnisses* (Würzburg, 1950); in English: *Archetype of the Church* (New York: Sheed and Ward, 1964).

Shoemaker, Stephen J. *Ancient Traditions of the Virgin Mary's Dormition and Assumption* (New York: Oxford University Press, 2002).

Söll, George. "Mariologie" in *Handbuch der Dogmengeschichte* III/4 (Freiburg/Basel/Wien: Herder, 1978), 193-215.

Soujeole, Benoit-Dominiq4ue. *Initiation à la théologie mariale* (Toulouse/Fribourg: Parole et Silence, 2007).

Stanley, David. "The Mother of my Lord," *Worship* 34 (1959-1960).

Strobel, August. "Der Gruss an Maria (Lc 1,28)" in *Zeitschrift für neutestamentliche Wissenschaft* 55 (1962) 86-116.

Szövérffy, Joseph. *Annalen der lateinischen Hymnendichtung*, Berlin (I) 1964 (II) 1965.

Thurian, Max. *Mary, Mother of All Christians* (New York: Herder, 1962).

Vagaggini, Cipriano. *Maria nelle Opere di Origene* (Rome: Pontificio Istituto Orientale, 1942).

Vollert, Cyrill. *A Theology of Mary* (New York: Herder, 1965).

von Balthasar, Hans Urs and Joseph Ratzinger. *Mary, the Church at the Source* (San Francisco: Ignatius Press, 2005).

INDEX OF AUTHORS

ST PAULS

This book was produced by ST PAULS, the publishing house operated by the Society of St. Paul, an international religious congregation of priests and brothers dedicated to serving the Church through the communications media.

For information regarding this and associated ministries of the Pauline Family of Congregations, write to the Vocation Director.

Vocation Director of the Society of St. Paul,
2187 Victory Blvd., Staten Island, New York 10314

Phone us at (718) 761-0047 ex 3211
E-mail: vocation@stpauls.us
www.stpauls.us

That the Word of God be everywhere known and loved.